The Cultural Maze

Complex Questions
on Native Destiny in Western Canada

John W. Friesen, editor

Detselig Enterprises
Calgary, Alberta

Canadian Cataloguing in Publication Data

Main Entry under title:
The Cultural Maze

Includes bibliographical references.
ISBN 1-55059-030-8

1. Indians of North America — Canada, Western.
2. Indians of North America — Canada, Western —
Government relations. I. Friesen, John W.
E78. C2C84 1991   971.2′00497   C91-091536-9

Detselig Enterprises Ltd.
P.O. Box G 399
Calgary, Alberta
T3A 2G3

Printed in Canada   SAN 115-0324   ISBN 1-55059-030-8

Other Books by John W. Friesen

Readings in Educational Philosophy, 1968
Cultural Change and Education (co-author), 1969
Religion for People: An Alternative, 1972
Profiles of Canadian Educators (co-author), 1974
Canadian Education and Ideology: Readings, 1975
People, Culture and Learning, 1977
Teacher Participation: A Second Look (co-author), 1978
The Metis of Canada: An Annotated Bibliography (co-author), 1980
Schools as a Medium of Culture, 1981
The Helping Book, 1982
Strangled Roots, 1982
The Teacher's Voice (co-author), 1983
Schools with a Purpose, 1983
A Multicultural Handbook for Teachers, 1984
When Cultures Clash: Case Studies in Multiculturalism, 1985
A Multicultural Handbook for Teachers, No. 2, 1986
Reforming the Schools - for Teachers, 1987
Rose of the North, 1987
The Evolution of Multiculturalism (co-author), 1988
The Community Doukhobors: A People in Transition (co-author), 1989
Introduction to Teaching: A Socio-Cultural Approach (co-author), 1990

Table of Contents

Part One: Becoming Familiar

Preface i
John W. Friesen

1. Introduction:
Highlights of Western Canadian Native History 1
John W. Friesen

2. Native Cultures in a Cultural Clash 23
John W. Friesen

3. The Role of Native Cultures in Western History:
An Alberta Focus 39
Hugh A. Dempsey

4. Explorations in Native Knowing 53
Joseph E. Couture

Part Two: Contemporary Frontiers

5. Indian Economic Development:
Innovations and Obstructions 77
James S. Frideres

6. Native Land Claims 97
Joan Scott-Brown

7. Metis Land Claims in Manitoba 111
Thomas Flanagan

8. Understanding Aboriginal Rights and Indian Government 135
John D. Snow, Jr.

9. The Challenge of Cultural Destiny:
The Role of Language 147
John W. Friesen

10. The Persistence of Native Educational Policy in Canada 163
Sonia Brookes

11. Community Educational Control Issues and the
Experience of Alexander's Kipohtakaw Education Centre 18
Joann Sebastian Morris and Richard T. Price

Part Three: Future Perspectives

12. The Role of Native Elders:
Emergent Issues . . . . 2(
Joseph E. Couture

13. Biculturalism:
Reflections on an Objective for University Education 2
Evelyn Moore-Eyman

14. Teaching in a University Native Outreach Program 2
John W. Friesen

15. The Role of Native People in Canadian Multiculturalism 2
John W. Friesen

Notes on Contributors

Sonia Brookes, M.A., has taught many years in Native schools and is currently a resource teacher with the Calgary Board of Education.

Joe Couture, Ph.D., (of Cree descent), is a former professor at Trent University and Athabasca University, and currently a freelance lecturer and consultant on Native matters.

Hugh A. Dempsey, DUC., is Assistant Director of the Alberta-Glenbow Museum and Adjunct Professor in the Department of History at the University of Calgary.

Thomas Flanagan, Ph.D., is Professor of Political Science in the Faculty of Social Sciences and Policy Advisor to the President at the University of Calgary.

James S. Frideres, Ph.D., is Professor of Sociology and Associate Dean (Research) of the Faculty of Social Sciences at the University of Calgary.

John W. Friesen, Ph.D., is Professor of Education in the Department of Educational Policy and Administrative Studies at the University of Calgary and editor of the *Multicultural Education Journal.*

Evelyn Moore-Eyman, M.A., is Professor Emeritus in the Faculty of Education at the University of Calgary.

Joann Sebastian Morris, M.A., is Director of Curriculum Development and Research at the Alexander (Kipohtakaw) Education Centre.

Richard T. Price, M.A., is Associate Professor and Director of the School of Native Studies at the University of Alberta.

Joan Scott-Brown, M.A., is an instructor at Mount Royal College and in the Department of Anthropology at the University of Calgary.

John D. Snow, Jr., B.A., is a member of the Goodstoney Band of the Stoney Indian tribe at Morley, Alberta, and works as a landman with Shell Canada.

Preface

There is a certain benefit in putting together a volume with many contributors. In the first place, such an enterprise usually involves a lot of consultation, and thus it simply becomes a way of providing learning opportunities for the editor. Second, the task requires patience, much more than is required when one writes a book alone. While I am not on a search for the "holy grail of patience," I have appreciated the spirit of exchange and cooperation which the various individuals whose work is represented in this project have exhibited during its incubation. I would like to take this opportunity to thank them all for sharing their experiences and insights in this way.

The concept of "maze," used in the title, sometimes carries a negative connotation in the sense that there may not appear to be "a way out" in a given situation. I hope that this impression will be absent from the reader's mind as these various essays are perused. It has been my experience that there is a strong hope for the future within the Indian community, and I believe this is true today more than ever. The signs are manifest for a resurgence of Indian cultural vitality, particularly in the areas of Native spirituality, higher education, schooling and language. These and other topics of a more complicated nature, such as land claims, are discussed in the pages that follow.

Caught up as we are in language, it might be helpful at the outset to clarify the use of some terms. In the strictest legal sense, the word "Indian" in Canada refers specifically to some 444 000 people (Status Indians), who have claim to that designation via the *Indian Act*. Many people are unaware of this and thus employ the more generic term "Native people" when they mean Indians. Of course, Native people or peoples should include Status Indians, non-Status Indians, Metis People, and Inuit. To complicate matters even more there is an implied legal or historic difference between Metis People and non-Status Indians. The Metis like to think of themselves as descendants of the former Metis Nation which in 1870 formed a government in the Province of Manitoba under the leadership of Louis Riel. In addition, some observers conceive of the Metis as a mixture of two specific races, specifically French male fur traders who took wives from Woodland Cree Indian tribes. Thus their children were the first Metis. Non-Status Indians can refer to people of mixed blood, Indian and non-Indian, as well as people who descended from disfranchised Status Indians, and others who do not trace their lineage to the Manitoba experience. They have little recognition under Canadian law.

Two other terms which have made their way into the literature are "Aboriginal peoples" and "First Nations" which in the strictest sense refer to "original inhabitants" or "the first ones." On the surface, these designations have reference to the Native people who had made contact with the incoming Europeans. However, there are Metis People today who make the same claim based on an interpretation of history that their ancestors were the first true people of the new nation, Canada. They were an admixture of two races, Indian and European, and as such deserve to be considered Aboriginal People.

In an attempt to avoid the implied technical and legal difficulties of the foregoing discussion, we have tried in these chapters to utilize the term "Native People," to emphasize the fact that the issues discussed generally affect the larger Native community. When the term "Indian" is employed in this volume, the wider implications of the discussion for the larger Native community should be borne in mind. Some of the chapters may be more related to a specific sector of the Native community, but not so as to detract from the fuller spectrum of the contemporary challenge for all Native people in Canada. As the following chapters will reveal, despite the complications of legalities or language or the issues to be resolved, the struggle to maintain Native culture may be complex and arduous, but the Native people will prevail.

This volume is divided into three main sections, the first of which provides a background to understanding some of the challenges with which the Native community is currently grappling. As might be expected, an historical perspective is taken, but an attempt is made to emphasize the role which Native people have played and their contributions to the development of this nation. A new dimension in interpreting Canadian (including Native) history is to attempt to understand traditional Native ways of thinking, and to incorporate both the process and content of that pathway into interpreting our past. This untried road may serve to frustrate the process somewhat, but that condition may be very effective in setting the stage to furnish a more wholistic perspective from which to understand and interpret past happenings.

The second section outlines six specific contemporary issues facing the Native community. These include economic development, land claims, Aboriginal rights, language, educational policy, and local control of education. As Native communities attempt to provide new vitality to their identity, the issue of economic development on Indian reserves becomes significant. Land claims comprise a long-lasting, yet ongoing battle, and our "bonus" feature is to include both an Indian as well as a Metis perspective so as to reveal some of the more subtle complications pertaining thereto. In the final analysis, the settlement of these claims may rely on a strict legal definition of the concept of Aboriginal rights, but that approach may be seen by some as a way to bypass the moral or ethical obligations of the nation.

Two themes dominating the quest for cultural maintenance in the Indian community are local control of Indian schools and the development of Native language programs. Traditionally, government policy for Native schools has been either blatant or subtle assimilation. That trend has at least been temporarily halted as Native parents have made their wishes known. They insist on having a part in the administration and operation of schools which enroll their children. Our case study of the locally-run school by the Alexander Band deals with the questions which have to be resolved in order to make such a transition effective.

As Native people continue to reflect on the cultural costs of the cultural clash with the Europeans to their way of life, many traditional ways resurface. One such renaissance is the strengthened role of Native Elders. Now, to a renewed degree, respected men and women who offer guidance and wisdom for the future of their tribe are being sought out and consulted. In turn, their enhanced role has served to provide a stronger spiritual base to the Native community. Simultaneously, with the movement to revive past strengths, Native leaders are aware of the need for the next generation to participate fully in 20th-century institutional life. Their youth are encouraged to enroll in institutions of higher learning with a view to obtaining the training essential to dealing effectively with government and surviving in a society fraught with political maneuvering. The point at which the "rubber hits the road," however, has to do with the attitude that Canadians generally have toward Native peoples. Many Canadians believe that Native people are simply part of the multicultural mosaic that makes up the nation. They perceive that the needs and wants of Native peoples should be handled in the same way as those of other cultural minorities or immigrant groups. Native people disagree, contending that their claims have *a priori* status, based on a number of considerations, not the least of which is the fact of first occupancy. Only the future will reveal the extent of success by Native people in this regard.

As is always the case when one puts together a book of this nature, one builds up a long list of the names of people to whom one becomes "beholden." At the risk of overlooking someone, and hoping in advance for their understanding, I would like to thank my friends in several different Indian communities where I have had opportunity to work for sharing their insights about Indian culture with me. This would include individuals in the Blackfoot, Cree and Chipewyan communities, but particularly members of the Stoney Indian Tribe at Morley, Alberta, who have taken time to teach me something of their ways over the many years that I have had opportunity to work with them. They have been patient and kind, and if this volume in any way reflects fairly on their concerns and hopes, they deserve the credit for it.

I would like to thank my secretary, Martha Loeman, for typing the various drafts of this work with dedication and cheerfulness. I want to express appreciation to my wife, Virginia Agnes, for helping proofread the manuscript, but I also want to mention that her support and encouragement in so many other ways are of a far greater value than can be expressed here. On the practical side, I want to acknowledge a grant from the office of the Secretary of State which helped this project to its conclusion. Finally, I want to express appreciation to my students who have over the years furnished me with a "discussion laboratory" in which I might experiment with my ideas. I trust that these contents will inspire many more meaningful and fruitful discussions for them and for other readers.

J.W.F.
The University of Calgary

Becoming Familiar

1

Highlights of Western Canadian Native History

John W. Friesen

Casual observers of Native culture are not usually aware of the legal and cultural subcategories of the Native community, namely that several statutory distinctions are important. To begin with, there are about 444 000 Status Indians in Canada, that is, persons who are legally recognized as having a right to that position courtesy of the *Indian Act*. In addition, some experts estimate that there are at least a million other Native people who are considered non-Status in legal terms. Sometimes these people are also called Metis or "mixed peoples," even though the term has distinct historical origins during the fur trade era of the 17th century.

Metis people are actually the descendants of marriages between French fur traders and Woodland Cree Indian women. A shortage of women among incoming peoples, most of whom were male fur traders, prompted these men to turn their eyes toward Indian communities for mates. The bush (Woodland) Cree were a ready target of attention because of their involvement in the fur trade. Thus a new people was born for the new nation, comprising a mixture of the old and the new. In the words of Bruce Sealey, "These Metis are the true Natives of Canada. Indians and Europeans were immigrants — only the millennia separated their penetration into the New World. The meeting of the two races produced a mixture which was not from another land, but whose sole roots were in the New World" (Friesen and Lusty, 1980, vii).

Contemporary nomenclature fails to differentiate among the various designations of Native peoples, but the most popular choices are "Native peoples" and "Aboriginal peoples," the former applying to persons having some Indian bloodlines, and the latter referring to the original inhabitants of the nation, i.e., Indians, Inuit and (according to their leaders) the Metis. The latter group, with some exceptions, have been recognized as a legal entity by the federal government, only since 1972. The Dominion Bureau of Statistics, on the other hand, has not recognized the separate existence of the Metis, and there are no population statistics of birth, morbidity or death rates pertaining to the Metis in the territories. In effect, they may have been included in the categories of

"Native Indians, Eskimos, Whites and Others," but those designations would depend on the location of their residence. They were included in the 1941 census and again in 1981; however, for the most part, the identity of the Metis exists by implication in the annals of Canadian history. Too often, they are, as Sealey notes, "Canada's forgotten people" (Sealey and Lussier, 1975).

The Challenge of Public Image

"Everybody knows about the Indians," the saying goes, for they are one of the "problems" which the nation has to deal with. A Native writer, Gilbert Oskaboose, put it this way in answer to the question, "What's it like to be an Indian?"

> Well, . . . on one of my bad days I would say that . . . to be Indian is to be expected to be an expert on all things pertaining to the Great Outdoors. An Indian must be totally familiar with the Indian, English and Latin names of all Canadian flora and fauna, by fully cognizant of their medicinal properties . . . and aside from knowing most moose by their first names, be able to converse fluently with at least 15 separate species."

Oskaboose goes on to denigrate typical stereotypes about Indians namely that their religion consists of worshipping totem poles and rocks, their war losses were always heavy in early western movies, and their situation (or "plight"), is subject to endless commiseration by Canadians (Oskaboose, 1980).

Negative statistics about Indians also abound, many of them sadly grounded in fact. For example, in the 1970s it was reported that infant mortality among Native people was more than twice that of other Canadians, household incomes below the poverty level were almost three times that of the nation, and life expectancy was half that of the rest of Canadians generally. In addition, the suicide rate among Native peoples was 19.7 per 100 000 population while that of the nation generally (including Natives) was 9.7. Unemployment among Native people was 50 percent, while the nation was enjoying an unemployment rate of only 6 percent (*Maclean's*, May 1973).

Ten years later, things had not changed much in the Native community. Infant mortality among Indians specifically was still twice that of the nation, the average age at death among Indians was 43 years, while the nation generally lived to age 67, and nearly half of the Indian population was still living below the poverty line. In addition, 68 percent were on welfare, and the suicide rate for Indians was six times the national average. On another front, it could be noted that while Indians constitute about 2 percent of the Canadian population, 8.7

percent of them are in jail at any given time. Most of the crimes for which they are incarcerated are alcohol-related (Frideres, 1988).

Negative statistics emanating from conditions within the Native community have led many observers to encourage the quick demise of their culture as a means of resolving what is often envisaged as an unfortunate national dilemma. A Calgary newspaper, some 20 years ago, commented on a lecture given locally about Indians by Dr. Harry Hawthorn of the University of British Columbia. Hawthorn lamented the passing of Indian culture, while the paper reciprocated by suggesting that it would not be a bad thing if Indian culture became a part of the Canadian mainstream; after all, "too much of Indian culture is really nothing but a poverty culture in this day and age. It spells out human suffering and reserve degradation, and the sooner it disappears the better" *(Calgary Herald,* February 17, 1971). The paper did allow that certain elements of Native culture should be preserved, "the arts, the crafts and some of the traditions," and this should be undertaken in the same manner that other Canadians have remained conscious of their heritage.

Native peoples have not always fared well at the hands of well-meaning anthropologists either, many of whom have no doubt also been influenced by their own cultural perspectives. Grinnell, writing about Indians at the turn of the century noted that "The Indian has the mind of a child in the body of an adult . . . . his mind does not work like the mind of the adult white man . . . by this I mean that it is a mind in many respects unused, and absolutely without training as regards all matters which have to do with civilized life" (Grinnell, 1900, 7-8). Grinnell may have been correct in his observation that Indian cultures thrived on different kinds of knowledge than their European counterparts, for he did admit that in terms of matters familiar to the Indian he manifested insights that would astonish even the white man "who is here on unfamiliar ground," but Grinnell could not refrain from making remarks that implied the superior intelligence of his own colleagues.

Another early 20th-century writer, John MacLean, was less subtle, and named one of his books about Indians *Canadian Savage Folk*, thereby revealing his concept of their cultures as uncivilized communities. MacLean delineated six types of religion among North American Indians, namely: (1) Shamanism, (2) Totemism, (3) Sun Worship, (4) Sabianism or Sky Worship, (5) Hero Worship, and (6) Ancestor Worship. MacLean contended that Shamanism was the lowest form of religion to be found, and it was practiced by the Eskimos, the Tinne tribes of Athabasca and certain tribes in British Columbia. (MacLean, 1986). Today we marvel at MacLean's designation of any religious form as being the "lowest" and wonder if his own culture did not produce the scale which he employed to rank the various religions.

One of the pioneers of American anthropology, Ruth Benedict, sparked a minor furor when she decided that Indian cultures could be divided into modal personality types. She suggested that Northwest coastal Indians were "Dionysian" in personality, or aggressive, prestige-seeking and competitive, while southwest Indians were "Apollonian" or peace-loving, laid back and more reconciled to nature (Benedict, 1934). Benedict went further to denounce the potlatch feast of the Kwakiutl tribe as wasteful and observed that it ranked low on the human scale of values. She was brought up short by a colleague who demanded to know where she got the scale by which to evaluate that cultural practice and she was forced to admit that it was of her own making.

Of course, other anthropologists followed similar lines of thinking when it came to Native cultures; Robert Lowie entitled a book on Indian beliefs, *Primitive Religion* (Lowie, 1924), and Diamond Jenness could not resist describing Indian religion as "crude" and "curious" (Jenness, 1924, 181-183). These statements are not intended to denigrate the work of anthropologists as much as to point out that observers of Indian culture, regardless of their professional affiliations, have from the beginning tended to make judgements about Indian culture from their own ethnocentric perspectives. On the positive side, while it may be true that we have made some headway in this respect, there is still much to do in rectifying past misjudgements.

Some hope for setting the record straight about the Native way of life emanates from the Native sector itself. Today there are increasing numbers of published books which describe the traditional Indian way of life and their hopes for the future, penned by Native writers. It would be idealistic to suggest that these works will necessarily produce an accurate picture of Native cultures since at least a few of the writers will be tempted to paint a little brighter picture of that way of life if only as a means of retaliation (Friesen, 1985). Nevertheless, these writings comprise a step in the right direction, namely that the Native side of things is at last being told. Perhaps for a little while at least, observers will have to walk that thin line in between the two writing perspectives, Native and non-Native, in order to decipher a true picture of Native culture and philosophy.

The Fur Trade

Unlike other cultural groups in Canada, Native peoples have a heritage of political conquest. Often the targets of resource-hungry and insensitive governments and church politics of cultural domination, Indians have a history highlighted with politics and certainly not dry reading. In fact, most of the initial intercultural contact between Natives and incoming Europeans was fraught with a view to eradicating Native cultures if necessary to prepare the new world for "civilization."

When the fur traders arrived in the 17th century they established the parameters by which Native cultures would be viewed during the centuries that followed. First of all, the Aboriginals were seen as a common culture with little regard for the inherent diversity among them. In all, there were as many as 2 000 distinct Indian languages spoken by the original inhabitants at the time of European contact, with 22 separate cultural areas identifiable in North America. Canada alone comprised 11 separate language families with 50-58 separate languages spoken (Morrison and Wilson, 1986).

The cultural variations among Native peoples traditionally were as great as they are today among any other cultures — European, Asian or North American. This fact is somewhat difficult for outsiders to comprehend in light of the habit of describing Native cultures as an entity separate from the cultural mainstream. Another related misconception is the tendency to think of Indian tribes specifically as always having occupied the areas in which they currently reside. In reality, some of the tribes engaged in substantial migrations. For example, the two main Cree tribes today were probably of the same origins. They were all Woodland peoples. Today, however, the designation between the Woodland or Bush Cree and Plains Cree is commonplace. Originally this tribe came west with the fur trade and gradually subdivided into Woodland and Plains people. The former tribe comprised the mainstay of the fur trade, while the latter group became primarily a buffalo people. In making this adaptation, they developed a culture not unlike that of the Blackfoot who also came west with the fur trade (Patterson, 1972; Dempsey, 1979).

Initially, the Crees welcomed the fur trade because it gave them access to goods not locally obtainable. Moreover, they liked to hunt, and the added impetous of trading off their goods enhanced their motivations for that undertaking a great deal. The Blackfoot were less directly involved in trading, preferring instead to act as suppliers of food, chiefly buffalo meat, and sellers of horses to trading posts. The animosity ascribed to Cree-Blackfoot relations today originated in the fur trade, each tribe being very jealous of anyone hunting in their territory.

If there were differences in the way the Natives accepted the newcomers of the fur trade, there were even greater differences in the way the fur trading personnel regarded them. To the south, the Spanish attempted to conquer the Indians for economic purposes, resulting in a colonization of the Indians. Religious missions were an important element in "civilizing" the Indians and intermarriage between the two groups was commonplace. Further north, the French traders acted in a similar fashion, even encouraging intermarriage as a means of cementing relations for a continuing successful fur trade. As noted earlier, this attitude eventually led to the origins of the Metis people. The English traders were not as kind, preferring to hold their new acquaintances at arm's length, rarely allowing Indian hunters into their trading posts as visitors (Patterson, 1972, 92). Both the English and French, however, were interested in establishing permanent settlements in the new world, primarily as a means of obtaining lucrative economic rewards. Both needed the Indians as allies in their quest, and despite the more hospitable attitude on the part of the French, the English eventually dominated. Their success was largely attributable to the efforts of the Hudson's Bay Company established in 1670. After a series of clashes between the Hudson's Bay Company and the French-established Northwest Company, things came to head when the English officially gained control of the Hudson's and James Bays through the Treaty of Utrecht in 1713 (Francis, et. al., Vol. 1, 1988, 340-341).

The fur trade brought about a series of major cultural upheavals among Native peoples, characterized perhaps by intermarriage. Social, political and economic changes also came about, many of them subtle enough not to be noticeable at first glance. Other changes like the introduction of the horse and the gun were immediately obvious. The effect of cultural changes was significant, for example, in the redefinition of the role of the Indian chief or headman. Accustomed as they were to functioning according to European social structures, fur traders usually sought out persons in authority when beginning the bargaining process, and thus the office of chief soon took on an added importance among Natives. Traditionally, the authority of the chief was limited, and was maintained primarily on the basis of his/her successes as a warrior or hunter. When the traders concentrated their efforts on the chiefs as negotiators, and lavished gifts on them in order to enhance their chances of good trade, the office began to take on added importance. Trade negotiators preferred to deal with the same individual year after year, and thus the chief's office grew to be a political force not previously recognized as such by the Natives themselves (Ray, 1974, 137). That prestige has been maintained to this day, accompanied by the traditional expectation that a chief will also supply and care for his/her people.

Ascribing importance to the office of chief worked to the advantage of fur traders in another way as well. If a tribe brought in a lower number of furs than expected, company negotiators withheld gifts from their leader as means of motivating them to encourage their people to work up to quota. Unfortunately, some of the gifts used to increase fur production worked devastation among the Indians, namely tobacco and alcohol. As gift-giving became more important in motivating the fur trade, larger quantities of both were given out. As Ray notes, competition also encouraged larger gift-giving which in turn reduced the motivation for hunting and lured Indians to spend more of their time indulging in the "indolent lifestyle" (Ray, 1974, 142). Thus the attempt to obtain more furs through gift-giving contributed toward the weakening of traditional Indian culture. Traders tried to stock up and trade more liquor and tobacco to enhance the trade market while the Indians continued to rely increasingly on products which ultimately damaged the fur trade.

As indicated, the introduction of the horse and the gun caused significant changes among Native tribes. The horse culture actually began in the early 18th century in southern U.S.A. via the Spanish colonies domicile in northern Mexico and New Mexico. Later the horse migrated further north to the plains. The horse fit in well with the nomadic moves of the Indians since the animal was valuable for hauling loads of goods on the travois. It could carry enormously larger loads than the dog ever could, and it was much faster. It was also a valuable means of transportation for hunting.

By the 19th century, the demand for horses skyrocketed to unbelievable proportions. It became popular to steal horses as a means of proving one's qualities as a warrior; partially the deed was magnified in importance by the amount of danger involved. To steal the picketted horse of an enemy was a very brave act, to say nothing of the value which a good horse could bring in trade or as a sign of individual wealth (Driver, 1968, 233).

Social distinctions were also made according to the number of horses which a man possessed. Often horseless families would attach themselves to a family with horses, and a band or subdivision of a tribe was thus formed. Social mobility of a new sort became a reality when a young man of a poor family rose to wealth and status by acquiring horses. This was often done through raiding parties; even sons of wealthy families often participated because of being teased into joining a raiding party to show how brave they were (Patterson, 1972, 93). Undoubtedly, the interest shown in rodeos by Indians today is a carryover from the status and significance which the horse wove into the fabric of Indian culture.

The introduction of the gun was a boon to the eager Native hunter and afforded an immediate superiority over the gunless enemy. This was not necessarily the case when the gun was first introduced because of the complications which developed due to the gun's inadequate technology. However, as the instrument improved, its users got to the point that they could hardly live without it. American historian, Walter Webb of the University of Texas, surmised that elements seemingly as simplistic as the six-gun, the windmill and barbed-wire made the West inhabitable for emigrating settlers (Webb, 1931). Imagine the surprise on the enemy's face when he discovered that his foe had fired what he thought was his one-shot musket, only to discover that the enemy continued to keep firing — six times in all. This was the superiority of the new gun. Not only could the hunter continue to stalk his prey if he missed the first time, he could also count on hitting him from a much greater distance. To complete the account of the various elements of frontier development promulgated by Webb, he also postulated that the windmill made it possible to access water on the plains from deep wells, and barbed-wire made cattle ranches a reality.

Early guns introduced problems of obtaining ammunition and weapon repair. If a gun failed, it was useless to the owner until he could make a long trip back to the trading post, usually in spring when travel was possible. Repairing guns also made possible a new vocation for men at trading posts even though it was not easy to consult with repairmen during severe winters when travel was restricted. That was a problem confounded with technological ramifications which would require years of catch-up experimentation (Ray, 1974, 75).

The Crees were the first western tribe to possess the gun and soon after, the Blackfoot also obtained it. Each tribe was anxious to obtain firearms once they learned of their existence because of the subsequent superiority the gun would render them in hunting and war (Jenness, 1986, 254). However, it could also be said that its very existence also contributed to strife and warfare, particularly so if the enemy was known not to have guns.

Another bi-product of the fur trade was the transplantation of diseases from Europe, including diseases now viewed as "common household or children's diseases," i.e., measles, whooping cough and tuberculosis. A smallpox epidemic in 1781-82 almost wiped entire tribes out of existence. At the height of the epidemic, some family members lay unburied in their tents while the survivors fled, unfortunately to spread the disease further. It was a fulltime occupation of inland trading post staff to care for sick Indians without even having time to ply their trade (Rich, 1976, 158-159). In the West, another smallpox epidemic in 1837 wiped out two-thirds of the Blackfoot tribe, and again in 1857-58, the dreaded disease hit epidemic proportions. Up till the 1900s it was largely believed by government officials that Native peoples would eventually die out from these causes. Thus the reserves on which the Indians were placed were seen as convenient custodial areas in which services could be provided to the residents on a temporary basis while their most certain destiny could unravel (Melling, 1967, 39).

Partially, the fur trade faltered because of the demise of fur-bearing animals. By the late 1800s, the buffalo had vanished from the plains, and where huge herds of buffalo could once be seen all across the prairies, in just a few years there were only a dozen or so animals in a herd (Symington, 1969, 217). The reasons why the buffalo disappeared are more complex than merely laying blame at over-hunting. To be sure, that did occur; in fact, the Metis are credited with killing up to 100 000 animals in one season alone, exclusively for the purpose of the fur trade. They also killed additional animals for themselves. In addition, sport-shooting took its toll on the lumbering beasts. A Sunday pastime would be to ride a slow-moving train through a herd of buffalo and see how many could be eliminated from each sportsman's gun. Some buffalo actually died from a natural enemy, namely prairie fires, which were sometimes ignited by smoke-spewing, charcoal-spreading trains which rumbled across the prairies. Some animals died from starvation as landspace became increasingly scarce due to its occupation by incoming settlers. With a severe restriction of grazing lands, it became harder for the herds to follow their annual migration trek.

An important factor in causing change in Native culture was the coming of the railway. The national tie of the railroad was completed in British Columbia in 1885, but its effect on the Native community occurred earlier. During the earlier part of 1880s, Winnipeg was viewed as the "Gateway to the West." It was where the rail ended and newcomers to the nation migrated to points west on horseback and by wagontrain. By 1882, a total of 133 000 settlers had arrived in Canada, two-thirds of whom chose the West as a place to live. The settlers came in response to government advertisements offering free land in dryland areas reputed to be excellent for farming. Each homesteader could obtain 160 free acres if buildings were erected and half of the land was tilled within three years (Friesen, 1989, 29; Palmer, 1982). During the peak of immigration, as many as 2 500 settlers left the Winnipeg depot each week and no doubt promoted the expansion of the railway to points west. Two years later, in 1883, there were just 750 miles of track to be laid before the nation would be joined by a steel line.

There was, of course, another important reason for expanding the railroad, master-minded by William Cornelius Van Horne of the Canadian Pacific Railroad. He saw railway expansion as a way to make Canada rich by attracting opulent travellers of Europe's upper classes to experience the majesty of Canada's beauty by touring the prairies and mountain areas by train. He also supervised the building of luxury hotels in the West so that the visitors could be accommodated in style

(Hart, 1983, 28). Many of these still dot the downtown landscape of western cities and smaller centres such as Waterton and Emerald Lake in Alberta.

One can only marvel at the discrepancy in lifestyles which existed between incoming immigrants and touring millionaires. Many of the newcomers came from peasant cultures and undoubtedly their quickly constructed shacks may have fascinated the affluent tourists as an additional attraction of the Canadian wilds. The immigrants, however, were probably too involved in eking out a living to notice the extent of wealth of the passing entourage of opulence.

For the Native peoples, the railway had greater significance. It meant more people in the West, more restrictions on hunting areas, a diminishing number of buffalo for food, and a growing realization that the traditional way of life was fast coming to an end. It would mean an end to a golden age which had only recently been liberated by the white man's horses and guns and now suffocated by even more inventions. Soon the proud and fearless nomadic Aboriginal was transformed into a "pathetic, half-starved creature, confined to the semi-prisons of the new reserves and totally dependent on government for his existence" (Berton, 1974, 374).

Treaties and Reserves

It is sometimes confusing to the uninitiated reader of Native history to decipher the legal complexities of such phenomena as Indian treaties, the *Indian Act*, and the establishment of Indian reserves. A total of ten treaties were signed by the Crown (acting for the Canadian government) with Indian people, although to confuse the matter, it is estimated that after the 1700s, in the pre-treaty era, close to 500 formal "deals" were signed between the French and the Indians alone (Purich, 1986, 96). The first formal "Canadian" treaty, known as Treaty No. 1, was dated August 3, 1871, and signed by the British government with the Chippewas and Swampy Cree of southern Manitoba. Essentially the treaties were agreements about surrendering lands and government payments for such. The terms of Treaty No. 1, for example, included the following components:

1. the relinquishment of the Indian right and title to specified lands;
2. certain hunting privileges;
3. annual payments of five dollars as compensation to every Indian person involved in these dealings (head chiefs and councillors each received $25.00 and $15.00 respectively), as well as a suit of clothes, a British flag and silver medals;

4. certain lands were allocated as "Indian reserves" amounting to 160 acres per family;
5. agricultural implements, oxen and cattle to form the nuclei of herds were offered on a one-time basis to the tribes; and
6. provision was made for the establishment of schools for the instruction of Indian children.

It is of some interest to note that Treaty No. 6 made provision for "a Medicine Chest to be kept at the house of the Indian agent" for the care of Indian people (Burrell, et. al., 1975). Native leaders today have pointed out that the gist of that clause implies free medicare for Native people, while government officials have tried to interpret the phrase in a direct literal sense.

Native leaders point out that while their forebears engaged in these deliberations on a nation-to-nation bases, the full understanding of what it meant to "surrender land" was alien to them. Moreover, these leaders also point out that church leaders whose best interests were not for the Natives' benefit, were often involved in these deliberations, and therefore, the government came out the winner. The element of bias was certainly evident in subsequent actions, because the educational provision of the treaties was quickly relegated to the churches. Thus these institutions could now peacefully promote religious indoctrination along with cultural assimilation backed by government funds. Some religious leaders regarded this as a windfall of sorts, but their joy turned to consternation later on when it became evident that Indian culture was not so easily squelched.

The traditional Native concept of land was that it belonged to no one, and any benefits to be derived from Mother Earth, e.g., the spoils of hunting, were to be graciously received with appropriate thanks rendered. According to some sources, some Indian leaders thought they were signing peace treaties because, most certainly, "stewards of the land" could not bargain its ownership away (Snow, 1977, 28-29). Additional confusion about land negotiations arose because the Native stance of negotiation was rooted in the tradition which fur trading nations had established with Native people. These dealings were done in good faith between two mutually-respecting and independent nations. The fact that European fur companies, both French and English, regarded the Indian tribes as separate political entities is recognized in the literature (Driver, 1968; Jenness, 1986; Frideres, 1988; Josephy, 1968; and Patterson, 1972). This attitude was certainly not the position of government treaty negotiators who saw the Indian in a different light.

By the time of treaty negotiations, government attitudes toward the Indian had changed from positive to negative. Where at first Indians were basically seen as providers of fur, even that position changed to one of mutual negotiation when the fur trade developed its own institutional structure. Later, as the "handwriting was on the wall" about the necessity for economic change in Indian society (due to the diminishing produce of the fur trade), governments saw the Native peoples as victims of the times. The Indian should now be grateful for anything that the government could do for them. Thus, Native leaders negotiated the treaties with the concept of mutual trust and interest while government officials saw themselves as engaged in an act of reluctant benevolence. Suddenly, the Indian became the "White man's burden" who was in need of civilization and in need of His Majesty's Christian influence (Surtees, 1969). Thus was ushered in the missionary era among the Indians.

The first piece of legislation concerning Indians was passed by the British parliament in 1670. It was vague and patronizing in intent, essentially founded in the notion of the Crown wishing to "protect" the Indian. Additional legislation was forged in 1857 (An *Act for the Gradual Civilization of the Indian*), and in 1859 (*Civilization and Enfranshisement Act*). Canada as a nation passed her first Indian-related legislation in 1884, known as the *Indian Advancement Act*, which was followed by the *Indian Act* of 1876 (Frideres, 1988). Initial legal recognition of the Indian was hardly on a nation-to-nation basis with the government regarding them very much as children who needed to learn how to become self-sufficient and civilized. The *Indian Act* of 1951 was specifically utilized as a legal means of determining who would have Indian status in Canada, such recognition also awarding certain immediate benefits. The Act is now used as a basis for settling current land claims.

The distinctions inherent in the *Indian Act* are of great importance today and responsible for the creation of several subcategories of Native peoples. The combination of the implications of the Treaty and the *Indian Act* have created Treaty-Status Indians, non-Treaty Status Indians and non-Status Indians. Some of the latter group also claim the heritage of the Metis Nation and reject the nomenclature of being non-Status. Sometimes Status Indians are also called "Registered Indians" although historically that term refers specifically to the individuals who were enrolled at the first "Indian census." Additional legislation also designates some peoples of the north as the Dene Nation and the Inuit (who were formerly called Eskimos).

The impact of treaty-making on the Indian community jarred them severely when it was discovered that traditional hunting domains were now off-limits. Even after the tribes were ushered onto their respective reserves, many hunting parties in search of food drifted off the reserve and had to be rounded up and brought back by members of the Northwest Mounted Police. In some instances Indians were actually herded onto reserves like buffaloes and the police were charged with seeing to it that they stayed there. Little sensitivity was shown to tribespeople in this undertaking. It was simply announced that Indians would live on reserves and eventually assume a government-approved form of self-government (Wuttunee, 1971, 111).

The formation of Indian reserves was motivated by a series of factors, not necessarily free from paradoxical reasoning. One of the prime motivations for creating reserves was to place the Indians on lands which would not be designated for incoming settlers. The poorer lands, not readily suitable for farming were left to the Indians; after all, they did not make "proper" use of the lands. A more humane reason for the creation of reserves was that they would afford management ease in administering custodial care to the Indians. It was sometimes frustrating to try to "do something for the Indians" when they wandered nomadically across the plains in search of buffalo. One could hardly build portable schools or churches. One priest charged with working among the Indians remarked in frustration, "When the last buffalo is dead, it may be possible to do something for the Indian" (Friesen, 1983, 45-46; McDonald, 1974, 152).

Conceptualizations of the Aboriginal peoples which motivated the formation of reserves also varied. Some officials saw reserves as a temporary essential political necessity since Indian populations were dying out anyway. Others sincerely believed that European-like communities of civilization could actually be developed among the Indians once their new means of livelihood was stabilized. There were even those who regarded Indian people in the poetic way that the 18th-century French philosopher Jean Jacques Rousseau did, namely as the "noble savage." This creature should be saved as a remnant of the bygone days of pre-civilization when people were happy and carefree. It was the excessive use of reason, Rousseau argued, that had made man corrupt (Surtees, 1969, 90; Friesen and Boberg, 1990, 8-9).

The changes to Native culture brought about by the clash with European civilization were almost insurmountable. Most have not been resolved to this day as outlined in later chapters of this volume. The impending agenda for adjustment includes a variety of challenges ranging from land claims to spirituality (Krotz, 1990; Ponting, 1986; Richardson, 1989; York, 1989). However, as the past has shown, the Indian people will undoubtedly prevail, and handle the various threats and challenges to their existence with some measure of dignity and perpetuity.

Missionaries, Churches and Schooling

It would be simplistic to believe that the thrust of missionary activity among the Natives was singularly religious. As far back as the days of Sister Marguerite Bourgeoys, founder of the Order of Ursulines in 17th-century New France, the education of the Indians was a mixture of humanitarian acts with Christian teaching (Chalmers, 1974). Jesuit day schools founded in the 17th century introduced agricultural education and manual training as a means of helping the Indians adjust to the impending cultural shift to farming and as a means of preventing laziness among Indian children (Brookes, 1990, 12). When the success of these schools maintained dismal results, the Jesuits began residential or boarding schools. The idea was that with better attendance, students would experience better success in the classroom. Initially, parents were bribed to send their children to the schools, and they were reluctant to do so because of the long absences they experienced from their children. Learning opportunities for students of the manual schools included choices of mathematics, marine navigation and arts and crafts. The element of integration was also at play in these schools because, while most of the students attending came from non-Native backgrounds, a few Indian children did attend (Chalmers, 1972).

By 1830, the administration of the federal Department of Indian Affairs was transferred from military to civil authority and a new philosophy became evident in Indian schooling. Industrial schools were added to the agenda in Eastern Canada and such trades as blacksmithing, carpentry and cabinet-making, and tailoring were offered to the boys. Girls were taught sewing, knitting, cooking, and laundry work. An evaluation of the success of these schools was undertaken in 1858 and they were soon abolished (Brookes, 1990, 21).

In the West, Roman Catholic missionaries under the leadership of Bishop Alexandre Taché (1823-1896), dedicated themselves to a rejuvination of Indian civilization on the premise that while Indians had once reached an advanced stage of civilization they had lost it because they had abandoned the "traditions which bound them to God" (McDonald, 1974, 151). Industrial schools were part of the package, founded with the secondary objective of recruiting Natives for the priesthood. It was a matter of disappointment to the Bishop that during his administration not a single Native person was ordained to the priesthood.

Also in the West, a Methodist named James Evans began work among the northern Saskatchewan Indians in 1840, accompanied by the Rev. Henry Steinhauer, a Native convert. Evans is noted for his invention of Cree syllabics which gave the Indians the Scriptures and hymns in their own language. Rev. Robert Rundle worked further south among the

Blackfoot and Stoney Indians, largely learning their ways by accompanying them on their hunting expeditions. It was the work of missionaries George McDougall and his son, John, who worked among the northern Swampy Cree and the Stoney tribe near Calgary to build the first Methodist schools for Indian children. Their first mission school opened at Whitefish Lake in which they tried to effect a broader-than-religion-only kind of policy, i.e., "Christianize, educate and civilize." To "Christianize," of course, meant an infusing of the Gospel (Methodist version) into Stoney culture, "education" meant the three "Rs," and "civilizing" implied developing an allegiance to the British Crown. The latter also required the instilling of various "civilized practices" among the Stonies, including democratic procedures of operation and the abolition of certain unacceptable (barbaric) practices such as the Stoney wolf-feast (Friesen, 1974).

Many Native people remember with pain the experiences they went through at the ill-famed residential schools which once dotted the landscape of most Canadian Indian mission fields. This was particularly true in the north where the hardest part was being absent from one's parents and families for extended periods of time during the trapline season. Here families were accustomed to migrating to their traplines for the winter months and returning to trading-post settlements in the spring. An inadvertent benefit of the residential school is that it did provide education for many Native people who today rely on that training in making their claims known to government. There is also some evidence that a kind of fraternity exists among individuals who atttended a particular school, and when they meet on occasion they have meaningful experiences to share (Slobodin, 1966, 114).

The rules of dormitory life at residential schools were demanding and patronizing. Indian children were forbidden to speak their native languages, and they were told that their traditional religion was wrong. Also, the transition from trapline to dormitory life was simply too much for many students who often ran away and were punished severely for it. Boys and girls were divided from each other so that family members of the opposite sex in the same school were often not able to speak with one another. In one school, for example, older boys and girls who wanted to develop friendships could promenade and hold hands from 4:30 to 5:30 p.m., under the observation of dormitory matrons, but they could not step off sidewalks or lean against buildings during that time (McKinley, et.al., 1970). Stories are rampant about children who were caught breaking the rules and the strict punishments that were meted out in that regard.

The death of the residential school was not caused by any inadequacy in the system. Rather, it was a trend of the times toward secularism which ended the missionary era, and religious leaders were sometimes shocked to see their schools taken over by government bureaucrats. The takeover was designed by government officials and inaugerated without consultation with Native peoples. The move was typical of previous dealings with Native peoples premised on the notion that "we must do the best we can for them."

From Federal Involvement to Local Control

In 1949, a Special Joint Committee of the Senate and House of Commons recommended that "wherever possible Indian children should be educated in association with other children." Finally, the committee had solicited the advice of Native leaders and collected a total of 411 written briefs. The final report was distributed among Native people before action was taken (Indian Affairs Branch, 1952). It looked as though the government was finally listening to the Indians.

It was not long before action was taken on the Joint Committee's recommendations. Administrators and teachers hired by the Indian Affairs Department soon took over mission schools, and provincial departments of education were charged with looking after the education of non-Status Natives. In response, the provinces soon formed separate school districts for these purposes. In the West, for example, Alberta established the Northland School Divison in 1960, and Manitoba set up the Frontier School Division in 1965. Missionary domination was over and secularism had come to the Native community. As with most innovations, however, these arrangements introduced new challenges, i.e., establishing relevant training programs for teachers of Native children, developing appropriate curricula which would recognize Indian values and heritage, and formulating a workable pedagogy that would meet the needs of the Native student and afford a personally-satisfying success rate (Friesen, 1977).

The developments toward government-run Native schools opened the way for additional input into education by Native people, although at first this was initiated only on an advisory basis. The first Native education committees were basically charged with caretaking functions such as: attendance and truancy, care of school grounds, special disciplinary problems, scholarships and extracurricular activities. Realizing the limited nature of effect in managing these important but secondary responsibilities, Native peoples soon agitated for additional input. The result was locally-run Native schools. This development, along with other contemporary Native challenges is outlined in a later chapter of this book.

References

Benedict, Ruth. (1934). *Patterns of culture.* Boston: Houghton-Mifflin.

Berton, Pierre. (1974). *The national dream: the last spike.* Toronto: McClelland and Stewart.

Brookes, Sonia. (1990). "An Analysis of Indian Education Policy, 1960-1989." Unpublished M.A. Thesis, University of Calgary.

Burrell, Gordon, Robert Young and Richard Price, eds. (1975). *Indian treaties and the law: an interpretation for laymen.* Edmonton: Indian Association of Alberta.

Chalmers, John W. (1972). *Education behind the buckskin curtain.* Edmonton: University of Alberta.

Chalmers, J. W. (1974). "Marguerite Bourgeoys: Preceptress of New France," *Profiles of Canadian educators.* Robert S. Patterson, et. al., eds. Toronto: D.C. Heath, 4-20.

Dempsey, Hugh A. (1979). *Indian tribes of Alberta.* Calgary: The Glenbow Museum.

Driver, Harold E. (1968). *Indians of North America.* Chicago: University of Chicago Press.

Francis, R. Douglas, Richard Jones and Donald B. Smith. (1988). *Origins: Canadian history to confederation,* Vol. 1. Toronto: Holt, Rinehart and Winston.

Frideres, James. (1988). *Native peoples in Canada. Contemporary conflicts,* 3rd edition. Scarborough, Ontario: Prentice-Hall.

John W. Friesen, (1974). "John McDougall: The Spirit of a Pioneer," *Alberta historical review,* Vol. 22, No. 2, 9-17.

John W. Friesen. (1977). *People, culture and learning.* Calgary: Detselig Enterprises.

Friesen, John W. and Terry Lusty. (1980). *The Metis of Canada: an annotated bibliography.* Toronto: Ontario Institute for Studies in Education.

Friesen, John W. (1983). *Schools with a purpose.* Calgary: Detselig Enterprises.

Friesen, John W. (1985). *When cultures clash: case studies in multicuturalism.* Calgary: Detselig Enterprises.

Friesen, John W. (1989). "The Human Side of Prairie Settlement," *Multicultural education journal,* Vol. 7, No. 2, November, 28-36.

Friesen, John W. and Alice L. Boberg. (1990). *Introduction to teaching: a socio-cultural approach.* Dubuque, Iowa: Kendall-Hunt.

Grinnell, George Bird. (1900). *The North American Indians of today.* London: C. Arthur Pearson, Ltd.

Hart, E.J. (1983). *The selling of Canada: the CPR and the beginning of Canadian tourism.* Banff, Alberta: Altitude Publishing Co.

Indian Affairs Branch. (1952). *Annual report.* Ottawa: Department of Citizenship and Development.

Jenness, Diamond. (1986). *The Indians of Canada.* Toronto: University of Toronto Press.

Josephy, Alvin M. Jr. (1968). *The Indian heritage of America.* New York: Alfred A. Knopf.

Krotz, Larry. (1990). *Indian country: inside another Canada.* Toronto: McClelland and Stewart.

MacLean, John. (1896). *Canada's savage folk.* London: William Briggs Company.

McDonald, N. G. (1974). "Alexandre Tache: Defender of the Old Regime," *Profiles of Canadian educators.* Robert S. Patterson, et.al., eds. Toronto: D.C. Heath, 141-166.

(n.a.) "About Indians," *Maclean's magazine,* May, 1973, 29.

Melling, John. (1967). *Right to a future: the Native peoples of Canada.* Toronto: T.H. Best and Co.

Morrison, R. Bruce and C. Roderick Wilson. (1986). *Native peoples: the Canadian experience.* Toronto: McClelland and Stewart.

Oskaboose, Gilbert. (1980). "To be Indian," *Indian news,* Vol. 21, No. 8, November, 3.

Palmer, Howard. (1982). *Patterns of prejudice.* Toronto: McClelland and Stewart.

Patterson, E. Palmer. (1972). *The Canadian Indian.* Toronto: Macmillan.

Ponting, J. Rick., (ed.). (1986). *Arduous journey: Canadian Indians and decolonization.* Toronto: McClelland and Stewart.

Purich, Donald. (1986). *Our land: Native rights in Canada.* Toronto: James Lorimer.

Ray, Arthur J. (1974). *Indians in the fur trade: their role as trappers, hunters and middlemen in the lands southwest of Hudson Bay,* 1660-1870. Toronto: University of Toronto Press.

Rich, E. E. (1976). *The fur trade and the northwest to 1857.* Toronto: McClelland and Stewart.

Richardson, Boyce, ed. (1989). *Drumbeat: anger and renewal in Indian country.* Toronto: Summerhill Press.

Sealey, D. Bruce and Antoine S. Lussier. (1975). *The Metis: Canada's forgotten people.* Winnipeg: Manitoba Metis Federation Press.

Slobodin, Richard. (1966). *Metis of the MacKenzie district.* Ottawa: Centre Canadien de Recherches en Anthropologie, Universite Saint-Paul.

Snow, Chief John. (1977). *These mountains are our sacred places: the story of the Stoney people.* Toronto: Samuel-Stevens.

Surtees, R. J. (1968). "The Development of an Indian Reserve Policy in Canada," *Ontario historical society,* Vol. LXI, 87-99.

Symington, F. (1969). *The Canadian Indian.* Toronto: McClelland and Stewart.

York, Geoffrey. (1989). *The dispossessed: life and death in Native Canada.* Toronto: Lester & Orpen Dennys.

Webb, Walter Prescott. (1931). *The great plains.* New York: Gosset and Dunlop.

Wuttunee, William I.C. (1971). *Ruffled feathers.* Calgary: Bell Books.

2
Native Cultures in a Cultural Clash

John W. Friesen

A farm magazine once sponsored an essay contest which, on conclusion, awarded a prize to a young Indian boy. The contest featured a picture of a deserted farmhouse on a desolate sand-swept field. Contestants were asked to describe what the scene meant to them. The Indian lad outlined an unfortunate turn of events which culminated in devastation and loss. He described how the owner of the farmhouse, obviously a white man, had cut down too many trees and built too big a teepee. As a result, everything deteriorated. In his words, "Grass gone, door gone . . . whole place gone to hell." His implied solution was to have followed the Indian way instead. This would have meant keeping the trees and grass for the buffalo and then living off the buffalo. This plan would provide hides for a teepee and for mocassins. It would provide food and eliminate the need for job-hunting. In comparison to the white man's way of life, the boy observed, "Indian no hunt job. No work. No hitch-hike, No ask relief, No build dam. No give damn. White man crazy."

The essay underscores the fundamental and underlying difference between Indian and non-Indian cultures. The difference is one of values — capitalistic versus communal, a folk society orientation instead of that of a secondary society. Quickly forgotten by many observers of the Native way, the fact is that at one time pretty well everyone lived the way the Indians did at the time of the European invasion. It was a pre-industrial way of life in a pre-technological time period. In that primarily rural configuration, relationships meant more than career success, and machines did not dictate time-lines. Nature determined most of the vicissitudes of everyday living and religious beliefs determined the essence and direction of life. These observations are not intended to argue for the "superiority" of the traditional Native way (no matter how tempting that may be), but merely to provide what is unfortunately too simplistic a line of demarcation that will aide in differentiating Indian philosophy from that of contemporary dominant society.

Perhaps the most significant observation that can be made about Native cultures is that they survived quite nicely for thousands of years before the European invasion. The impact of this statement may easily be diminished when attention is diverted to the events which have transpired since the Indians and the incoming Europeans first made contact. For the most part, historians have concentrated on Native adaptation to the cultural impact of the incoming Europeans and the previous millenia of Indian history are either forgotten or glossed over. Some of the major features of the missing story which must be emphasized include the reality of the wide range of cultural and linguistic diversity within the Aboriginal communities, their tremendously intricate religious system, and their implicit, often covert social structure. Most importantly, reliance on the oral tradition among Native cultures often deluded the European invaders to believe that the Native peoples did not *have* a history.

The impact of the oral tradition must not be glossed over. As time goes on, the benefits and perplexities of this tradition are becoming better known. Although the practice does not foster a written documentation of the essence and activities of any cultural configuration, the underlying belief is that it encourages a living culture, one that is not dictated to by the past. The past *is* respected, even revered, but it does not determine change nor future growth. As time goes on and the impending social, economic and geographic forces in any culture entangle themselves with the people, the living pattern of a culture changes. Social commentators enjoy documenting these changes, and leave them for succeeding historians to analyze. In Native settings, neither the documentation nor the analysis of activities is of special significance; only reality of life at any given moment is important.

The fundamentals of Native culture were traditionally perpetuated through the process of relating legends. In the Stoney tribe, for example, these legends existed for several purposes, but primarily they had three purposes: they were told because they transmitted cultural information, they were told for amusement, and they were relied on for the impartation of moral and spiritual truths. The legends which were perpetuated for *spiritual* teaching were regulated by a series of special rules, namely that they could only be related by a recognized spiritual Elder, and the particular version told by that person *belonged* to that individual. Changes in a storyline were readily acceptable from one storyteller to another as well as to changes made to a particular story by the same individual at different tellings. Variations in the storyline could be affected by time and place as well as by the perception of the storyteller. If he or she perceived that a particular version was appropriate to a particular situation, changes would be made (Friesen, et.al, 1989; Snow, 1977).

Current attempts to record some of the legends told by Indian tribes have been subjected to criticism from Elders who believe that once they are put into written form they may become public property and lose the vitality which the oral tradition tends to preserve. It is often surprising to outsiders just how much strength legend telling has in the structure of Stoney Indian culture.

Piecing together the various aspects of even one of the various traditional Native cultural configurations is at best a somewhat dubious process. The diversity of patterns among the tribes of any given geographic area are considerable. Plains cultures vary vastly among themselves, and cannot easily be compared with southwestern tribes or tribes of the Pacific West Coast, etc. Nevertheless, for the purpose of trying to fulfill the mandate of this chapter, it might be justifiable to attempt to: 1) foster *some* appreciation for the vast differences between traditional Aboriginal cultures and those emanating from other continents; and, 2) provide a general historical background of Native cultures which may encourage a better understanding of the contemporary challenges facing Native peoples outlined in the balance of this volume.

Anthropological Perspectives

It is intriguing to compare the orientation of the anthropologists who provided the first detailed writings about Indian cultures with those later expounded by Native writers. For the most part the early anthropologists offered a picture of Indian cultures which incorporated an admixture of admiration and curiousity. Mainly they were impressed with the survival techniques of the Indians, but they could not refrain from describing elements of the Native society as "problematic," particularly with regard to schooling (Wax, et. al., 1964; Hanks and Hanks, 1950).

As time passed, however, the objectivity of the anthropologist appears to have increased, although it may also be said to reflect the social values of the time of each writing. At the turn of the century, Grinnell, for example, expressed surprise that the Indians he encountered lived so close to nature. He indicated that their observations about nature were so astute as to astonish "the civilized man" (Grinnell, 1900, 8). Grinnell allowed that the Indians were certainly not feeble-minded, but when they came into contact with the superior technology of his European counterparts, the Indians were certainly outwitted. Maclean was a bit kinder, and although he entitled the first chapter of one of his books about Indians as "Some Queer Folk," he *did* emphasize that a faithful study of Indian languages and customs would compel the student to acknowledge that " . . . under the blanket and coat of skin there beats a human heart . . . . there is beauty, sweetness and wisdom in their traditions and courage, liberty and devotion in their lives" (Maclean, 1896).

In his study of "primitive world religions," Robert Lowie detected many similarities or universals among cultures, whether they could be labelled "primitive" or otherwise. He noted in 1924, for example, that when Native people grappled with the problems of everyday life, they often employed precisely the same psychological processes of association, observation and inference that their white counterparts did. Lowie stated, "When a Hopi Indian in Arizona raises corn where a white tiller fails . . . he is solving his everyday problems, not only competently but with elegance" (Lowie, 1924, xvi).

In 1932, Jenness compared the social and political organization of migratory and stable Indian tribes and attributed the "success" of the latter groups to enhanced contact with other societies. He postulated that less migratory tribes manifested a more complicated society and more complex political organizations (Jenness, 1986,133)

Driver dared to be more specific about describing aspects of Native social structure, for example, when he referred to the potlatch ceremony which was practiced among West Coast Indians. This ceremony was outlawed by the British government because it did not complement British cultural ways. Driver noted that while the ritual involved the destruction of property, it could be partially justified as better than the loss of lives which occurred through intertribal feuding. He suggested that the practice served as a substitute for physical violence and could be deemed acceptable, " . . . in the stage of transmission from aboriginal to Canadian society" (Driver, 1961, 228).

Hoebel, a contemporary of Driver, expressed admiration for the way of the Cheyennes, particularly their "Great Ceremonies." He could not, however, refrain from making the observation that "the legends that ascribe band names are trivial and trite, often ambiguous and uncertain" (Hoebel, 1960, 32).

Commenting on the role of the Indian Shaman or medicine man, Roland Dixon observed that "in the *lower stages* of culture . . . the medicine man was at once healer, sorcerer, seer, educator, and priest . . . (Dixon, 1908). This is the kind of comment that may at first appear innocuous, but on closer scrutiny it yields the underlying implication that criticisms which appear valid in one cultural context may be entirely invalid in another.

Two other anthropologists, Hanks and Hanks, undertook a longtitudinal study of the Blackfoot tribe in Alberta involving lengthy visits over a period of several years. They premised their study as an administrative problem which would have implications in similar situations where a conquered people are ruled by a foreign regime. Essentially, the problems pertained to the tendency of housing dwellers to allow willful deterioration of their premises and to lose their incentives by living on relief (Hanks and Hanks, 1950). While skillfully executed and exemplary of "true" academic objectivity, the Hanks study contributed to the stance that studying other cultural forms as "problematic" is acceptable anthropology.

Josephy contends that it is essential to know about Native cultures if one is to understand the civilization of the Western Hemisphere. He attributes the negative stereotypes about Indians to this lack of knowledge, stating that what is written about Indians is often superficial, distorted or false (Josephy, 1968, 4). Trigger notes that much of the information about Indians today originated for the purposes of propaganda first, and only secondly as works of history (Trigger, 1969, 5). Many North Americans who read such source books are surprised to learn that contemporary Indians are citizens with a right to vote and many of them participate in the country's activities in the same manner as other citizens. With the exception of living on a reserve, where treaty arrangements make exceptions, Indians earn a living and pay taxes just like anyone else. In addition, instead of diminishing in population, their numbers are rapidly increasing. As their long history has demonstrated, they are capable of a wide range of maneuvers and adaptations, even those induced by the impending forces of assimilation and modern technology (Couture, 1985).

Native Perspectives

Written descriptions of traditional Native cultures by Native writers are of considerably more recent origin than anthropological sources and they promulgate an entirely different perspective. Relying heavily on information from contemporary Elders, it must be acknowledged that much of this information is speculative and in alignment with the oral tradition, not necessarily on written historical documentation. Much of the past is clouded with mystery and informants can only guess at the meaning of traditional Indian values. The extent of preserved knowledge also varies from one community to another. Further, most of that which *was* recorded, and is currently utilized by Native writers, was accomplished by individuals who neither spoke Native languages nor understood their cultures (LaRoque, 1975, 29). Writings by Indians, recent as they are, also paint a more positive picture of the old way of life rather than presenting a purely descriptive view or analyzing seeming inconsistencies or deficiencies therein. Perhaps this stance is adopted as a means of arguing against the negative stereotypes postulated about Native peoples. A few examples may illustrate this observation.

Writing at the time of the formulation of the infamous federal White Paper of 1969 which advocated the breakup of Indian reserves, Harold Cardinal called the policy pertaining thereto as a " . . . thinly disguised program of extermination through assimilation," based on the philosophy that "the only good Indian is a non-Indian" (Cardinal, 1969, 1). He argued that the "good old days" of Indian life featured effective institutions of every kind and fostered a series of corresponding values. For example, Cardinal postulated that the educational system in traditional Aboriginal communities worked because it was designed to prepare the child for the life he was to lead. The end result was that the child knew who he was and how he related to the world and the people about him. Like other Native social institutions, the underlying currents of motivation were spiritual and based on "the philosophy of brotherly love, the principle of sharing in the purification of giving, in the good sense of forgiving . . . " (Cardinal, 1969, 81). Cardinal contended that many Indian leaders believe that if society returns to the old values, ethics and morals of Native beliefs, their social institutions would be strengthened. Unfortunately, there are only deaf ears to this pleading; today's leaders still prefer sectarianism to faith.

Writing two years later from the standpoint of comprising a rebuttal to Cardinal's work, a fellow Cree, William Wuttunee strongly denounced the concept of the Indian reserve as an outdated mode of living typified by "wearing a feather and dancing on one foot." Wuttunee contended that modern Indian culture must move past traditional notions of "buckskin and feathers" and become flexible and relevant. However, like Cardinal and other of his counterparts, Wuttunee believed in the glory days of the buffalo hunt and in the virtues of traditional Indian life — peace and contentment, a sense of relaxation in their concept of time, an appreciation of living close to nature without polluting one's surroundings, and a deep concern for fellow members in the community (Wuttunee, 1971, 117; Snow, 1977, 16). No race of people ever had a stronger love for their families. They never punished their children by corporal punishment, fully recognizing the harmful effects that come from manhandling children (Red Fox, 1971, 21; Pelletier and Poole, 1973). Even the conditions of their physical health has been enshrined as excellent, for the Indian was healthy and strong and seldom sick. The great outdoors provided him with dependable remedies for his few ailments, and he enjoyed life fully even though the rigors of the northern winters brought many hardships (Dion, 1979, 5).

Observers of Native cultures sometimes fall into the trap of believing that because the nature of the structure of those cultures is so different, and often invisible to the outsider, there is no inner structure. In fact, nothing could be further from the truth. In addition to having very specific rules governing every aspect of their way of life, there were very strong foundational spiritual bases on which these rules were designed. Promulgated by the oral tradition, many of the interpretations of the various rituals and practices changed with the times and with the practitioner, but their persistence even in modified form gave structure and meaning to the culture. In the final analysis, the strength to fulfill oneself lay within the individual. Religious purity was a state of being within the self. "If you cannot be honest with yourself, you will never be honest with anyone else" (Manuel and Posluns, 1974, 36).

There are a number of Native writers who convey a note of negativity and disenchantment through their portrayals of traditional Indian lifestyle, particularly with regard to its chances to endure. Frustrated with what they consider to be a relentless campaign of assimilation for the Indian, they describe as purely paternalistic, past and present institutional efforts to intervene in the Indian community, particularly governmental, educational and religious (Sealey and Kirkness, 1973, 198). They assert that efforts by Native peoples to improve their lot on these fronts are thwarted or hindered by interfering government officials and outside do-gooders (Campbell,1973, 156).

The future looks bleak, and the options for Native people are sometimes portrayed as limited and negative. Some writers cast an air of despair about them (Cardinal, 1977, 219); others, disillusioned even with the leadership emanating from within their own communities, predict the possibility of violence as an option (Adams, 1975; Sealey and Lussier, 1975, 194).

Events which transpired in 1990 in the Mohawk community at Oka, Quebec, are but one example of this reality. This happening also resoundly underscores the fact that circumstances which birth conflict and discord find their origins as much in the non-Native world as they do in the Native community. Cultural misunderstandings emanate from two sectors just as meaningful dialogue and conflict resolution comprise a two-way street. The roots of misunderstanding are buried deep in Native history, usually thoughtlessly perpetuated by outside powerbrokers who see no need to understand the Native point of view. The resultant disregard for and manipulation of Native values are often propelled by an impatience for traditional (slower) ways which are seen to impede progress.

Some Native writers, though much aware of the atrocities worked against their people in the past, still manage to postulate an air of optomism and hope (Campbell, 1973, 156-57; Manuel and Posluns, 1974; Snow, 1977). These are not the writings of poets, but of realistic philosophers and politicians who work together hoping for a renaissance of Native ways (Lincoln, 1985). They are well aware that any changes to be effected in their communities will be the result of cooperative effort between Natives and non-Natives working side by side (Erasmus, 1989, 42). This will mean that "ruling class Canadians" will have to give up something for cooperation to be birthed, psychologically as well as in material means, if justice is to be effected (Riley, 1984, 163). Thus, the future of Native hopes for a better world is fraught with a painful kind of challenge for all Canadians, all North Americans in fact. The question remains, "Do we possess enough of the human spirit of goodwill that we can 'move over' sufficiently, even though heavy costs may involved, and assist Native people in attaining their just due in our society?"

Fundamental Components

One of the basics of Native culture is its inherently religious nature (Driver, 1961; Friesen, 1977; Vogel, 1990). This is a feature that was overlooked or misunderstood by the Europeans who first came into contact with Native cultures, perhaps because they concentrated on the *differences* between Indian beliefs and practices and their own. Had they but paid heed to the similarities of inherent faith structures, they might have concluded that the two systems were not that far apart. Certainly the reward of more recent studies has been just that realization (Seton,1963). Had the first missionaries to the Indians taken the time to develop a more tolerant perspective, it might have occurred to them why the Natives could so readily adopt Christianity; it was precisely because of the similarities that existed between the two belief systems that this uncomplicated adoption could take place (Snow, 1977).

Analysts of the Indian religious scene have debated for centuries the exact nature of the underlying theological postulations. Father Wilhelm Schmidt, for example, argued that the Native system was monotheistic in origin although subsequent departures originated belief in additional spiritual beings (Schmidt, 1965). Anthropologists have been more likely to describe Indian religions as polytheistic in nature, affording greater attention to the concept that lesser gods and spirits were of equal importance to belief in the Great Spirit.

The theological structures of traditional Native religions cannot be ascertained with any degree of specificity because of adherence to the oral tradition. Undoubtedly these structures have often changed to fit the times, but consultation with revered Elders has always been and still is a major avenue for the perpetuation of dominant beliefs (Kirk, 1986; Medicine, 1987). In addition, the many rituals and ceremonies which are still practiced in many Native communities testify to the duration of those belief systems. Space does not permit an elaboration of even the most important celebrations, and only a few will be highlighted. Undoubtedly the most important ceremony among Plains Indians was the Sundance which is still observed by many tribes, supplemented by an almost endless series of pow wows. In addition, many other rituals like dances are held. The Plains Cree still observe a variety of dances, e.g. prairie chicken dance, buffalo dance, horse dance, witigo dance, bear dance, medicine dance, ghost dance, giveaway dance, calumet dance, tea dance, etc. Similar dances are practiced by other tribes although by other names.

A number of important distinctions about Native dancing persist. Generally speaking, some dances are for men only, others for women only. Some are traditional dances while others are "fancy dances." Traditional dances represent the "old ways" and feature movements related to elements of traditional culture, e.g. hunting and gathering and warfare. Fancy dancing originated as a form of competition when ancient tribes used to gather, by chance or by arrangement, and engaged in competetive games. Sometimes the dances formed the summit of the festivities, fostering contests about appearance, agility and endurance (McArthur, 1987, 49-51). These gatherings formed the basis of today's pow wows which are highlighted by the performance of many different dances, backed up by Native singers and drummers and sporting a variety of costumes.

Changes *do* occur in the pow wow ceremony, as the history of the "jingle-dress" demonstrates. Comprising a form-fitting, brightly-colored dress decorated by an array of attached tin cones, the dress makes a striking "jingle" sound in process. Originally inspired by the vision of a holy man on the Mille Lacs Reservation in Minnesota in 1919, the dress spread rapidly through the Chippewa and Ojibway tribes to the Sioux and further north. Still, its popularity eventually waned, and by the 1960s it was rare to see the anyone wearing a jingle dress. By the 1980s, the dress was back, and its users were performing in the proper style of step which resembles the Charleston. A similar revival has occurred in men's clothing featuring a grass dance costume (Horse Capture, 1989).

Explanations regarding the origins and nature of the Sundance vary among its descriptors. Snow suggests that the purpose of the ceremony was "an expression of the joy and ecstasy of a religious life, of being thankful for life, the beautiful creation, the rain, the sun, and the changing seasons." The ritual comprised an expression to the Great Spirit with a prayer for a good future, health, strength and prosperity for the tribe (Snow, 1977, 111). Hanks and Hanks interpreted the ceremony as an occasion for joyful renewing of acquaintance, exchanging property and feasting with bosom companions. In addition, they identified a corollary preventative aspect implying that the Sundance was performed as a form of insurance to guard the people against disaster (Hanks and Hanks, 1950, 25). Hoebel, in describing the Cheyenne Sundance, observed that its purpose for all Plains tribes was world renewal, even though its corollary aims varied from tribe to tribe (Hoebel, 1960, 11).

For the non-Native and unsympathetic observer, the Sundance was a complex and cruel event because of the self-torture aspect which some male participants inflicted on themselves as part of the event (Erdoes, 1972, 105-6). Some anthropologists promoted this position; Jenness observed that the sensational element of the Sundance was unessential and labelled the participants, "misguided devotees" (Jenness, 1986, 316). For this reason, beginning in 1890, the Canadian government outlawed the ceremony, pressured by missionaries who interpreted the practice as barbaric (Friesen, 1983). In symbolic terms, the sacred Sundance tree was torn down and replaced by the cross and a flagpole (Lincoln, 1985, 173). Then, without any attempt to understand the background to Indian rituals, the Christian church service and chapel services of the residential school were touted as the desirable spiritual festivities of the tribe. This attitude forbode an objective understanding of the Sundance, and its basic features survived mainly through secretive practice and reliance on the oral tradition. Several North American tribes omitted the torture element from their Sundance, namely the Kiowa, the Ute and the Shoshone; other tribes included it as a voluntary component while the Dakota and the Ponca tribes celebrated it as a theme (Lowie, 1963, 199).

The traditional commencement of the Sundance in the Blackfoot tribe was announced by a holy woman (Lincoln, 1985, 115), and generally consisted of a formal three or four day ceremony. Jenness argued that the three day event consisted of the following program: the first day was for dancing, the second for spiritualism and the third for feasting (Jenness, 1986, 316). Its initial step involved the building of a sacred lodge for the centre of the camp where the main activities would take place. The call for a Sundance by the holy woman was that the ceremony would be a dedication to a prayer request by the woman. The request might be for the recovery of a sick loved one or for the return of someone who had undertaken a dangerous mission. The woman would offer her thanks in the form of the Sundance in which the whole tribe would participate. The event also gave opportunity for socializing; old warriors could recount their deeds of bravery and young people could learn the sacred ways of their people (Dempsey, 1976, 66).

Elements of the Sundance ceremony were quite structured, for example, among the Blackfoot, the cutting down of the tree for the centre pole of the sacred lodge at the centre of the camp followed very specific dictates. Once cut, the tree could not touch the ground again until it was carried to the lodge site. Among the Stonies, one or more men were selected by the medicine man or woman to make the centre lodge ready for the ceremony. When the structure was completed the medicine man or woman would start the sacred fire. On the fire they would burn sweet grass, cedar branch needles and boughs and other incense dedicated to the Great Spirit. Like all sacred events, the Sacred Pipe would be smoked, its participants seated in a circle, always holding the stem of the pipe in a northerly direction (Snow, 1977, 11).

Even a cursory study of Native ways will underscore the uncanny similarity of religious practices in the Christian (and other major religions) tradition. The elaborate stress on prayers, fasts and visions are universal religious activities. The symbolism of the four directions and the sacred circle are distinctly Native, emphasizing their oneness with nature. Underlying all activities and symbolism was the ultimate and continual dedication to the Great Spirit, undoubtedly the Creator God of the Christian world. If these things do not portray the markings of parallel belief systems, then the indubitable brotherhood of peoplekind is indeed a myth. Had the early bearers of European religion made note of these phenomena they might have eliminated a significant portion of the frustration which the resultant cultural (and religious) clash effected.

The Plains Indian cultural configuration, like many other traditional or folk societies, functioned according to an extended family format. Some tribes had names to designate every branch of kinship from aunt and uncles to the furthest "shirt-tail relative." This also meant that age gradations were important, and older people were respected, children were revered as the precious potentialities of the new stage in the endless circle of life, and the middle group was charged with carrying out the functions of maintaining and preserving life. Children were nurtured into cultural ways through careful verbal guidance and modelling. When it was necessary to offer a more firm form of discipline, it was enacted through ridicule or joking by a relative, not by the parents or grandparents. Often the intended direction of behavior was guided through the telling of a story, perhaps even made up for the occasion. In any event, it was an effective arrangement (Couture, 1985, 7).

The concept of respect was deeply embedded in Native cultures, and individuality was revered as a supreme orientation. It was at the same time operationalized in terms of a form of self-centredness and caring. As Couture observes, the Indians have a sense of ". . . self-reliance, easily perceived as stubbornness; an aloofness that is really a reluctance to ask for or receive help other than in an emergency or crisis; a tendency not to interfere, on a basis of live-and-let-live . . . " (Couture, 1985, 9). At the same time, elderly people who had outlived their usefulness were well provided for. Among the Crees, a place was reserved for them at the left side of the fireplace in the teepee. Thus, the visitor who entered the teepee had to pass directly in front of the older people. The right side of the teepee was reserved for the owners so that the visitor never had to pass in front of them (Dion, 1979, 8).

One may easily be overwhelmed by the nuances of a particular cultural configuration when some of the idiosyncrasies or finer points are sought out. Dion points out, for example, that Plains Cree women had a different form of speech from the men; thus the "same" phenomenon might be identified by using different words (which had the same meaning), depending on whether the describer of the phemonenon was male or female (Dion, 1979, 2). A variety of other strict practices were also observed; for example, a man was never to speak with his mother-in-law, and children were never to pass in front of an older person. In positive terms, these societies also fostered many supportive features for their membership even though their strictures would seem harsh to the uninitiated. A child was never without an advisor, particularly as the teen years were approached. Marriage was a simple ceremony, but rooted in a tradition of solidarity and permanence. Each age level featured selected privileges and responsibilities, and though the society was primarily concerned with survival, it offered an abundant share of the "good life" for its participants.

There is a tendency for observers of Native culture to overlook the fact that the traditions of their own cultures were once parallel in many ways to the lifestyles of their Native contemporaries. Sometimes the simplicity of the traditional Native lifestyle seems exotic or extraordinary to the casual observer unless it is realized that every culture is meaningful to those who call it home (Friesen and Boberg, 1990, 154). Still, the intracacies of the various cultures include a vast range. For example, many Native cultures in Central and South America developed very elaborate cultural forms compared to the hunting and gathering lifestyle of the North American prairies (Seton, 1966, 27). In many ways, the Central and South American cultural forms surpassed those brought by the incoming Europeans.

Cultural complications comprise more than structural forms, however; many of them are covert. When the Native and European cultures met on the Canadian prairies, they experienced the shared but difficult challenge of trying to make meaning in the harsh reality of the raw frontier. To accomplish this, the Native peoples developed inner strengths to overcome the harshness of the geographic obstacles. True, for the most part, life consisted of caring for the family by gathering food, and making clothing and trying to soften the blows of northern winters. On the other hand, there were also good times, characterized by socializing, playing games and engaging in various other forms of recreation. Games played an important part in the Native world in more terms than merely having fun. They also played an underlying purpose. For example, when two tribes met unexpectedly on the prairies, their men might engage in a series of competetive games, the object of which was to prove warrior superiority. Many were games of bravery and daring, including taxing horse races and foot races of endurance, often accompanied by forms of gambling. As the games increased in intensity it became obvious that the losing side stood to lose much in terms of honor. This loss was deemed much more important that any physical component of the event.

Dion relates an incident which resulted in the death of a young man whose horse accompanied him to his death in a daring leap over a buffalo jump. By deliberately riding to his death, the young man saved face for his tribe and drew such admiration from his opposition that all could leave the games area with their dignity intact. In fact, in that particular incident, a landmark was named after the episode and the location was avoided for some time, until the ghost of death no longer lingered in the vicinity (Dion, 1979, 15).

The Cultures Clash

The first intention of the incoming Europeans was to trade with the Native people and thus make great gain for themselves. As the invaders turned their attention to agricultural pursuits, however, the perceived role of the Indian began to change. Suddenly the old cultural forms were viewed as inconvenient to emerging society and the newcomers sought desperately to amend the scene with various programs. Within a few decades, settlers were given claim to Indian lands, government officials took care of the legalities of settling the Indians on reserves, and the missionaries began the process of forced assimilation through religion and schooling. As is easily the case in assessing a somewhat one-sided situation, antithetical behaviors can be overlooked. Even in those times, there were also individuals who took the time to study Indian cultures and make note of the obviously positive inherent attributes.

There were some missionaries, for example, who admired the Indian way, describing it as an honorable and religious civilization. In 1636, a Jesuit company said of the Iroquois that it would be useless to erect hospitals for the poor among the tribe since there were no beggars among them. The villagers shared everything, and the whole community would have to be in distress before any individual would be left in necessity (Seton, 1966, 36). One Jesuit missionary with 25 years of service, Father A. M. Beede, described the Sioux as a "true Church of God" with a religion of truth and kindness. He suggested that the tribe had no need for a missionary, so he abandoned that role and studied law so as to become their legal advisor and advocate. He was defrocked, of course, but he spent his last days in service to the downtrodden race of America (Seton, 1966, 38).

The repercussions of the cultural clash between Indian and non-Indian cultures are very much manifest today. The conditions in most Indian communities, economically and socially, are in many instances devastating. The fact that the original cultural "clash" resembled the takeover of one culture over another hindered a genuine exchange or even clash, but recent developments tend to manifest elements more indicative of the latter. Backed by a newly emerging sophistication and experience in the realities of the political world, the Indian people are fighting back. Mingling hope with political reality, their future conquests will undoubtedly find success in a bridging of the gap between theirs and the dominant culture. Quoting from the prophet Isaiah, Chief John Snow prognosticates that the Indians will "mount up with wings as eagles" in claiming their rightful destiny (Snow, 1977, 160). A Lakota Elder, Beatrice Mcdicine, hints at an Indian cultural revival based on the inherent qualities of traditional Indian philosophy combined with the "best of the white world," namely their educational system (Medicine, 1987). Other writers are more persistent and suggest that Native peoples *demand* support for a rebirth of their way of life, socially as well as politically (Cardinal, 1977; Lincoln,1985). If the current drive by Indian people to regain a rightful toe-hold in the forthcoming annals of Canadian history is any indication, that hope will be much more than an illusion. Its achievement will necessarily force a restructuring of the Canadian mainstream, but that occurrance will result in a new form of cultural enrichment.

References

Adams, Howard. (1975). *Prison of grass: Canada from the Native point of view*. Toronto: New Press.

Campbell, Maria. (1973). *Half-breed*. Toronto: McClelland and Stewart.

Cardinal, Harold. (1969). *The unjust society: the tragedy of Canada's Indians*. Edmonton: M.G. Hurtig.

Cardinal, Harold. (1977). *The rebirth of Canada's Indians*. Edmonton: Hurtig Publishers.

Couture, Joseph E. (1985). "Traditional Native Thinking, Feeling, and Learning," *Multicultural education journal*, Vol. 3, No. 2, November, 4-17.

Dempsey, Hugh A. (1976). *Crowfoot: chief of the Blackfeet.* Edmonton: Hurtig Publishers.

Dion, Joseph F. (1979). *My tribe: the Crees.* Calgary: Glenbow Museum.

Dixon, Roland. (1908). "Some Aspects of the American Shaman," *Journal of American folk-Lore,* Vol. XXI, 7. Quoted in Virgil J. Vogel. (1990). *American Indian medicine.* Norman, Oklahoma: University of Oklahoma Press.

Driver, Harold E. (1961). *Indians of North America.* Chicago: University of Chicago Press.

Erasmus, George. (1989). "Twenty years of Disappointed Hopes," in *Drum beat: anger and renewal in Indian country.* Boyce Richardson, ed. Toronto: Summerhill Press, 1-42.

Erdoes, Richard. (1972). *The sun dance people: the plains Indians, their past and present.* New York: Random House.

Friesen, John W. (1977). *People, culture and learning.* Calgary: Detselig Enterprises.

Friesen, John W. (1983). *Schools with a purpose.* Calgary: Detselig Enterprises.

Friesen, John W. (1985). *When cultures clash: case studies in multiculturalism.* Calgary: Detselig Enterprises.

Friesen, John W., Clarice Kootenay and Duane Mark. (1989). "The Stoney Indians Language Project," in *Effective language and education practices & Native language survival.* Jon Reyhner, ed. Proceedings of the Ninth Annual International Native American Languages Issues Institute. Choctaw, Oklahoma: Native American Languages Issues, 30-38.

Friesen, John W. and Alice L. Boberg. (1990). *An introduction to teaching: a socio-cultural approach.* Dubuque, Iowa: Kendall-Hunt.

Hanks, Lucien M. Jr. and Jane Richardson Hanks. (1950). *Tribe under trust: a study of the Blackfoot reserve of Alberta.* Toronto: University of Toronto Press.

Hoebel, E. Adamson. (1960). *The Cheyennes: Indians of the great plains.* New York: Holt, Rinehart and Winston.

Horse Capture, George P. (1989). *Pow wow.* Cody, Wyoming: Buffalo Bill Historical Center.

Jenness, Diamond. (1986). *The Indians of Canada.* Seventh Edition. Toronto: University of Toronto Press in association with the National Museum of Man.

Josephy, Alvin M. Jr. (1969). *The Indian heritage of America.* New York: Alfred A. Knopf.

Kirk, Ruth. (1986). *Wisdom of the elders: Native traditions on the northwest coast.* Vancouver: Douglas and McIntyre.

LaRoque, Emma. (1975). *Defeathering the Indian.* Agincourt, Ontario: The Book Society of Canada.

Lincoln, Kenneth. (1985). *Native American renaissance.* Berkeley: University of California Press.

Lowie, Robert H. (1924). *Primitive religion.* New York: Grosset and Dunlap.

Lowie, Robert H. (1963). *Indians of the plains.* New York: The Natural History Press.

Maclean, John. (1896). *Native tribes of Canada.* Toronto: William Briggs. Reprinted in 1980 by Coles Publishing Company.

Manuel, George and Michael Posluns. (1974). *The fourth world: an Indian reality.* Don Mills, Ontario: Collier Macmillan.

McArthur, Pat Deiter. (1987). *Dances of the northern plains.* Saskatoon: Saskatchewan Indian Cultural Centre.

Medicine, Beatrice. (1987). "Understanding the Native Community," *Multicultural education journal,* Vol. 5, No. 1, April, 21-26.

Medicine, Beatrice. (1987). "My Elders Tell Me," in *Indians education in Canada, volume 2: the challenge.* Jean Barman, et. al., eds. Vancouver: University of British Columbia Press, 142-52.

Pelletier, Wilfred and Ted Poole. (1973). *No foreign land: the biography of a North American Indian.* Toronto: McClelland and Stewart.

Red Fox, Chief William. (1971). *The memoirs of Chief Red Fox.* New York: McGraw-Hill.

Riley, Del. (1984). "What Canada's Indians Want and the Difficulties of Getting It," *Pathways to self-determination: Canadian Indians and the Canadian state.* Leroy Little Bear, Meno Boldt and J. Anthony Long, eds. Toronto: University of Toronto Press, 159-63.

Schmidt, Wilhelm. (1965). "The Nature, Attributes and Worship of the Primitive High God," in *Reader in comparative religion: an anthropological approach.* William A. Lessa and Evon Z. Vogt, (eds.). 2nd Edition. New York: Harper and Row, 21-33.

Sealey, D. Bruce and Verna J. Kirkness. (1973). *Indians without tipis: a resource book by Indians and Metis.* Vancouver: William Clare.

Sealey, D. Bruce and Antoine S. Lussier. (1975). *The Metis: Canada's forgotten people.* Winnipeg: Manitoba Metis Federation Press.

Seton, Julia M. (1963). *The gospel of the redman.* Sante Fe: Seton Village.

Snow, Chief John. (1977). *These mountains are our sacred places: the story of the Stoney Indians.* Toronto: Samuel Stevens.

Trigger, Bruce G. (1969). *The Huron: farmers of the north.* New York: Holt, Rinehart and Winston.

Vogel, Virgil J. (1990). *American Indian medicine.* Norman, Oklahoma: University of Oklahoma Press.

Wax, Murray L. et. al. (1964). "Formal Education in an American Indian Community," *Social problems,* Vol. 11, No. 4, Spring, 1-126.

Wuttunee, William I.C. (1971). *Ruffled feathers: Indians in Canadian society.* Calgary: Bell Books.

3

Role of Native Cultures in Western History: An Alberta Focus

Hugh A. Dempsey

The above title is rather ostentatious, and does not necessarily reflect exactly what is written here. What I want to do is to tell how the Indians got into the situation they are in today. I will be referring primarily to the Indians of southern Alberta, for this is the area in which I have had the most experience. I want to show why Indian people differ from the rest of society today, and what the reasons are for some of these differences. The Indians have good reason to be proud of themselves and yet this pride is all too often lacking. I feel very strongly that if the Indians are going to progress as a people, they must have this pride or they must regain it. There are many reasons why they should and many ways in which this can be done. And I have no doubt that this lack of pride is one of the most serious problems facing the Indians today.

For example, some time ago, on the Cote Reserve in Saskatchewan, a survey was made among the school children. They were given a list of 10 racial or national groups — English, German, Black, Indian, Chinese and so on, and they were asked to list these in the order of preference of which they would like to be. When the final totals were made, the Indians were at the bottom of the list. Now, when you have a group of people who consider themselves so inferior that they place their own race at the bottom of the list of what they would want to be, you can be sure that there is a very serious problem.

A few people, both Native and non-Native, have attempted, over the last several decades, to do something about this lack of pride, without too much success. But within recent years there has been a stronger movement, particularly on the part of Indian people, to regain some of this pride, and much of the success that they are attaining is through their own efforts. A few years ago I had the pleasure of attending a National Indian Cultural Conference which brought together Native people from all parts of Canada to discuss what could be done and what has been done in the area of cultural preservation. Frankly, I found this to be one of the most encouraging Native meetings that I have attended in many years. I will give you a couple of examples of the discussions I heard. One person told of a school in Quebec where they were dissatisfied with having religious instruction once a week either for the Protestant or for the Roman Catholic faith. Finally, some of the people said, "We have our own religion." After some discussion, it was agreed that a third course would be offered in the Longhouse religion. So the students had the choice of weekly religious instruction in either Roman Catholic, Protestant, or Longhouse religion. Now one of the senior people on the reserve who is involved with the Longhouse religion voluntarily comes to the school each week to present information to the students. And from what we can gather, this has been quite successful.

There have been a number of other attempts to introduce cultural training in integrated schools. One example was given in Manitoba, where the Indians asked for and received permission to have a course in Indian folklore at the integrated school. They selected several Elders from the reserve to come to the school and tell various stories of Native folklore. This had some very interesting results. At first, the Indian students themselves were rather leery about the whole idea. They wondered what they might have by way of cultural knowledge that white students would be interested in. But their attitudes changed after the program had been going for a while and were replaced by the feeling that maybe they did have something. This led them to think that maybe everything docs not have to be done the white man's way; maybe they do have a way of their own.

The white students, to a certain extent, tempered the ideas they previously had about the Indians. Living close to a reserve, there were negative feelings that had developed toward Native people. The course gave them some insight into the culture that existed, and still exists, and yet was something of which they were completely unaware. Finally, the Elders who were giving this course started out with a strong feeling of shyness, but as they continued with the course and measured the reaction, it changed their attitudes. In some small way it had an effect on their own feeling of pride in doing something that makes them equal partners of the white man, rather than being on the receiving end.

So there are programs like this underway. There are certainly not enough of them, but there does seem to be a trend to provide Native people with information about their own culture. Much of this, and I speak here as an historian, can come through a knowledge of history.

Indian - White Encounter

I would like to deal with a few points of history that reflect some of the reasons for the loss of pride of the Indian. When the first white man arrived in this part of the country he was given a name, and among the Blackfoot this was "napekwan." If you examine this word, you find that it means "Napi's people." Napi was a mythical person, a minor Creator, among the Blackfoot. It is obvious from the choice of name that the first Indian who saw the white man in this area thought he was some sort of a supernatural being. His skin color was different; he had such things as guns and metal tools, and a technical knowledge that far surpassed anything that the Indians themselves had. So they started, right from the beginning, with the white man in a superior role and the Indians as their inferior. Over the years, the fur trade perpetuated this attitude as the white man dominated the Indian through his superior technology. Later, when the missionaries arrived, they discovered that the Indians had their own religious beliefs which, of course, were at variance with the teachings of the missionaries that Christianity was the only religion and that it should be practiced to the exclusion of any other. The result was considerable confusion in the minds of many Indians. Father Desmet encountered this problem in 1846 when he passed through this region and spoke to a Cree Indian who had been a nominal Christian but had renounced Christianity. Father Desmet went to him and asked him why he had given it up. This man claimed that he had died and then he told Father Desmet the following story:

> Immediately after my death, I repaired to the heaven of white man or Christians where the Great Spirit and Jesus Christ dwell. But they refused to admit me on account of my red skin. I went then to the country where the souls of my ancestors are and there too I was refused admission, on account of my baptism. I therefore came back to this earth to renounce the promises I made in baptism, and to resume my medicine bag.

You can see the confusion that existed and it was a type of confusion that went on for many, many years. Some people, however, were able to rationalize. I can remember a friend of mine, Jack Blackhorse, telling me that he was a good Anglican, a good Mormon, and a good follower of the Sundance religion. When I asked him for his rationalization on this his answer was quite simple. "Well," he said, "there is only one God." To him there was no confusion but to many other Indian people there was, particularly when the missionary was constantly hammering at the theme: "Your religion is wrong. Your religion is evil." Among Native people, religion was not something that was practiced once a week, but it was a part of everyday life. When a person ate, when a person hunted, when a person moved camp, when a person did almost anything, there were religious undertones to his or her actions. If this was wrong, if the Native religion was wrong, then what was left? Again, this stripped away some of the independence and some of the pride of the Native people.

By the time the treaties were made in the 1870s, there was no doubt in the mind of the Indian or the mind of the white man that the latter was dominant. He was the leader. This brought about an interesting situation about Indian attitudes at the time of treaties that even to this day has escaped many people. A missionary, a couple of years after the signing of Treaty Seven in 1877, said that the understanding of the Indians at that time was that they were giving up their rights to their hunting area on the understanding that the white man would look after the Indian from that time forward. This was a logical way of thinking, for the white man had taken the role of domination in a similar way that the chief would take over as the leader of his camp. And the chiefs were leaders because they were generous and kind and because they helped their people whenever they were in need. Leaders were seldom rich because they were constantly giving away what they had in order to help their followers. The white man had taken this role of leadership over the entire Indian people so he, to the Indian mind, took over the same responsibility of a chief. If there was no food, the white man would provide it. If there was no shelter, the white man would provide it. It was a logical line of thinking that grew out of the attitude toward leadership.

After the buffalo were wiped out in southern Alberta and after the Indians had settled on reserves, there was no recourse for the government but to issue rations. Their policy was that there would be an interim period between the time when the Indians lived by depending on the buffalo and the time when they would become self-supporting through farming, ranching and other activities. In the interim, the government would help the Indians by giving them food.

This was the government's attitude, but the Indians' attitude was that they looked after themselves when there was the buffalo but now that the buffalo are gone, their grandfather (which was one name for the Indian agent) "will look after them." He will given them food because there are no more buffalo. The Indian did not look upon this as a temporary measure but as a permanent change. Many of the early Indians could not visualize a type of life that would have them scratching the ground, sticking seeds in, and waiting for things to grow. Many Indians went into the ration system with the idea this was not a privilege that was being given by the government but that it was their responsibility. Then, as the rationing continued, it became permanently engrained in the Indian way of life and developed into the welfare system as we know it today.

Indian Reaction

During this period, the feeling of inferiority among Indian people increased greatly because it was obvious that the white man was a success and that he had many things that he could give the Indian, while the Indian had very little, if anything to give in return. The white man passed laws against Native ceremonies, laws against polygamy, laws against warfare, and so on. At the same time, he said, in effect, that the only way the Indian can be a success is by being like a white man, by dressing in the clothes of a white man, and by gardening and farming like a white man.

Another problem of this period was the steady decline in numbers of the Indian population. By the mid-1870s there were about 18 000 Indians in Alberta, but by the time they settled on the reserves there had begun a steady decline which reached its low ebb after the influenza epidemics of 1918. By 1920 there were less than 6 000 Indians in Alberta. I might add that they are well beyond the 40 000 mark now, but in the 1920s they had reached a low ebb. For a while there was a fatalistic attitude among many of the Indians that the race was going to die. The white people talked about the "vanishing American" and this attitude also existed among the Indians. They felt there was no way that they could stop this decline, that disease was carrying them off, that the buffalo were gone, that there was no future for them, and that they were, in the course of time, going to be wiped out. There was not a feeling of antagonism about this, rather it was a fatalistic feeling.

In spite of this, there were some Indians who were able to retain a certain degree of pride in themselves and in their race. One of the reserves that I have been most closely involved with, the Blood Reserve, had this attitude. In 1889, for example, a Mounted Policeman making his report told about some of the problems he was having with the Bloods. "The Bloods think they are the cream of creation and it is about time they were imbued with some modification of this idea." The pride had not been knocked out of them, but it had been retained. This is perhaps one of the reasons why the Bloods today have such successful programs. The Kainai Industries plant, which has been in operation for more than 20 years, is a good example. You must have a certain degree of self-assurance and pride before you can embark on projects of this magnitude.

A number of individuals during the latter part of the 19th century also did well. For example, Chief Moon from the Bloods saw the market for hay, so he borrowed mower and equipment from the Indian Agency, and began filling hay contracts for the local ranchers, the Mounted Police and others. He did so well after the first year that he could buy his own mower and equipment and for some 15 or 20 years after, he was an independent hay contractor. Similarly, on the Peigan Reserve, a man with the name of Big Swan observed that the trail between Fort Macleod and Pincher Creek passed through the reserve, and that the midway point was very close to a small creek. So he built a stopping-house at that point and operated it. His wife served meals; they provided sleeping space for the freighters and other people who were travelling the road, and operated a successful, independent business. In the north, a leader by the name of Pakan, at Saddle Lake, saw the problems of his people. There were no direct employment opportunities in the 1880s, so he arranged that his best hunters would pool their resources and he operated something comparable to a soup kitchen so that the needy could come to a central point and receive assistance that was completely apart from anything that was being done by government.

Probably one of the most dramatic cases of independence was that shown by a man called Black Horse of the Bloods. In the early 1890s he applied to the council for permission to work a coal seam that was up at the north end of the reserve. He hired a number of other Indians as pick-and-shovel people and began mining coal. He obtained contracts, initially from the Indian Department itself, and from the local mission schools, but later he branched out and was soon filling contracts for the Mounted Police. Later he provided much of the coal that was being sold in Lethbridge, Raymond and other towns. Then he brought his son, Chief Mountain, into business with him, and they successfully operated a coal-mining industry on the Blood reserve for some 30 to 35 years. He had Indians hired as freighters to haul the coal and had Indian pick-and-shovel workers. And, interestingly enough, we have at the Alberta Glenbow Museum two examples of his printed letterheads. Even though Black Horse and Chief Mountain could not read or write, they had a regular printed letterhead and also printed invoice forms. They had a young Indian boy who was a recent graduate from the local mission school do their writing for them as well as the work of invoicing and entering into correspondence. There is little that is comparable to this among the Indians in Alberta today, to my knowledge, but it was a very successful operation and continued on until about the 1920s when an unfortunate incident occurred that caused the closing of the mine.

So, during these years there were people who were making the transition. There were some people who accepted ranching because it had some comparable features to the buffalo hunt. Looking after four-footed beasts, travelling around on a horse, and moving from place to place had some of the aspects of their earlier life. Many Indians became quite successful ranchers, and others, particularly those who were graduates from the mission schools, were beginning the first steps of successful farming operations.

Change and Technology

Early in the 20th century an incident occurred which spelled disaster for the Indian people. It has been said that the world went into the First World War on horseback and came out in tanks. I think this is true, and it marked the beginning of the machine age. Until the time of the First World War, the horse was an important beast. A man could successfully operate and live on a quarter-section of land and had to be able to work with his hands. He did not have to be a scientist, or bookkeeper, or pharmacist, or mechanic, or financier; he just had to be able to work with his hands and know the business of farming. Many Indians were doing this, but after the First World War, there came the automobile, the truck, and various tractors, chemicals, complex machinery and mass production. This rapidly changing situation left the Indian people far behind.

Many of the white people had difficulty at this time too. But they had centuries of acculturation to draw upon, so that although they may have had difficulties at first, they were able to adapt to the situation. They could, like a modern farmer of today, become a chemist, a machinist and expert in so many of the fields that are important to agriculture today. But the Indian did not have this. He had his horse, which he was familiar with, and his small plot of ground which he could work manually. But when all the new demands arose and when the cost of farming became high, the Indian found that he was being left further behind. This, of course, became a source of great discouragement and today you do not see this same type of individual success as was so evident prior to the First World War. This was a tragedy of the machine age.

Contributions of Indian Culture

This brings us to the present. The situation started from the onset of the machine age and continued to deteriorate from that point on. At the same time that it was deteriorating, the welfare system became more evident, not only in the Indian community, but in the whole of Canada.

On the subject of pride, there are many contributions that the Indians made to the history and development of Canada. I have had a number of arguments with people about these contributions and have been challenged to name something that the Indians did that is important in history. If I name one item, they say it is not important and, very often, individually, these things are not too significant. But when you put them together, you find that the contribution is quite noticeable and should be a source of pride for the Indian people. Some of these activities were not the sole responsibility of the Indian people but certainly their actions were quite important.

For example, unlike the American West, we had a peaceful confrontation between Indians and whites that was unmarked by bloody wars.

One of the reasons for this was the type of leadership that was available. For example, among the Blackfoot in the 1830s and 1840s, one of the leading chiefs, named Many Swans, was noted as a powerful warrior and a merciless man when it came to dealing with the enemy. This was at a time when the white man was still very much a minority, but other pressures were being felt. The Blackfoot were being pressed by the Assiniboines, the Cree, and other tribes, who were often in closer contact with the traders and were better armed. The tribe needed a strong leader who had his people geared for war. If a more peaceful person had been a chief at that time, the inroads of the Crees and the Assiniboines would probably have been much greater than they were. Many Swans also hated the white man and looked upon him as an interloper. He died in the smallpox epidemic of 1869-70, and the leadership of the tribe was taken by Crowfoot.

Again, Crowfoot was the right man, in the right place, at the right time. He also had been a great warrior and had an excellent war record. But he was the type of man who could see what was happening to his country. If Many Swans had been the chief at the time of the coming of the Mounted Police in 1874, he probably would have opposed them and we could have had a very different picture of western Canadian history. Crowfoot, on the other hand, saw that to fight the white man would end only in the tragedy of his own people. It was a realistic approach and it was one which resulted in a peaceful settlement of the West.

A similar situation existed with the Bloods, where Calf Shirt had been chief. He had a reputation of being a wild character who received his holy power from the grizzly bear. He wiped out the small town of Ophir in Montana and generally opposed the presence of the white man in his territory. He, too, did not survive until the settlement period; he was killed in the winter of 1873-74. He was the only man who might have competed with Red Crow, the head chief of the Bloods, for leadership at the time of the coming of the white man. Red Crow had been a great warrior, but also was a man who recognized the situation and treated the white man as a friend rather than as an enemy.

There were a number of other people who also are important to the history of Canada simply through the role that they played. The history of Canada would not be the same if it lacked the Crowfoots, the Big Bears, the Poundmakers, the Red Crows, the Bull Heads, and the others who were an important part of our history. This gives us something unique in Canada, something that should be a source of pride both for the Indian and the non-Indian. In terms of another contribution, we have also received from the Indian much of the folklore that has been incorporated into parts of the school system, again giving us something that is unique in our country. We have tales of origin and tales of the land that are important to Canadians as a whole. We also have a wealth of place-names. The word "Canada" itself is a Native term. Ottawa, Saskatchewan, Wetaskiwin, Ponoka, Winnipeg — there are many places that have Native names which are now incorporated into the English language. And many other places have names which have been translated into English which are of Native origin. Often they have an interesting and colorful history.

The Indians have also provided us with many cultural artifacts or objects, such as the moccasin, snowshoe, tee pee, canoe, and so on. How important is it to be plodding around the country in a pair of Indian moccasins? Perhaps very little, but when you put this together with the other contributions, I think it becomes significant. Even such things as the Native costumes are important. You will recall a decade or so ago attempts were made to use Indian costumes for modern clothing that were sold in shops as far away as New York. Some features, such as the headbands, have been widely accepted as a part of the dress of younger people.

All of these things together become significant in weaving the Indians into the framework of Canadian culture. Natives are important and should be proud of the contribution of their people to Canadian life.

One of the problems about this situation is that many Indians are completely unaware that their people have made these contributions. There is a feeling on their part that nothing they could offer would be desirable or useful to the white man, and yet this is far from the truth. I think it is important that the Indians, particularly at the school level, be given much more information about their own cultures and history. I do not mean white man's history. I do not know how many times I have picked up an article that purported to be an Indian history, for example, of an Indian reserve. It may say the reserve was set up in 1881; the first Indian agent was appointed six months later; the first missionaries arrived in such-and-such a year; they built their church in such-and-such a year; they established a residential school five years later; and gradually the agency and school became focal points of the reserve. What you end up with is not the history of the Indians, but a history of white administration of an Indian reserve.

I have also read histories, supposedly dealing with Indians in western Canada, that say that Paul Kane, the artist, came west in 1847-48 and painted portraits of certain chiefs. What does this have to do with the Indians? The history goes on to say that Reverend Rundle, a Methodist missionary to the Indians, came west in 1840. This is great news for the Methodists, but I cannot suggest what it did to the Indians. So you see these so-called Indian histories have been written from the standpoint of the white man and what he considered to be important, not from the standpoint of the Indians and what they would feel was important.

Need for Indian Heroes

I think the Indians need their own heroes. I will not deal with Louis Riel because this can be a very touchy point, among both whites and Indians. I have heard more anti-Riel comments from Indians than I have from whites. These are mostly from the Blackfoot, who do not have much use for the Crees anyway. But there are many heroes that could be significant to all Indian people.

I will give you one example of the type of Indian hero that the Indians really do not consider meaningful. He was Maskapatoon, the "martyr of peace." If you go along the highway to Edmonton, you will see a sign about him along side the road on the Hobbema Indian reserve. There have been books written about him; Kerry Wood has written a book called *Maskapatoon* which is available in most schools. Who was Maskapatoon? He was a Cree who converted to the Methodist church, and once converted, became a strong proponent of Christianity. This happened in the 1860s, which was not exactly the best time to be opposed to warfare. In 1869 he went to a Blackfoot camp to talk peace and the Blackfoot killed him on the spot. He thus became the martyr of peace, but to the Methodist church, not to the Indians. I say let the church have its heroes, but do not try to foist them on the Indians. Maskapatoon was not a hero that is meaningful to the Indians; rather I would have someone like Big Bear who was involved in the Riel Rebellion and was part of the Frog Lake massacre.

Big Bear was a man who refused to sign a treaty in the early years because he felt the deal was not good enough. He did not want a one-sided proposition where the government offered a proposal for the treaty and everybody signed it. He wanted to negotiate. He felt that some of the provisions of the treaty were not good enough and he talked other leaders into supporting him. This immediately made him a villain in the eyes of the Canadian government and he was considered to be a troublemaker mainly because he refused to go along with them.

When the Frog Lake massacre occurred, Big Bear was not the instigator and, as a matter of fact, the massacre was about the last thing that he would have wanted. He was still negotiating at that time and was using every peaceful tactic that he could bring to bear to get a better deal. He was smart enough to know that violence and bloodshed would destroy the very thing that he was working for. It was the young people in his camp, Four Sky Thunder and others of this type, who really led off the massacre. But it *did* occur, and it wiped out Big Bear's hopes for success. Here was a man who was a real hero in the eyes of his people.

Then there was another man by the name of Big Rib of the Bloods. I started gathering information about him and another man by the name of The Dog because the Mounted Police said what awful characters they were. Their reports in the 1880s and 1890s emphasized that these men were criminals who were in and out of jail, escaped en route to Stony Mountain Penitentiary, and were at large for over two years.

When I began my research on these two, I asked myself, "How could Big Rib live in a camp of Bloods for two years and not be turned over to the Mounted Police if he was a real villain?" Obviously he was not, as far as the Indians were concerned. My research, and discussion with Elders of the tribe confirmed this. I learned that Big Rib had fought hunger and starvation in the tribe by leading young men in killing white man's cattle. He got nothing out of this, except perhaps a war record, but wanted to provide beef for the hungry camps. This is why he was arrested and this is why he was sent to jail. When he escaped, he was able to remain free for as long as he wished. And while he was free, he still played the role of warrior and on one occasion he went right into Fort Macleod, which was the Mounted Police headquarters, and did some shopping right under the eyes of the Mounted Police. This was an act of sheer bravery that the Indians would recognize as being the actions of a hero. The Mounted Police tried to stop him and took a shot at him but another Indian nearby knocked the gun to one side and Big Rib escaped. He finally surrendered to serve out the remainder of his sentence. When he came back, he was arrested for wounding a Mounted Policeman. He was sent back to prison again and died there of tuberculosis.

I tried to find out why he had been sent to prison, and I finally found an account of the trial which stated that he had attempted to stab the Mounted Policeman who was drunk and was trying to rape Big Rib's wife. The Indian was sent to jail and died there.

These are stories that are rarely told. They deal with a type of people that could be the basis for study by Indians and perhaps provide the type of heroes that the Indians need.

The Contemporary Indian

Finally, I would like briefly to mention another subject — how the Indians of today are different from their white neighbors. An Indian person who comes to a city may be successful in our eyes and yet he may be a failure by Indian standards, or he may not be successful in our eyes and yet be successful in the eyes of the Indian community. There are some obvious differences in the two cultures and these can affect the reactions of people to given situations.

From time to time I have been asked to explain certain questions, a few of which I would like to mention here. First, why are Indians not competitive and why don't they try to do something with their reserves? They have the land and could establish good farms. The opportunities are there, why don't they take advantage of them? With the Blackfoot and probably with other tribes, one of the worst insults you can give a person is to tell him he is "trying to act like a white man." There is a lot of meaning behind this phrase. In the nomadic period, the Indians led a communal lifestyle where everything was shared. A man might go out hunting one day, kill a couple of buffalo and share the food with the others in the camp. The next week his neighbor might go out and hunt buffalo and while he got none, he knew that his neighbor would share with him. This type of life was accepted and still is important today.

So if an Indian comes into the city and gets a job, his relatives may move in with him. Now this man is faced with a choice; he either accepts the way of life in the white community, or he shares what he has. Of course, he will not progress if he shares, in the eyes of the white community — he'll never have the money. Many Indians are faced with this situation in the city and it becomes so impossible that they give up and return to the reserve. On the other hand, if the man turns his back on his relatives and says, "I'm sorry, you can't live with us. I got paid today, but this money has to last me all month," he rejects his relatives, his relatives reject him and he ends up with a very difficult situation.

Another question is about the Indian attitude toward saving. Why don't Indians have bank accounts? Why don't they save their money? Again, one must go back to the nomadic culture, to a people who were living off the buffalo. All they owned they carried on a travois. Could they kill 10 buffalo and carry them around for the next three months? That was not very practical, so they became fatalistic about the future, eating today and perhaps starving next month. This was a way of life and elements of it have carried over to today.

Another problem is that landlords sometimes will say, "I am not going to rent to Indians any more because they leave the place a shambles." Here again, if you go back to the nomadic period you will find definite laws and definite controls. There were certain types of punishment meted out to those who violated the rules. When these people settled on reserves, the government, instead of using the existing policing system to its advantage, stamped it out. This left a situation where the white man's laws were to be followed but there was no punishment that was meaningful to them. A good example of this is the punishment for infidelity. In our society this deviation was often controlled by the attitudes of the community and by religious instruction. In the Indian community, it was controlled by cutting off a woman's nose. But the white man outlawed the practice and believed that women would be prevented from being unfaithful by giving them a good Christian background. But what really happened was that effective Native controls were taken away and were not replaced by any meaningful form of punishment.

People also talk about the Indians' lack of motivation. Why don't they want to succeed? Why don't they try harder? But success by whose standards? By Indian standards or by ours?

In our society the leaders of our people — the mayor, the premier, a leader in business, a leader in industry — are often equated with somebody who is wealthy. This was not the situation among the Indians. Chiefs were chosen because of their ability to look after their people. Very often they were not wealthy people, because they gave everything away to help the needy. For example, in 1881, the Governor-General of Canada visited the Blackfoot Reserve, where he saw Chief Crowfoot. There he observed the chief:

> ... with his finely chiselled countenance and bright smile as, leaning heavily on his staff, and worse clad than any of his followers, he moved forward to his place; the shabby clothes, which the poorest artisan would be ashamed to wear, contrasted sadly with the Victoria medal which he wore on his breast.

The Governor-General saw this very shabby man and recognized him only because of his reputation. Wealth was not important to the Indian leader, nor was the way he dressed. If he was a wealthy man, he used his wealth to help his people in time of need. If Crowfoot had been in a white community with that attitude, people would say that he was not a success because he appeared so poor. I have seen similar situations today where leaders in Indian communities are not considered to be successful by white people because they have no money. Yet they are a success in the eyes of the Indian people.

There are many other problems such as drinking, the time factor, and so on. I will not go into these now, but I do repeat that Native culture has been important to the history of Canadians and that the Native culture is important today to the Indian people themselves, both for having a pride in themselves and for understanding why they may be different from other Canadians. These differences are not necessarily bad, for some of them are quite desirable; but I think it is important that every effort be made to enable the Indians to understand these differences and to understand and to appreciate their own culture.

4

Explorations in Native Knowing[1]

Joseph E. Couture

It is . . . difficult to find a people who over such a long period of time have undergone such destructive influences, yet have survived and preserved their identity so firmly as the American Indian.[2]

The Indian . . . has established a creative response rooted in his ability to sustain life in its moment of high tragedy and to continue the basic path of his human development in its most distinctive aspects.[2]

With our overemphasis on mental activity we are apt to think that the Indian, without any written language, lacks something important or necessary in not possessing a scholastic or dialectical type of doctrinal presentation.[3]

A Story

It began during the first "round" of my first sweatlodge ceremony. Jammed in with many others in the dark, swirling hot steam jetting over my face and body, mistaken stoic warrior I strove to sit straight and unflinching. My ignorant posturing unnerved me, for I panicked, no longer able to inhale the sharp, scalding air. I remained aware that I might bump others onto the hot rocks in any dash to the door, so I frantically grabbed the base of lodge boughs on each side of my hips, and set myself to uproot them. In that split-second of grabbing and bracing to pull up, the lodge flaps opened. As craved lungs lunged at the air, my eyes fell into the full, steady gaze of the ceremonial leader. There, on the backside of a bright twinkle, something told me that he knew what had happened to me. His gaze reassured me, midst extremes of feeling and thought. However, I remained particularly stunned and startled, for, how did he know . . . ?

Since 1971 that intriguing question has kept me in pursuit of the answer. That event began a demanding and arduous quest, a relentless facing of necessary changes, the learning of ways to release blocks to developing a Native mindfulness. A number of rigidly entrenched, myopic assumptions were obstacles within my mind. I didn't understand at first, for example, the key importance of reliance on subjectivity in the learning process, nor did I know how to think paradoxically. A radical reshaping of conventional university induced, scientific thinking was required. From that incipient event, through phases of seeking and discovery, I came to discern the objective validity, paradoxically, of a full subjectivity, thereby expanding my capacity for knowing and my range of knowledge. It has been an extensive exercise in patient eradication of fears, in experiential discovery of Life-Force, of Energy as Isness and Oneness, of my individuality in relationship with self, with others, and with the Cosmos. This personal journey has led me to a strong and growing appreciation and admiration of why and how remarkably enduring the original human of this continent is. I'm grateful for those unyanked boughs. The Exercise, shaped as it is by a Metis-Cree, male life experience, and limited to my present level of attainment in Native medicine ways, continues now through this exploratory essay which seeks to delineate some cognitive dimensions of that experience.

The reader must keep in mind a standing *problematique*, an ongoing learning and communication difficulty stemming from the fact and nature of oral tradition. For example, Elders and their teachings must be experienced and perceived in that context, so that a "right" perspective and direction is maintained. Enlightened grasp of that reality is normally the business of a lifetime, and so this essay can be no more than a wayfarer's report, an inherently tentative enterprise. Elsewhere, difficulties in writing about Elders and tradition-related issues are discussed (Chapter 12). Comments in that chapter hold here as well, perhaps more acutely. Primarily in social science language, without sentimentalism and as carefully as I can, I wish to identify some components of Native thinking, based on the assumption that that is both possible and useful to attempt.

An Encouraging Context

My own attraction to the subject is reason enough to want to hold forth. However, there are signs of late, emergent and compelling socio-cultural signs, which seem to warrant a forthright assertion of who we are as spiritual people, possessors as we are of an unique spiritual heritage and experience. It is true that the Elders who "know" have been reticent, most discreet about sharing and teaching their "knowledge."[4] However, those same Elders now point to an unfolding prophecy, which states that "... the time has come to share the secrets ..." And so, Elders are a first sign.

A second sign is the contemporary ecological movement, and the related current dialogue between physicists and mystics. The analyses and considerations of such internationally known eco-philosophers and eco-investigators as Berry, Swimme, Suzuki, and others are another indicator.[5] Prevalent conditions in many Native communities, where there is loss of language and spiritual culture, might incline an observer to conclude that tradition is gone, irretrievable. This apparent absence is also a sign, an invitation to walk where we can to learn the ways of "indigenous knowledge," without piecing together from scraps, bits and pieces of the past. Rather, what we can and are looking to most sharply is, in Boissiere's words: " . . . the ancient purity and integrity of the ceremonies, the ancient knowledge of early humanity."[6]

After the shot-gun intensity of the 1970s socio-political start-up, followed as it was by a brief catch-breath phase, a pause that triggered a first return to Elders, as a People we now find ourselves encouraged and affirmed from within ourselves. The meanings of the dramatic details of our survival are being revealed, becoming clearer, and impacting upon us. Berry is right in declaring that the Indian is aware of having won a " . . . moral victory of unique dimensions during the past five centuries."[7] And so now, as Native writers Hausman and Highwater each observe: "We are returning to our Native place, after a long absence."[8] " . . . to celebrate those multitude of things that make us distinctive and unique."[9] As a People, it seems to me, Aboriginals, custodians of centuries-old skills and understandings, are positioned with honor. Berry notes that the Indian:

> . . . has this position . . . not merely by his temporal priority, but by his mystical understanding and communion with the continent. . . . He has realized that life tests the deepest qualities within himself, qualities that emerge in heroic combat not merely with others, but with himself and with the powers of the universe.[10]

An analysis of Native knowing and knowledge somehow now seems necessary, and is certainly now possible. My contention is that indigenous knowing and knowledge, as in past eras, remains necessary to the survival and enhancement of Native personal and communal identity. Also, now that most barriers to secrecy have fallen away, it is possible to access, as it were, some aspects of the characteristic content and mode of Native thinking, and to accede thereby to some of its power. Through a mode of existential positioning virtually ignored hitherto by general Western culture, we can attain to some understanding of how non-dualistic knowing balances all relationships, individual and "communitarian." There is an alluring uniqueness to this possibility, and it parallels the possibilities underscored by such contemporary investigators of human consciousness as Ornstein who comments with regard to East/West psychologies that a bridging between the two will allow man to develop in ways not contained in either.[11]

It is most plausible to me then that from within our Native struggle, we affirm ourselves now, *as we are*. We have been pulled by a disruptive, humiliating experience of age-old cultural carnage against a Western experience in transcending the limits of personal knowledge through external objective sciences, and also against an Eastern experience in inward studies to overcome, in Ornstein's words, ". . . the shifting biases of personal awareness . . . "[12] The Native American has skill and an understanding to share with North Americans, and so with all humankind. The fundamental Native American experience perhaps demonstrates to mankind a way to human development not contained in many other spiritual cultures. It deeply stirs our sense of self therefore to consider, as Berry concludes, that the Native American is an expression of ". . . genius that cannot be denied."[13] With Berry I regard the humanness of the Native American as an unique human mode of being, and see him standing with the other great spiritual traditions of mankind. In this view, the Native American spiritual tradition ranks along with, for example, the respective emphases on divine transcendence in India, on mystical humanness in China, and on a sense of an historical divine savior in Europe. Berry declares that ". . . the American Indian has his own special form, numinous mode of *nature mysticism . . .*" or *earth mysticism*, ". . . a mystical sense of the human amid other living things."[14]

Purpose

Framed as it is by an intense, ongoing personal experience, this paper attempts to indicate characteristic dimensions, such as the nature and conditions of acquiring indigenous "earth knowledge." This sensitive undertaking is complex, multi-faceted, multi-leveled, and difficult. Nonetheless, the intention is to begin some assorting by focusing on what are for me several interrelated factors. A first section describes facets or dimensions of process and content, understood as core principles in Native knowing. That description leads to proposing assumptions as critical guidelines to further reflection and research in this area, and to suggesting some implications of this for university programs. A third section serves as a conclusion.

Dimensions of the Issue

A number of Native and non-Native writers attribute an inclusive meaning to the term "Native knowledge."[15] I agree with that view, for one must hold in hand a number of concepts, such as mode, mind as agent, mind processes, oral literate mind, relationships, primal experience, laws of nature, Elder sayings, and what contemporary psychology has to offer.

Mode and Capacity

The mode of indigenous knowing is a non-dualistic process — it transcends the usual oppositions between rational knowledge and intuition, spiritual insight and physical behavior. It is inclusive of all reality. As a process of thinking and perceiving, it is irreducible. Its scope and focus are on what goes together. For example, sense of self-esteem and competence and sense of control over life events are together with sense of internal and external conflict, and over the compelling influences of both Native and dominant society cultures; sense of space and sense of time are together.

Mind Agent

The agent or subject of this comprehensive, multi-dimensional knowing is the mind. A fully developed Native mind is one that is aware, and fully conscious. This mental awareness "organizes" the entire Native bio-system, i.e., it accomodates the complete range of world components, apprehended through the sensory systems. This mental awareness is the ground of conscious life. It is that from and through which, for example, all ceremonial impact proceeds. It underlies, is behind thought, perception, and feeling. And, it remains active when these are not present.[16]

Mind Processes

The "seeing" mind discovers in self-reflection that it is an ongoing activity that generates, in Diekman's words ". . . a process of felt-meaning . . . "[17] In other words, the mind is a living context for thoughts and perceptions, a relational movement. Like all minds, Native mind manifests in functions or operations which are ways of organizing relationships, perceptions or forms of interconnectedness.

Meditation, whether as a formal discipline, as in Eastern spiritualities, or informal consciousness expansion as in Native areas, is the tool or the means which Native mind uses to arrive at "seeing" through experience. It is, as Bass says: ". . . the effort of timeless, open, still, and concentrated listening to what goes on within, to the root melody of all being, *instead of a straining of the intellect.* "[18]

Central in this processual mode is the imagination activity. Imagination in Native mind, as I experience it, is the route or the means via which the spiritual world influences creatively the development of individual and group cultural life. In other words, imagination is a capacity, a power which enables, as Steiner states ". . . the true spiritual world to light up within the individual soul."[19] In sum, traditional Indian knowing is an experience in matter and spirit as inseparable realities, nondualistically apprehended. Characteristically, because Native thinking is inclusive, it resists simple, abstract, objective definition. There are several other interrelated components to consider.

Oral Literate Mind

Traditional indigenous mind is an oral literature dependent mind, as compared to a mind that is print literature dependent. Polanyi and Prosch in their study of primitive mind state that "... basic archaic thought tends to be based on more *far-reaching tacit integrations* than are acceptable to the scientific mind of modern man."[20] Native traditional mind is openly and sharply impressed, in my view, by sensory qualities of relationships, all perceived as inherently meaningful. Native thinking, to transpose a Steiner phrase, may be referred to as "pictorial thinking."[21] Elder teaching of concepts is therefore characteristically and understandably directly visual or "pictorial." Brown reiterates this view in observing that Native mind expresses "... through the symbol, which includes the auditory word or echo, all of which have reference always to the forms, forces, and variations of nature."[22] Brown also observes that: "There is a fluidity and transparency to the apperceptions of the phenomenal world which permits no absolute line to be drawn, for example, between the world of animals, men, or spirit."[23]

Native capacity to form "far-reaching tacit integrations" is manifest in its extensive use of symbology, e.g., journey symbols, heroic personalities, symbol of quartered circles, mandala symbolism of the self, various transformative symbolisms, the Great Mother, creation myths, initiation ceremonies, sacred pipe, sun dance, ghost dance, vision quest.

In reference to what to learn and where to learn it, Abe often exclaimed: "It's all deah. Een de sareemonees! Dat's awr Bybool."[24] Native ceremonies are the primary oral literature, and remain the main traditional source of psychic energy for thinking, for identity development and control, for survival and its enhancement.[25] The oral literate mind displays a capacity to integrate, to form patterns, a process that penetrates and transforms the experiences obtained in and through a dynamic, non-print environment. According to Bateson, "patterns" interconnect the components of process and content, of knower and known, and thus provide context and meaning.[26]

Primal Experience

Huston Smith considers that: "... there is, first, a Reality that is everywhere and always the same; and second, that human beings always and everywhere have access to it."[27] The perennial experience of that "Reality" constitutes the primordial, abundant foundation of Native traditional existence. It is the accumulated knowledge, rooted in that experience, that is carried forward by oral tradition. Within this experience, reality and meaning are found and held. To be in this experience and to be skilled in sustaining it, and in initiating others into it, is the normal and natural activity, the knowing and doing of evolved Elders. The primal "experience" embraces the inner and outer worlds. In Native cognition, these are together and are equally real and functional. The sense world, as well as the spiritual world, each has something to reveal which only each can express. The spiritual and the physical are both acknowledged as inseparable, and recognized as belonging centrally to the sphere of Native, human knowing. It follows that such primal experience is the basis, as well, of traditional Native culture. As Berry says:

> These experiences, which generally present themselves as divine revelations, are irreplaceable. They form the foundations upon which the cultural system of various peoples are established. They also determine the *distinctive psychic structure* of the individual personalities within the culture. Together these revelations form the ultimate psychic support for the human venture itself.[28]

In sum, the Native North American experience suggests, again in Berry's words, that there are:

> . . . extensive human resources that are available to these original inhabitants of this continent . . . intimate communion with the depths of their own psychic structure is one of the main differences between the psychic functioning of the Indian and the psychic functioning of the Euro-American in modern times.[29]

Relationships

As initimated earlier, being in relationships is the manifest spiritual ground of Native being. In traditional perception, nothing exists in isolation, everything is relative to every other being or thing. As Indians are wont to exclaim: "And all my relations." Native thinking in its modality precludes dichotomous categories. In other words, traditional awareness, as Brown states, is characteristically one of ". . . inter-relatedness across categories of meaning, never losing sight of ultimate wholeness."[30]

Native mind is therefore a mind-in-relational-activity, a mind-in-community. This personal-experience-within-a-community-of-beings-and-cosmos, subtle and elusive in quality, is not the same as the concept of "belief," for it does not derive from a declarative authority. This qualitative principle is not an *a priori* doctrinal point, a *lex credendi*, but is a direct result of consciously experienced process.[31] This "knowing" in its "workings" is also irreducible, for it is, in the final analysis, entirely subjective, absolutely personal. This is simply so, in turn, because that is the way it is.[32] This mode is as irreducible as is one's sense of identity and self-understanding of a culture. Min states that:

> In the final analysis, the identity of a person cannot be objectified or imposed from the outside. It is a matter of the self-description, self-definition, and self-understanding of the person himself or herself. The self-understanding of a culture is likewise irreducible, unique and should be taken without attempts at reduction and objectification. As the ultimate collective self-understanding of a culture, a particular religion should be accepted as an entity *sui generis*.[33]

Laws of Nature

Elders consistently refer to the "laws of nature." This means that in the inner and outer worlds, occurrences are according to "perduring" patterns (integrations), which are "laws" of time and space, of now and then, of here and the universe. There is a classical activity, a matrix of "laws" at work in Native mind, connatural with those which govern the universe. For example, perception of relationship between time and space is fundamental. It is noteworthy that, as Brown points out, "Most Native languages . . . reflect a perennial now."[34] Also, the experience of "space" is not entirely physical, as an anonymous Indian aptly states: "Everybody has a song to sing which is no song at all: it is a process of singing, and when you sing, you are where you are."

Summary

Non-dualistic thinking develops a physical image of the spiritual. The thoughts of the "world" are as creatures, and processes of growth and becoming, and not as abstract concepts and explanations. Native awareness and perception is of the spiritual as belonging to this world, and not to some beyond. This is the stuff of "earth spirituality." Native knowledge is of what is behind inner and outer phenomenon, and is acquired and developed in a grasping of it — the phenomenon — by entering into it, according to the "laws of nature." And, this is normal.[35]

Elder Sayings

Elder sanity, the "normal and natural" behavior of Elders ". . . arises from living in accord with the natural process and freely relating to the dynamic impredictability of every moment . . . "[36] Elder process of becoming a balanced human being lies in the attainment of being able to go to the further reaches of human nature (as Maslow has often declared regarding general human capacity). It is this developed capacity that is the constitutive basis of Native spiritual uniqueness. There is an observable Elder "psychology" implicit in what they do and say. Elders, as highly aware persons, and as carriers of oral tradition, are the examplars, the standing reference points. When guided by Elders, the apprentice learns to perceive and understand something of such dimensions as the nature itself of their knowledge, of the centrality of primal experiences, of the "laws of Nature," and this in Elder sayings.

A quick reference to frequent sayings suggests a body of evidence that highlights Native process and content. For example:[37] "Everybody has a song to sing which is no song at all: it is a process of singing, and when you sing, you are where you are." "There are only two things you have to remember about being Indian. One is that everything is alive, and the second is that we are all related." "It's up to you." "You have all the answers within you." "What is Life but a journey into the Light." "At the center of Life is the Light." "There is within me a voice which tells me who I am and where I am." "And all of my relations."

Evolved Elders arrive at and preserve a sense-rooted thinking which knows the world as a spiritual reality. He who "knows," experiences a spiritual nature in the perceived world. Reality is experienced by entering deeply into the inner being of the mind, and not by attempting to break through the outer world to a beyond. This positions the Native person in "communion," within the living reality of all things. His "communion" is his experience of the ideas within, concentric with reality without. Thus, to "know," to "cognize," is experiential, direct knowing.

Contemporary Psychology

An earlier reference implied an important role for contemporary psychology in the study of non-Western epistemologies. At first glance, it may seem improbable that contemporary science, and psychology in particular, can address indigenous cognition, given the latter's instrumental penchant and preoccupation with analysis and behavioral quantification. Although the difficulties and shortcomings of the Western mode of knowing are manifest in mainstream psychology, there are recent signs, nonetheless, as frequent reference to Welwood in this essay attest, of a promising shift in theoretical development. The very structure of Western technological civilization which seems to deny and destroy the inner meanings and mysteries of everything it touches, may tempt one to conclude that a communication in depth with Native peoples is most difficult, if not impossible. However, it may be mostly for want of effort, as Brown declares:

> Rarely is the prerequisite effort made to understand the alien tradi-
> tion *on its own terms*, through the categories of its proper language,
> and thus for what it really is in all its profundity and complexity, and
> with all its impelling and sacrificial demands.[38]

Western psychology cannot yet address non-dualistic experience, i.e.,
awareness, for there is a complexity and a depth that psychology is not
able to comprehend fully, let alone articulate.[39] However, Ornstein
provides a toe-hold. For example, he considers that the identification of
the metaphors, e.g., unconsciousness/conscious (the surface dualism
notwithstanding), and their translation into those of Western
psychological thought, and vice-versa, could be helpful.[40] There are, as
well, other promising endeavors. Within the sub-areas of cognitive
psychology, despite the latter's significant relationships with be-
haviorism, one notes encouraging developments.[41]

Feuerstein's concepts of human cognition, for example, in my view,
are amenable to extension, that is, they could move to the identification
of further reaches or dimensions of mental capacity and function to
reveal and articulate congruence with characteristic dimensions of the
Native mode of cognition.[42] Recent Western studies of oriental
psychologies are most suggestive.[43] Equally promising are recent investigations by feminist psychologists and philosophers. Belenky and associates, for example, conclude from their research findings to the
importance of drawing on intuition and feelings, and of stressing
"'responsibility of caring orientation' (interdependence, intimacy, nur-
turance, needs, context)," in contrast to a "'rights orientation'
(autonomy, independence, abstract critical thought, morality of
rights)."[44] A provocative review of feminist and womanist literature, by
Sandra Friedman and Alec Irwin, features several conceptual congruen-
cies, such as relationality, power and empowering.[45]

Relative to several facets of the issue of Native mind mode, current
work in Asian psychology provides several attractions. One is that its
concepts are rooted in actual experience rather than in concepts forming
a theoretical system. A second attractive feature is that Asian psychology is primarily concerned with humans and their experience as a whole
process, studied in relation to the whole of the environment. Third and
finally, Asian psychological perspective includes the transcendent, i.e.,
is primarily taken with human experience in an awakened state of
mind.[46] Wilber illustrates how virtually all of Western therapeutic
theories and methods may be applied to several levels of awareness.[47]
His descriptions have implications, I would suggest, for issues of Native
learning, personal change and development. He contends that his
model of consciousness is of "universal" application, for it includes the
ample insights from both non-Western psychologies, and from amongst

a plethora of therapies of such typical Western disciplines as ego-psychology, psychoanalysis, humanistic psychology, Jungian analysis, interpersonal psychology, cognitive psychology, and behavior modification.

Summary

These several Western insights are promising. However, none are explicit about primordial "earth experience." Once again, central to Native knowledge is the concept of a direct experience of nature, the principle of the spiritual immanent in creation, in direct relationship with Nature. In a word, behavioral science in general has not yet developed a "psychological geology" to reveal those underlying activities which shape the mind's topography. A pluridimensional approach is needed if we are to understand Native mind and knowledge, and thereby discern the roots of Native identity and survival. The challenge to Western researchers and theorists, and to educationists as well, is therefore one of awakening to the comprehensiveness of this awareness — to conceive ultimately of limitless awareness, to become able to perceive and to establish the experiential unity of all that is. In other words, how awareness of being interconnected on the basis of a high sense of self-worth and dignity beyond conventional notions of "normal behavior," derived from a matured capacity for direct experience, awaits psychology's attention.

Another aspect of our quest is to discover, in Western terms, how an "idea," i.e., Indigenous knowledge, is moving or can move about in a sophisticated technological world, and shape the way people think and feel about themselves.[48] We need to appreciate both how the completely subjective conditions of Native conscious experience have objective validity, and how the experience of sense perception is allied with the experience of ideas, experiencing through the sense world its objective reality. Steiner writes that there is a step ". . . from the unessential external aspect of the sense-world to its essential inner reality . . ."[49] Whatever the conceptual means, I think we are looking for what the anthropologist Bateson identifies as ". . . the pattern which connects . . . ," the context which yields the meaning(s), in aliveness, and not just as a "structure."[50] Native mind is dynamic, is in a oneness that includes the biosphere and humanity. There is a meta-pattern, immanent, embodied in all specifics, amenable to Native mind. Intellectually, it is a question, in Bateson's words, of . . . *looking to this to arrive at that by which one can apprehend what is as it is.*[51] The Native sense-world is spiritually patterned, and the mind lives within this recognized spiritual world by widening the consciousness to encompass it. This mind state is one of clear consciousness in its process, like that of a

Western mind entering mathematics, or analytical physics, for example. I think that in the name of science and its method, one can get to that kind of awareness.

Discussion

Critical Assumptions

Sifting through from the above section are a number of concepts. The following are critical givens which I propose as givens to a further exploration of the indigenous mind.

1. It is possible to "know."
2. A high sense of self-deprecating humor is needed in the acquisition of Native knowledge.
3. Characteristically, Western culture values rationalism and objectivity vs. intuition; mastery vs. relating to; and having vs. the doing of becoming-being.
4. Characteristically also, Western culture tends to regard intuitive knowledge as "primitive," therefore unsophisticated, and therefore less "valuable" than so called objective modes of knowing.[52] This is not the case. The issue of oral literature is one of subtlety and sophistication.
5. There is no difference between mental and spiritual activity and development—they are two sides of the same, transparent coin. Both constitute an arduous and complex development over time.[53]
6. Native thinking is predominantly "pictorial," manifest in key metaphors, and constitutive of the "substance" of Native oral literature.
7. Investigators must continuously question assumptions they make about themselves as persons and as professionals, about others, the cultural-socio-political world, the environment, and the cosmos.[54]
8. It is not clear, at this time, whether the issue of knowledge is really one of Native vs. non-Native, rather than one of male vs. female, or is a question of the nature of humanness with male/female, masculinity/femininity dimensions, or is an issue of objective vs. subjective knowledge—or, is one with elements of all of those.[55]
9. Holism is holism, and the source for a fresh paradigm. The older conceptions are too narrow.

University Relevance

The difficulty of acquiring indigenous knowledge is of some relevance, if not of crucial importance, to such university programs as Native Studies. One aspect of the difficulty stems from the nature and requirements of the knowing process itself; a second derives from an inescapable role which many Native-related university programs assume, consciously or not.

Universities are obviously purveyors of culture. The attainment of this goal, in programs about and for indigenous students, is understandably conditional on the experience of the faculty itself. Native Studies' faculties, knowingly or not, are prime agents of aboriginal culture preservation and development. They draw critically on many disciplines and methodologies, as on tradition, in order to define and deliver programs and courses in response both to the wide spectrum of Native need, and to university learning requirements.

Within that endeavor however, oral tradition factors fare unevenly, whereas, in my view, oral tradition should be a central concern in program and course development. But, that requires faculty members who have a developed sense of oral tradition, and a prolonged experience in ceremonies. That challenge is in turn compounded by the forces of traditional university intellectualism vs. Native intuition; of academic vs. colloquial languages; of elitism vs. people-in-communities; of knowledge of the professional vs. knowledge of the People; of direct knowledge vs. indirect knowledge ; and of written tradition vs. oral tradition.

It is a standing question as to whether Native ways of knowing can be fostered in a university environment. Stated ideals to the contrary notwithstanding, universities historically have rather tended to develop critics and not artists/poets, scientists/controllers and not facilitators. To formulate questions of what is necessary, what is possible, what should be possible, might make that possible. Perhaps the recent work of women social scientists is suggestive. As mentioned earlier, Mary Belenky and associates affirm that learning has to be personalized in order to develop the intuitive and the analytical aspects of human mind to prize and to affirm, to evaluate. Their basic assumption is that: "... the nature of truth and reality and the origins of knowledge shape the way we see the world and ourselves as participants in it. They affect our definition of ourselves, the way we interact with others, our public and private personae, our sense of control over life events, our views of teaching and learning, and our conception of morality."[56]

Anthropologist Vera John-Steiner, who is doing work in Navajo cognition, insists that university-level learning requires craft, logic, mastery and commitment.[57] She is also emphatic about the need for "dialectical movement" between process and product, person and society, modality within modality, intention and expression, as all these are thought processes at the core of the creative process.[58]

Conclusion

The concern of this essay is with a core knowledge translated by oral tradition, in its nature and in its process (notwithstanding the pragmatics of discernment thereof, both within personal experience, and within a tradition strongly influenced inwardly and outwardly since contact with Euro-American culture. My focus precludes consideration of several other significant areas. For length reasons, this paper does not address related religious questions, attendant at various points throughout. The same reason prevails also with regard to the consideration of healing, "bad/good" medicine, and the spectrum of psychic phenomena. The exclusion of lower levels of knowledge is intentional, such as may be observed in social attitudes and customs in contemporary Native communities, regarding health and education, for example. I have concentrated on the principle that the traditional "world" of indigenous knowledge is a sense-world which is in truth spiritual. My ambition to discern this phenomenon here is predominantly intellectual and, admittedly that is a limiting factor. The reader who "studies" what I have written here, without any sense of direct knowing, will not understand.

Indigenous knowledge and Native American survival somehow go together. However, as Berry observes, after five centuries of contact, there is yet ". . . no adequate interpretation of this event. . . . It remains, however, *one of the most significant events* in the total history of the earth."[59]

Notes

[1]This paper expands on the substance of a lecture delivered to the annual Conference on Indigenous Peoples' Education, sponsored by the School of Native Studies, University of Alberta, November 18, 1988. I am indebted to Thomas Berry and to Rudolf Steiner for helpful words and phrases in this reflection on content and process of my "knowing" and "seeing." Berry is insightful in his interpretation of the Native American presence. Steiner is a scientist and epistemologist.

[2]Berry 1976, p. 135.

[3]Brown 1982, p. 31.

[4]Regarding the general difficulty facing the Native writer, Highwater states: "It is my educational duplexity in two completely contrary sets of values that

gives impetus to what I have to say." (p. xi) It is this duplexity of sorts, an inner sense of "irreconcilable differences" which compounds the need for appropriate words and phrases. But, perhaps this is not so at deeper levels of mind . . .

I would also emphasize that this inner struggle is rendered more difficult by a process of breaking out of the cramping confinement of acquired Western thoughts and thought processes, through a complicated and problematical process of "going back."

Regarding the "sharing of secrets," there are those who fear and object that the white man will take over Native spirituality, were he to learn the "secrets," and again, one ultimate time, leave the Native absolutely bereft. This is a most understandable and significant apprehension which, on closer examination however, falls away because the requirements of the "learning" of the "secrets" are such that, were non-Indians to acquire the "knowledge," they would be "trustable" — for, in a sense, they would no longer be non-Indian!

It is sobering to keep in mind that significant numbers of Natives across the continent abuse their "gifts" through "bad" medicine. We have perhaps more reason to fear our own. See E. James for an account of "medicine" misuse and corruption.

Boissieres writes:

". . . the Indian visualizes the mysteries of life without the need to express them consciously to anyone." (p. 22)

[5]David Suzuki in public presentation, 1988. Also see Koestler, p. 54.

[6]Boissieres, o.c., p. 21.

[7]Berry, o.c., p. 134.

[8]Hausman, p. 5.

[9]Highwater, p. xiv.

[10]Berry, o.c., p. 136.

[11]Ornstein, p. 136.

[12]Ornstein o.c., . p. 136.

[13]Berry, o.c., p. 136.

[14]Berry, o.c., p.136. The emphasis is mine.

[15]See, for example, Battista and Youngblood-Henderson, Berry, Brown, Brumble, Bruteau, Buller, Cordova, Erdoes and Ortiz, Gould, Gravely, Grof, Highwater, Jilek, Johnson, Jules-Rosette, Obonsawin, Shafer.

[16]This paragraph is based on Welwood in J. Welwood (ed.), pp. 30, 34, 151.

[17]Diekman in Welwood, p. 47.

[18]Bass in Welwood, p. 190. The emphasis is mine.

[19]Steiner o.c., p. 251; see also p. 191.

[20]Polanyi and Prosch, p. 150.

[21]Steiner 1977, p. l04. The emphasis made here is not exclusive. In my view, Native mind, as exemplified by evolved Elders, manifests highest order intellectual activity, both discursive and analytical, as well as the range of intuitive and metaphoric capacity. I do not observe this mind has having less of any human mental capacity, but that, in the context of this paper, when compared with Western mind, traditional Native mind displays highly developed "pictorial thinking"

[22]Brown, 1982, p. 69.

[23]Brown 1983, p. 9.

[24]The late Abe Burnstick, Stoney Elder, Duffield Reserve, Alberta.

[25]To Couture on Elders, o.c. pp. 5-6, I would add the following comments.

> Oral literature is and must be considered as a medium in its own right, apart from textuality, if one wishes to "study" indigenous knowledge. That is a starting point requirement. Addressing this issue under that condition is a major challenge to the print-based academic researcher.

The question of grasping another interpretive system, especially when rooted in the culture — and as a social scientist — is never complete, as is it never complete for the individual. However, I assume that there is some process of communication and evaluation possible across Native and Western forms of thought. (See Geertz, and Jules-Rosette for caveats and possibilities).

[26]Bateson, pp. 12-13.

[27]Smith, pp. 276.

[28]Berry, o.c. p. 136. The emphasis is mine.

[29]Berry, o.c., p. 137.

[30]Brown 1982, p. 71; 1983, p. 9..

[31]See Fontinell in Couture, o.c., pp. 18-19.

[32]Fontinell p. 130.

[33]Min, p. 273.

[34]Brown, o.c., 1982, p. 50.

[35]The relevance and the serious practical difficulties of discernment regarding Elders are addressed elsewhere (see Couture 1991).

I would like to add that a Native Elder, is a person who says what he/she thinks himself entitled to say according to his own experience from within a spiritual world — and, there is much evidence regarding this ineffable behavior.

Also, in the teaching of Elders bearing on stages of learning—clearly there are steps which can not be skipped, for each situate the necessary competency (comprising content, skill, attitude), i.e., the means of "organizing," to make "sense" of it all. This model of sorts reflects the insight that traditional Native personality is a multileveled manifestation, or expression of a single consciousness.

Noteworthy also, as Cordova states is 1) "Our thinking is in the mainstream of human thought." (p. 24); and 2) "Native American beliefs contain some of the most abstract notions in any philosophical system." (p. 26)

[36]Transposed from Welwood, p. xiv.

[37]This list, in my view, is a characteristic sample of Elder axioms.

[38]Brown, 1982, p. 110. The boldface emphasis is mine. Ornstein points out that:

> Our culture is the best educated, wealthiest, most "emotionally aware" in history. It is also one of the most spiritually illiterate. We are, I think, near the end of this illiteracy. (p. 136)

[39]Welwood states that:

> Oddly enough, this central aspect of everyday consciousness has rarely been observed, much less studied, in Western psychology, which has chosen instead to analyze mind as though it were an object independent of the analyzer, consisting of postulated structures and mechanisms that are not directly experienced. The Eastern approach to mind sets out to examine different aspects of immediate awareness, how we relate to things, and to understand mind in a very direct, personally relevant way. (p. xii)

[40]Ornstein in Welwood, p. 149.

[41]Slife and Barnard clearly delineate the behavioral roots of cognitive psychology, and present a useful comparison between cognitive and existential psychology.

[42]See Feuerstein writings in bibliography; cf. also Jensen and Feuerstein.

[43]See Grof, Ornstein, and Welwood.

[44]Belenky et al., p. 8.

[45]Friedman and Irwin, pp. 387-405.

[46]Transposed from Welwood, p. xiii.

[47]Wilber, pp. 7-8.

[48]In a manner, parallel perhaps, to what Turkle has discovered about how a basic culture is shaped by an idea, e.g., Freud on contemporary culture — and now computers. (p. 23)

[49]Steiner, o.c., p. 215.

[50]Bateson, p. 8.

[51]Our emphases, based on Bateson, p. 8.

[52]See Belenky et al., Feuerstein, John-Steiner. Feminist researchers stress a personalized way of knowing vs. the rationality and objectivity of Western technological society, with its prevailing assumption that intuitive knowledge is more primitive, lacking in sophistication, less valid therefore than so-called objective modes of knowing.

[53]See Peck, Progoff, Steiner 1986.

[54]I do not wish to underplay the significance of obvious obstacles to acquiring a non-dualistic mode of knowing. I would liken the characteristic Western

way of knowing to a "cultural addiction." Morrow claims cultural addiction to be as pernicious as chemical addiction. The latter takes over the role of primary integrating force in a person's life. As such it distorts his/her perceptions and actions to a degree which is very limiting. Cultural addiction has a similar effect.
This is an addiction that we may not readily admit to. Morrow points out that the remedy is to develop "acute self-awareness" in order to free ourselves of our own cultural addictions. (p. 32)

Another example of cultural addiction is what Berry calls "compulsive savior instincts," a characteristic of some professional religious people. (p. 134) See Couture 1989a.

[55]I have contrasted Native with Western for the sake of as simple a presentation as possible.

[56]Belenky et al., p. 3.

[57]John-Steiner, p. 5. She also states that:

> The conventional conception of "scientific method" slights the intuitive, imagistic side of creative thought and ignores the place of passionate dialogue — has not addressed the reality or realness of "direct experience." (p. 5)

Her statement is complemented by Bateson's observation that:

> Logic and quantity turn out to be inappropriate devices describing organisms, and their interactions and internal organization. (p. 22)

[58]John-Steiner, o.c., p. xii.

[59]Berry, o.c., p. 133.

References

Bass, M. (1979). "Eastern Wisdom and Western Psychotherapy," in *The meeting of the ways: explorations in east-west psychology*. J. Welwood, ed. New York: Schocken Brothers, 184-191.

Bateson, G. (1979). *Mind and nature, a necessary unity*. New York: Bantam.

Battista, Maria, J. Youngblood-Henderson. (1979). *The medicine circle and cognitive imperialism*. Berkeley: Native American Studies, University of California. Unpublished; for use in course N.Am.St. 102. 48 pp.

Belenky, Mary Field, Blythe McVicker Clinchy, Nancy Rule Goldberger, Jill Mattuck Tarule. (1986). Women's ways of knowing. *The development of self, voice, and mind*. New York: Basic Books.

Berry, T. (1976). "The Indian Future," *Cross currents*, Summer, 133-142.

_____ (1987). "Creative Energy," *Cross currents*, Summer/Fall, 179-186.

_____ (1987). "The New Story: Comment on the Origin, Identification and Transmission of Values," *Cross currents*, Summer/Fall, 187-199.

_____ (1987). "The Dream of the Earth: Our Way into the Future," *Cross currents*, Summer/Fall, 200-215.

_____ (1987). "Twelve Principles for Reflecting on the Universe," *Cross currents*, Summer/Fall, 216-217.

Boissieres, R. (1986). *Meditation with the Hopi*. Santa Fe, N.M.: Bear & Co.

Brown, J.E. (1982). *The spiritual legacy of the American Indian*. New York: Crossroad.

_____ (1982). "The Bison and the Moth: Lakota Correspondences," *Parabola*, May, 8, 2, 6-13.

Brumble, D. (1980). "Anthropologists, Novelists and Indian Sacred Material," *Can. rev. Amer. st.*, Spring, 11, 1, 31-48.

Bruteau, Beatrice. (1985). "Global Spirituality and the Integration of East and West," *Cross currents*, Summer/Fall, 190-205.

Buller, G. (1980). "New Interpretations of Native American Literature: A Survival Technique," *American Indian cultural research journal*, 4, 1 & 2, 165-177.

Cordova, Viola. (1988). "Philosophy and the Native American," *The people before Columbus*. Albuquerque, N.M.: University of New Mexico, Southwest Indian Student Coalition, 23-26.

Couture, J. (1987). "What is Fundamental to Native Education? Some Thoughts on the Relationship Between Thinking, Feeling, and Learning," in *Contemporary educational issues. The Canadian mosaic*. L. Stewin, S. McCann eds. Toronto: Copp Clark Pitman, 178-191.

_____ (1989). "Native and Non-Native Encounter. A Personal Experience," in *Challenging the conventional - essays in honor of Ed Newbery*. W. Cragg, ed. Burlington: Trinity Press, 123-154.

Erdoes, R., A. Ortiz eds. (1984) *American Indian myths and legends*. New York: Pantheon Books.

Feuerstein, R. (1979). *Dynamic assessment of retarded performers: the learning potential assessment device, theory, instruments, and techniques*. Glenview, Illinois: Scott, Foresman & Company.

_____ (1980). *Instrumental enrichment: an intervention program for cognitive modifiability*. Glenview, Illinois: Scott, Foresman & Company.

Fontinell, E. (1988). "Faith and Metaphysics Revisited," *Cross currents*, Summer, 129-145.

Friedman, Sandra, A. Irwin. (1990). "Christian Feminism, Eros and Power in Right Relation," *Cross currents*, Vol. 40, 3, Fall, 387-405.

Geertz, C. (1973). *The interpretation of cultures. Selected essays*. New York: Basic Books.

Gould, Janice. (1988). "A Review of Louise Erdrich's *Jacklight*." *The people before Columbus*. Albuquerque, N.M.: University of New Mexico, Southwest Indian Student Coalition, 11-14.

Gravely, W. (1987). "New Perspectives on Nicholas Black Elk, Oglala Sioux Holy Man," *The illif rev.*, Winter 44, 1, 1-19.

Grof, S. (1985). *Beyond the brain. Birth, death, transcendence in psychotherapy*. New York: Suny Press.

Hausman, G. (1986). *Meditation with animals.* Santa Fe, N.M.: Bear and Co.

Highwater, J. (1981). *The primal mind. Vision and reality in Indian America.* New York: Harper & Row.

James, E., ed. (1956). *Thirty years of Indian captivity of John Tanner.* Minneapolis: Ross & Haines.

Jensen, M., and R. Feuerstein. (1986). "Cultural Difference and Cultural Deprivation: A Theoretical Framework for Differential Intervention," in *Cultural diversity and learning efficiency.* R. M. Gupta and P. Coxhead, eds. London: MacMillan Press.

Jilek, W.G. (1971). "From Crazy Witchdoctor to Auxiliary Psychotherapist - The Changing Image of the Medicine Man," *Psychiatrica clinica,* 4, 200-220.

Jilek, W.G. (1978). "Native Renaissance: The Survival and Revival of Indigenous Therapeutic Ceremonials Among North American Indians," *Transcultural psychiatric research review,* XV, October, 117-147.

Johnson, T. (1988). "The Four Sacred Mountains of the Navajos," *Parabola,* Winter, 40-47.

John-Steiner, Vera. (1985). *Notebooks of the mind. Explorations in thinking.* New York: Harper & Row.

Jules-Rosette, Benetta. (1978). "The Veil of Objectivity: Prophecy, Divination, and Social Inquiry," *Amer. anthrop.,* September, 80, 3, 549-570.

Koestler, A. (1976). "Cosmic Consciousness," *Psych. today,* April, 52, 54, 104.

Min, A. (1988). "The Challenge of Radical Pluralism," *Cross currents,* Fall, 268-275.

Morrow, D. (1972). "Cultural Addiction," *J. rehabilitation,* May/June, 30-32, 41.

Obonsawin, R. (1979). "Traditional Indian Health and Nutrition. Forgotten Keys to Survival in the 21st Century," *Indian news.* Ottawa: Department of Indian and Northern Affairs, 6-7.

Ornstein, R. (1976). "Eastern Psychologies: The Container vs. The Contents," *Psyc. today,* September, 36, 39, 43.

Peck, M. (1978). *The road less traveled.* New York: Simon & Schuster.

_____ (1987). *The different drum.* New York: Simon & Schuster.

Polanyi, M., and H. Prosch. (1975). "Truth in myths," *Cross currents,* Summer, 149-162.

Progoff, I. (1975). *At a journal workshop.* New York: Dialogue House Library.

_____ (1980). *The practice of process meditation.* New York: Dialogue House Library.

Shafer, Carolyn R. and Dr. Leslie Grey. (1987). "Bridge Between Two Realities," *Shaman's drum,* Fall, 21-28.

Slife B., and Suzanne Barnard. (1988). "Existential and Cognitive Psychology," *J. hum. psych.,* Summer, 119-136.

Smith, H. (1953). "Philosophy, Theology, and the Primordial Claim," *Cross currents,* 28, 3, 276-288.

Steiner, R. (1977). *Rudolf Steiner, an autobiography.* New York: Multimedia Pub. Corp.

_____ (1986). *The philosophy of spiritual activity. Basic features of a modern world.* Bell's Pond, Hudson, New York: Anthroposophic Press.

Suzuki, D. (1988). *World environment and indigenous peoples.* Edmonton: Lecture presented to Yellowhead Tribal Council conference.

Swimme, B. (1984). *The universe is a green dragon. A cosmic creation story.* Santa Fe: Bear & Co.

Turkle, Sherry. (1984). *The second self: computers and the human spirit.* New York: Simon & Schuster.

Welwood, J. ed. (1979). *The meeting of the ways. Explorations in east/west psychology.* New York: Schocken Brothers.

Contemporary
Frontiers

5
Indian Economic Development: Innovations and Obstructions

James S. Frideres

The economic development of Natives in Canada has long been held as a goal of Canadian public policy. However, most will also agree that few effective programs have been implemented and the efforts to achieve this goal have not been very successful. For example, the number of Natives with incomes below the poverty line has remained at about 60 percent for the past three decades. Why this lack of success? Usually the explanation is that insufficient funds have been set aside to support Natives or that the funds set aside for economic development are inadequate. Given that over three billion dollars were spent on Native Affairs last year and by the year 1992 the cost is expected to be over five billion dollars, it would seem that financial constraints are not the answer. (This represents a per capita payment of well over $14 000 per year.) However, there are three major factors that might contribute to the failure of policy related to Native economic development.

1. Failure of policy to reflect the economic realities of reserves.
2. The adoption of conflicting goals in attempting to achieve economic development.
3. An emphasis on a singular strategy to achieve economic development.

However, before we begin to assess these explanations, we first need to look at the physical, demographic and cultural characteristics of Natives.

Geographical Region of Reserves

The physical characteristics of each of the regions of Canada create constraints to economic development strategies. The location of the reserve also affects the development plans, e.g., remoteness of a reserve will affect transportation costs and thus impact the import/export price of a commodity and ultimately the viability of the plan.

Indian land is comprised of approximately 2 242 reserves that are spread throughout Canada from east to west, with the smallest less than

50 hectares and the largest covering 900 square kilometres. Altogether, Natives reside on nearly 26 000 square kilometres of land. Much of the land set aside for reserves lies in the subarctic region although a considerable amount of land lies within the productive Great Plains region of western Canada.[1]

Reserves in the eastern woodlands are comprised of deciduous forests in the south and a mixed deciduous-coniferous canopy in the western boundary. To the north, the boreal forest zone comprised of spruce, fir, pine and larch cover the landscape. This northern terrain is characterized by many small lakes and extensive parklands. The climate of this area has short, cool summers and long cold winters. Generally, the Canadian shield dominates this area and has determined its lack of resource potential both renewable and nonrenewable.

The plains area covers the provinces of Manitoba, Saskatchewan and Alberta. This region has a continental climate with few trees. Most of the vegetation is grasslands. Over half of the area is under crop, summer fallow or communal pasture. The Northwest coast environment varies from mountains to deep fjords. Temperatures in this region are moderate, usually above freezing and receive at least 65 cm of precipitation per year; some areas receive over 600 cms per year. Heavy coniferous forests dominate this region with dense undergrowth.

Cultural Characteristics of Indians

In general terms, there are six broad cultural areas which differentiate Indians. They are: Algonquian, Woodlands, Plains, Northwest Coast, Subarctic and Arctic. In addition, there are 10 major linguistic groups which cross-cut these cultural areas. Culture is important in determining people's behavior. While this is an exceedingly simple statement, the complexity underlying such a statement is indeed worth addressing. People's behavior, attitudes and modes of thinking (mind sets) are determined by the cultural context surrounding an individual as he / she is growing up. These early socializing experiences set the stage for behavior in later life. Hence, whether you see something or not, what you see, how you interpret what you see and what action you take, is determined by the cultural ethos within which you are raised.

Even today, Indians tend to be categorized as a culturally homogenous group of people, different from non-Indians. At a macro level this is correct and at such a level of abstraction, the statement or generalization will go unchallenged. However, to assert that the category "Indian" is a homogeneous social group is incorrect and to implement policies and programs on the basis of such an assumption poses many problems which, until recently, have gone unchallenged.

Demographic Characteristics of Indians

There are an estimated 444 000 Indians in Canada, of which about 65 percent live in approximately 577 bands of varying sizes. Approximately 50 percent of Indians are treaty Indians, i.e., have signed a treaty with the federal government. The Indian population is significantly younger than the national population. Over half of the Indian population is under 20 years of age compared with less than one-third for Canada. Only 3.5 percent of the Indian population is 65 and over compared with over 10 percent for the nation. The age structure has important short and long term labor force implications, e.g., the annual increase in the working age population for Native people will be about three percent, three times that of the remainder of the population. Seventy percent of the Indian population has less than a high school degree compared to 45 percent for the national average. Of those attending school, less than 20 percent of Indian students complete high school compared to the national rate of 75 percent. In addition, accessibility to secondary schools is constrained for much of the aboriginal population because they live in remote or rural communities.

Unemployment is chronic in Native communities, with an average of 35 percent employed; those who are employed are underemployed or employed as seasonal or part-time workers. The types of jobs taken by Indians generally fall in the service and nonskilled jobs. Related to employment is the income of Indians. The average individual Indian income is less than half of that of the national average. A considerable proportion of this small income derives from transfer payments, e.g., old age pension, social welfare, child allowance. Housing units on the reserves are crowded and in poor condition. In addition, few houses have the facilities which are taken for granted in other houses, e.g., indoor plumbing, electricity, etc.

Indian health is affected by the poverty conditions in which they live. As a result, they use hospital facilities more than two times that of the general population; particularly younger children. This has produced a mortality rate for young people three times that of the general population and an average age of death at 46 compared to over 70 for the national average.

Indian Dependency

Reserve Indians occupy a position of "domestic dependency" (Jorgensen, et al, 1978). Dependency means that the major decisions which affect socio-economic progress within the reserve, e.g., decisions about commodity prices and investment patterns, are made by individuals and institutions outside those areas. This domestic dependency is a special form of domination that is both political and economic.

Initially, Indians were treated as "domestic" nations with whom only the federal government could deal. The relationship was primarily limited to the establishment of treaties. The creation of the Department of Indian Affairs continued the federal primacy over Indians. This department controls and monitors every aspect of Indian people's lives through the implementation of the *Indian Act*.

Today, Indians are further controlled by provincial governments.The development strategy employed by Canada over the past century encourages the engines of growth, investment, production and consumption. Thus, the industrial sector is given prime consideration in plans and programs; usually concentrated in cities. While the industrial sector is being promoted, the more traditional sectors, such as agriculture and cottage industries are ignored. Even when agriculture was promoted, it has usually never been integrated into a development plan. It only has been viewed as a way of increasing exports and balancing our trade as well as supporting the increasing urban population (Kuznets, 1972). Reserves, characterized by subsistence agriculture and domestic production, became integrated as a dependency into the larger national market through the establishment of various patterns of trade and development. As a result, the national demands determines what Indians produce.

Role of Technology

The role and commitment to technology in modernization is crucial. Technology implies a systematic approach to control of production through labor saving devices and a sophisticated communication and transportation operation; technology's influence is not a neutral investment. If technology is embraced, then certain societal structures and orientation must be accepted. Thus modern technology brings with it certain values, and challenges existing traditional values. Three major values of modern technology have had particular importance when introduced to reserves. First is the belief in rationality. This means that an idea or phenomenon can be broken down into component parts, put together again and verified. Related to this is the belief that if we change things, we will be able to extract more out of nature. A second value is efficiency. This means that by organizing all human efforts, we will be able to increase our productivity. In short, the final output is all important. Finally, modern technology promotes problem solving. In other words, technology does not view nature as something to live in harmony with; rather, the goal is to manipulate and dominate nature (Wilber, 1977).

When technology is brought to undeveloped areas or traditional cultures, value conflict points emerge. For example, there is a difference in how technology is viewed. Developed economies view it as a marketable commodity while in undeveloped areas it is considered a free good. There is also a conflict with regard to developing autonomy or purchasing imported technology which means one can lose their autonomy. A third conflict focuses on the issue of standardization. Developed economies want to standardize everything in order to take advantage of economics of scale and efficiency. Undeveloped areas prefer cultural diversity and pluralistic social patterns which can accommodate individual needs. Finally, underdeveloped areas generally want to develop "low tech" which is inexpensive, labor intensive and small scale, while developed areas want "high tech" which is expensive, large scale and capital intensive (Schultz, 1972).

The Decision to Modernize

How should Indians allocate their scarce resources to modernize? Perhaps even more important is the question of whether Indians should modernize! Contemporary evidence suggests that reserve Indians continue to evaluate land as space where livelihoods are obtained and places where present and future generations will reside. They believe that spaces are part of nature and are of special consequence and meaning to past, present and future. In addition, Indians treat resources different than non-Indians, i.e., non-Indians view resources as commodities, Indians do not (Jorgensen, et al, 1984).

The object of modernization (development) for Indians is to raise their level of living and to provide them with the opportunity to develop their potential while still being able to retain the more salient components of their traditional culture. The disenchantment Indians have with industrial growth has been based on a disenchantment with the form that economic growth has taken. In most cases, the production and modern technology has produced an income distribution and a style of development that is out of tune with the above definition of development (Whyte and Williams, 1968).

Industrialization and modernization brings about a radical change in the social structure and Indians are very aware of this. Because social institutions encode information, they allow us to make routine decisions, solve routine problems and carry out a considerable amount of regular thinking on behalf of individuals. The question Indians face is whether or not they want to (or need to) move from a traditional set decisions, solve routine problems and carry out a considerable amount of regular thinking on behalf of individuals. The question Indians face is whether or not they want to (or need to) move from a traditional set of institutions to those created out of the industrialized society. Indians are faced with two questions which affect their decision to modernize.

1. How difficult or costly it is to obtain needful information about society and,
2. How many institutions are there which provide the individual with information (Douglas, 1986).

Obstacles to Modernization

Factors creating resistance to modernization are more complex than the dead weight of tradition, customs suppressing individual initiative, and the lack of work ethic (Myint, 1972). They are usually a combination of contradictory desires including an unbridled enthusiasm for economic development and exaggerated expectations from modern technology, and the resistance to the necessary changes to accommodate technology.[3]

Specific obstacles to economic development have differed from one context to another as well as from one time to another. It is generally accepted that economic and technical advancement depend upon social mobility. Native people are not mobile in the social sense. While they move from reserve to city, their mobility is best characterized as a sojourner. This unwillingness to move permanently to the city or another area of Canada is an impediment to Indian economic development.

A second factor impeding Indian development is the fact that many economic plans developed by both Indians and the federal government are not realistic, given the needs, resources and productive capacities of Native people. Until recently, any chance to inject money into a local reserve economy was thought to be a good thing. A conflict between short-run and long-run aims are a third stymying factor. Because different strategies are required for short-term and long-term development, these may come into conflict. Indians want greater diversification in production in the long run, but the short-run activities, "agriculture," must be supported at the same time. Finally, Indians need to develop new social institutions and to educate people to new habits and values, e.g., changes in methods of work and skill levels to accommodate the new technology. For example, Indians need to increase their rate of capital accumulation. They must widen the margin between consumption and total output. This means they must reduce consumption of urban centres. In doing so, they aggravated regional disparities and rendered the exploited areas uninhabitable, e.g., deforestation and the destruction of wildlife in the area. Generally, Indian people have not been allowed to participate in the development because of their lack of capital and skills. These developments have disrupted and displaced Indian people in many regions. If Indian people have been involved in resource development, they have played a subordinate role such as low-paid transient labor (Barsh, 1987). Egbahl (1983) calls this process "development exclusion" and notes that anytime the developed segment of society initiates a large-scale project, peripheral groups have little choice to participate and at what level.

Experience has shown that rising prices and ecological deterioration make Indian people more dependent on cash and food imports (versus food off the land) (Waldram, 1985; Collins, 1986).The results of such a development strategy is threefold. First, these projects enrich multinational organizations as well as a large cadre of personnel that are supported by this structure, e.g., consultants, banks, contractors. Second, regional and ethnic economic disparities widen. Indigenous people become impoverished, powerless, and are never able to break the cycle of underdevelopment. Third, these development strategies increase ethnic tensions by adding highly visible economic factors to already real or imagined cultural and historical grievances (Hoselity, 1972).

Indian Communities

The current Indian economy is a unified entity of a complimentary set of small-scale productive activities vested around stable production, e.g., agriculture, cottage industry, fur production. Indian people are at the edges of the industrialized world, although they participate in the modern economy at several, albeit small, junctures (Asch, 1987). Nevertheless, their involvement is minimal but increasing. Today, they have a large subsistence and a small capitalistic sector. This marginality in modern technology has kept them from entering middle class and engaging in such activities as saving. Their poverty does not allow them to alter their way of life — their income remains fixed since most of their income is directed toward fixed customary expenditures (Henriot, 1977).

Economically, Indian communities have been stagnant for decades. Personal and tribal resources are allocated in much the same way they have been for years. Over time, members of the community have, through experience, developed a body of information about how to produce goods and the contribution each will make to one's income.

Similarly, people have adjusted to certain consumption and saving preferences (Chartrand, 1987). How does a community free itself from this very unproductive equilibrium in which it is caught? The turn to more land or more money will not solve the problem. Superior skills and equipment, e.g., education, training and equipment are available and must be incorporated into the Indian way of life. Indians can no longer use an apprenticeship model to develop their skills; they must use education (Owen, 1978).

The Need for Control

In order for Indians to meet long-term as well as short-term needs, they must maximize their control over the events that take place on the reserves. This means that jurisdictional, financial and managerial control must be exercised. It also means that they must create a diversified and stable reserve economy (Cox, 1987).

Jurisdictional

This is the ability to regulate activities of people and businesses on the reserve through the enforcement of appropriate laws and codes. This means that Indians must have control over both Indians and non-Indians on the reserves. This also means that they will not undertake developments that increase the number of non-Indians on the reserve. Finally, this means that they must control all business activity that takes place on the reserve.

Financial

This is the ability to generate capital for investment and control the rate of return for Indians. As noted previously, no multiplier effects have been created on the reserve. This is particularly characteristic of an export economy. Taxation also falls under the rubric of financial control. Taxation allows a government to finance its own activities by requiring businesses that are not producing wealth to share the costs of government services that support the needs of both business and the general population. Taxation also gives the government the ability to regulate the economy on the reserve. Two types of taxes have been identified as potentially appropriate for reserves.

(a) Possessory-interest tax is a tax on the value of leased property, and

(b) business-activity tax is a tax on the gross receipts of a business. Indians should be able to provide incentive reductions to these taxes. For example, if a non-Indian business buys Indian goods and services, taxes are reduced.

Managerial

This is the ability to conduct research, promote and manage business activity and provide training programs. History has shown that when Indians have given up control of their resources to outsiders, they have lost economically in the long run. Large-scale developments also mean that Indians will have to set up non-Indian organizations and institutions.

Tribal

This is the ability to create a stable and diversified economic base. The multiplier effect has been absent for past reserve developments because most purchases (at any stage of development) are made from off the reserve. In addition, nearly all businesses on the reserve are owned by non-Indians. There is a need to develop vertical integration of tribal economics. For example:

timber
finished wood product
houses, furniture.

Indians need to emphasize production for local needs not for export (although some export may be undertaken). Furthermore:

- Development must be of a scale that can be controlled by the tribe.
- Development should be labor intensive not capital intensive. It is better to create more jobs at moderate pay than few at high wage.
- Jobs should be consistent with Indian lifestyle and kinship obligations.
- Development should be oriented to the "inner economy" of the reserve.
- Development should not focus on individual businesses but rather on tribal businesses.

Tribal members must be encouraged to relate economically to the tribe so that the tribe can relate to the larger economy. As such, the tribe will have more power and be able to compete against outsiders. It must be remembered that humans are not passive individuals acting under more or less complete constraint. Individuals are not totally caught up in the complex machinery which they do not make. Rather, they are an active part of it (Douglas, 1986).

Indian Affairs: The Problem

The short introduction to the present paper suggested that there are variations in the resources, needs, and goals of Indians residing in different parts of Canada. Each group's history, regional milieu and contact with the capitalist system has had a differential impact on the needs, resources and goals of each.

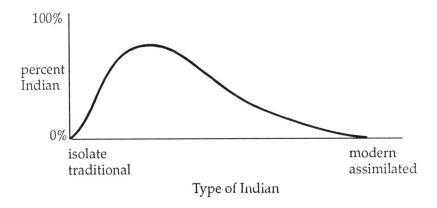

Type of Indian

The figure above illustrates the wide distribution and cultural diversity of Indians in Canadian society. It also demonstrates that the largest number of Indians fall at the isolate, traditional end of the continuum. The federal Department of Indian Affairs has failed to acknowledge this diversity. In addition, Indian Affairs has, persistently, taken the position that there is only one "type of Indian" and has promoted only one type of program to help Indians develop and modernize. The one program type developed by Ottawa has assumed that Indians are at the "modern-assimilated" end of the continuum and all policies and programs emanating from Indian Affairs are developed for this type of Indian community. What needs to be developed, at minimum, is a dual strategy with policies and programs geared to Indian communities that represent both types of Indians depicted in the above diagram. Finally, Indian Affairs is unwilling to be innovative in developing alternative programs for Indian people. It has long been *sine qua non* of Indian Inuit Affairs Program (IIAP) procedures to interpret policies/programs for the convenience of IIAP personnel, not on the basis of reality.

Natural Resource Development Strategies:

Some Alternatives

The following section will identify several approaches that Indians might take in the development of one component of their economy — natural resources. It clearly demonstrates that there are many alternative development strategies. Furthermore, given the diversity of Indian communities, they must have the option of choosing the right development plan. In doing so, they will be able to generate a modest cash flow and further develop their overall economy. However, as in any development, a cost is incurred. The actual cost of developing the natural resource is directly related to the type of agreement Natives enter into with government or private industry in order to develop the resource.

What can Indian people do to deal with their marginal state in the Canadian economy? How can they deal with the increasing pressure to develop their natural resources? Indians ask when the resources are gone, will the reserves be even more impoverished? What will be the fate for our children and grandchildren? On the other hand, the need to support the present population is great, how can they resist the promise of jobs and money? We now take a closer look as to how Indians might be able to develop their natural resource potential.

While we focus on one aspect of the economy for illustrative purposes, it should be remembered that the present paper takes the position that there is a need to develop selected aspects of various sectors of the economy. This rejects the notion of balance growth. Why?

1. It is too costly and politically impossible to develop all sectors of the economy equally.
2. Even a developed economy is not balanced so why would you want to artificially create it on a reserve?

Undeveloped areas such as reserves must search for and invest in some intermediate or basic industry whose products are distributed as inputs through industrial sectors. That is, set up heavy/capital goods industries rather than consumer goods industries (Anders, 1980).

Most reserves do not have the ability to undertake large-scale natural resource development on their own. The capital requirements are too high, economic funds are not enough and banks won't loan reserve Indians money.[4] Tribes don't have the necessary expertise to manage large-scale developments. In addition, the energy industry is tightly controlled by existing multinationals and it is difficult for Indians to cut into the market. Finally, access to major transportation routes from many reserves is problematic (Robbins, 1984).

There are many different types of agreements that Indians could utilize in order to develop their economic base. Because of a limitation of space, we will discuss six of these: the concession, the joint venture, the service contract, the management agreement, the development corporation, and the local producer's cooperatives.

The Concession

This strategy has been the traditional way in which Indians (through the federal government) granted a company mineral production rights. The company makes a direct equity investment for the sole purpose of extracting a resource (Bankes, 1983). Asante (1979) claims that, in many cases, the concession amounts to a virtual assumption of sovereignty over the Indians' resources by transnational corporations. Under these conditions the corporation asserts ownership of not only the fixed assets but of the natural resource itself (Bankes, 1983).

Under a concession agreement, there is very little direct "up front" cost for the Indian community nor are there operating costs. In addition, these agreements are easy to administer, since the need for supervision, auditing and training is minimal. All of this is provided by the Company agreeing to exploit the minerals. In short, the cost for the band is minimal. Correspondingly, the return to the Indian community is also minimal. Indians have also found that this type of agreement does not encourage the training of local residents to assume jobs in the industry; thereby introducing them to the wage economy.

Another cost for Indians is that companies determine royalties by the price received by a wholy-owned subsidiary from a refining or distribution subsidiary of the parent company. Evidence in court cases in the United States also shows that many other ruses have been used to cheat Native people. The following list identifies only a small sample of techniques employed by companies over the past decade: bypasses on wells, adjustable metres, unreported oil sales, unapproved "sales" that are fed directly into pipelines, and movement of oil from a higher royalty lease to a lower one.

The Joint Venture

This means that there are two (or more) parties which pool their interests (e.g., money, technical expertise, land) in order to develop a project. There are two variations we will identify. The first is where a separate legal entity is created which would be jointly owned by the parties involved, e.g., Indians and development company. The second type does not involve the formation of a separate company but, rather, the parties to the venture have a direct undivided working interest in the project, (Bankes, 1983).

The joint venture type of agreement requires that Indians: (i) have some technical expertise and (ii) have some "interest" which is considered valuable by the other party, e.g., land, mineral rights. There is both a direct and indirect cost to this type of development. Conversely, the joint venture generally presents an opportunity for the local people to increase their control over the development, may increase revenues to Indians, and allows for a flexible method of collecting revenues (Bankes, 1983; Asante, 1979).

The Service Contract

Under agreements of this type, the status of Indian ownership over the natural resource is reaffirmed. Thus, rather than transferring the title of the resource (as in concession) to the developing company, the Indian community simply hires the corporation as a contractor or business partner to perform a specific task for a specified amount of money. A major implication of utilizing this strategy is that Indians have to have a substantial cash flow in order to pay for the "up front" cost of the development. Given that mineral exploration and production is highly capital intensive, substantial monies would be necessary and available to Indians prior to the actual development. Both Zakariya (1976) and Bankes (1983) point out that under this type of agreement, the band would have no internal control over the project, and there would be minimal opportunities for Indians to gain employment or technical/administrative skills, and careful monitoring of the project would be required by the Indians to ensure that maximum benefits would be derived. The benefits of such an arrangement would be that Indians would retain total ownership and jurisdiction over the natural resource. In addition, other firms would supply the technology (and risk capital) to explore, develop and market the resources.

Management Agreement

This is a strategy whereby Indians purchase expertise for a specified period of time. The contracted consultants can act as advisers while management (Indians) retains sole control of the company or it can relinquish control to the consultants.

Regional Development Corporation

These corporations are created to help to plan and implement the development goals of a community or region and assist business development. The corporation may involve itself in risk capital or it may be an advisory body. A variation of this strategy is referred to as a local producers cartel. This is a business strategy which involves the formation of a syndicate or trust that is able to take over a business venture from the original developer and carry on all negotiations with developers. The cartel takes over from the traditional developers and controls the operation. When 25 American Indian tribes created CERT (Council of Energy Resource Tribes) in order to control all mineral development on the reserves, they established a cartel.

Cooperative

These are usually voluntary, nonprofit societies incorporated to run a business. The members of the cooperatives own shares of the business and have one vote at each general meeting. A Board of Directors usually is elected to operate the business and carry out day to day activities. In effect, a cooperative is a business owned by its customers.

In 1959, the government began to encourage and support a number of locally owned and operated cooperatives. This idea seems to fit particularly well with one of the elements of Indian culture-sharing. The first Native cooperatives were producer-oriented art and fishing. Then, consumer cooperatives emerged where both importing and exporting activities were carried out. In many communities, cooperatives and other private enterprise businesses, e.g., Hudson Bay Company, exist side by side selling and buying many of the same products.

The Native cooperatives have two major problems in continuing their operations. First of all, they lack managers with good management skills. Secondly, they find it difficult to engage in direct competition with other integrated multinational companies. Nevertheless, they have provided employment for Native people and are the largest employers of Natives in the North, with annual sales of $30 million. Today there are about 50 co-ops employing about 600 people and generating nearly $10 million in income.

Nevertheless, an infusion of government monies is still required for many co-ops to continue operation. Over time, various government departments have contributed over $10 million to the development of cooperatives. In 1983, the federal government set aside an additional $10 million for a continuation of its Co-op Development Program. Much of this has been directed toward the training of directors, managers and staff to ensure their competence in running the co-ops. An additional two million dollars was set aside to help with the new production techniques and marketing strategies.

Conclusion

To date, the concession has been the most widely employed development strategy used by Indians. However, recently the joint venture has become a more attractive alternative arrangement by Natives by which they can participate in the ongoing modern economy. This strategy has been made possible because of the federal government's involvement. They have loaned money to Native companies and have guaranteed their backing. However, with no control or ownership of the natural resources and little capital to invest in backward and forward linkage, it is unlikely that these joint ventures can continue or be made a viable economic strategy by Native people.

Each of the development strategies discussed will have both benefits as well as costs. Hence, the type of agreement that a Native group might wish to make is ultimately determined by the group's needs, resources and goals. For example, if the Native group wanted to maintain a subsistence way of life (e.g., Cree of James Bay) and still allow development of natural resources, the concession type of agreement might be appropriate. On the other hand, if they wanted to become involved in the project, then a joint venture would seem more appropriate. For example, a joint venture called Shehtah Drilling was formed among Esso (50%), the Dene (25%) and Metis (25%) Development Corporations in 1983 to conduct drilling and service rig operations in the Northwest Territories. The ATCO/EQUTAK drilling venture organized between Atco-Mustang Drilling, the Inuivaluit Development Corporation (with the assistance of Petro Canada) and the Beaufort Food Services, and a joint venture between Beau-Tuk Marine and the Inuvialuit Development Corporations are other examples of joint ventures that have been relatively successful.

Notwithstanding the above goal, Indian people have three major problems that confront them in trying to make a decision as to whether or not to develop their natural resources. First of all, and unique to our case study, these resources are nonrenewable and thus are a one shot event.

A second major concern for Indian people is the impact of the development (both short- and long-term) on their communities.There is increasing evidence and awareness of environmental damage, pollution and disruption of Indian ways of life by industrial activities and recent major resource development projects: (DIAND, 35).The effects include an impact in rate and nature of cultural change, e.g., a change to a wage economy from a subsistence economy, the forcing of Indians to relocate (both individuals and communities), the disruption of fish and game populations and, in some cases, the creation of serious health hazards.[5]

A third concern relates to the view that Indians have of their reserve communities. Reserves are viewed by many Indians as their homeland. As Pendley and Kolstad (1980) point out "... it is impossible to separate tribal attitudes and actions related to their homelands. To tribal members these are part and parcel of the same thing. Once the development occurs, the residents must live with the consequences."

Finally, Indian people are concerned about their ability to negotiate agreements with private enterprise for the development of their natural resources. There is a great deal of suspicion on the part of Indians when dealing with private enterprise and a feeling often exists that the government cannot be trusted to act on their behalf. Hence, Indians themselves must obtain expertise in the area of development in order to insure that they receive the best deal and are aware of the impact of the development.

The above concerns (plus others) have forced Indians to be cautious when making decisions about natural resource development. It is an "ethos" that neither government nor private enterprise have taken into consideration when approaching Indian peoples. As Fudge (1983) points out, Indians are conservative in strategic outlook, emphasizing loss avoidance rather than risk taking. Indian community leaders are, therefore, often caught in a dilemma. On the one hand they are urged by local residents to asset a public desire for change, and yet at the same time they are cautioned to express an intense scepticism about any specific proposal to achieve change.

Indian people must convince federal and provincial officials that they are not a single homogeneous group. Indian communities must be afforded the opportunity to develop according to their need. In addition, Indian Affairs must develop alternative programs to match the needs, resources and goals of different Indian communities.

Today, most reserves have variations on a theme of "dual allegiance economic development." These adaptations have been made primarily as a result of nondirected adjustments by local residents over time due to opportunities made available by expanding economies. All were a result of dramatic human population decline, resource decimation or forced relocation by government. Few developments have been created because they fit the needs or goals of Native people. Assessing long-term impacts of various developments is likewise a rare event. Until long-term implications are considered and local community needs/resources are taken in account in the development plan, most economic ventures on reserves are doomed to failure.

Notes

[1]The brief statement of the major areas of Canada refer to the biogeoclimatic zones which refer to a large ecosystem that is geographically limited and controlled by a special single macro climate. Within these areas one will find the same predominant soil-forming processes which determine the zone's soil, vegetation and animal life.

[2]The issue of income distribution is not discussed at the beginning of development because leaders argue that it will curtail projects for investors, lower the rate of savings of those most likely to invest and decrease the choices people have. The hope is that the trickle-down effect will distribute the income at a later time.

[3]Some say that "group mindedness" inhibits development. People in traditional society think that individual improvement can take place only at the expense of somebody else. Therefore no change should occur unless the group is benefitted equally. But these same stagnant conditions may give rise to excessive individualism. If people think you can't change society, the best thing to do is to act as an individual and pursue selfish and short-term gains.

[4]The Tax Department seemed to take the position that the source of the income, not the residency of the Indians, was the basis on which liability for income was to be determined (Daugherty, 1978).

[5]The federal government has identified 20 Indian communities (involving 10 000 poeple) as facing impacts free from industrial development. In addition, the government has identified an additional 22 areas in Canada where "industrial development" may have serious and irreversible impacts on Indians and their communities.

References

Anders, G. (1980). Indians, Energy and Economic Development," *Journal of contemporary business*, 9:57-74.

Asante, S. (1979). "Restructuring Transnational Mineral Agreements," *American journal of international law*, 73, #3, 335-371.

Asch, M. (1987). "Capital and Economic Development: A Critical Appraisal of the Recommendations of the Mackenzie Valley Pipeline Commission," *Native people, Native lands*. B. Cox, ed. Ottawa: Carleton University Press, 232-240

Bankes, N. (1983). *Resource Leasing Options and the Settlement of Aboriginal Claims*. Ottawa, Ontario: Canadian Arctic Resources Committee.

Barsh, R.L. (1985). "Evolving Conceptions of Group Rights in International Law," *Transnational perspectives*, 13, #2, 6-11.

Chartrand, J. (1987). "Survival and Adaptation of the Inuit Ethnic Identity: The Importance of Inuktitut," *Native people, Native lands*. B. Cox, ed. Ottawa: Carleton University Press, 241-255.

Collins, J. (1986). "Smallholder Settlement of Tropical South America: The Social Causes of Ecological Destruction," *Human organization*, 45:1-10.

Cox, B. (ed.). (1987). *Native people, Native lands.* Ottawa: Carleton University Press.Daughtery, W. (1978).

Discussion report on Indian taxation. Department of Indian and Northern Affairs, Ottawa, Treaties and Historical Research Centre.

Douglas, M. (1986). *How institutions think.* Syracuse: Syracuse University Press.

Egbahl, A. (1983). "Ethnicite-Etat et Strategie de Developppment en Afrique ou le Development-Exclusion." *International Foundation for Development Alternatives.* Dossier, 36, 18-29.

Henriot, P. (1977). "Development Alternatives: Problems, Strategies, Values," *The Political economy of development and underdevelopment.* C. Wilber, ed. New York: Random House, 5-22.

Hoselity, Bert. (1972). "Social Implications of Economic Growth," *Readings in economic development.* W. Johnson and D. Kamerschen, eds. Cincinnati: South-Western Publishing Co., 53-85.

Jorgensen, J., R. Clemmer, R. Little, N. Owens, L. Robbins, S. Davis, R. Mathews, eds. (1978). *Native Americans and energy development.* Cambridge, Massachusetts: Anthropology Resource Centre.

Jorgensen, J., S. Swenson, D. Bomberry, J. Mohawk. (1984). *Native Americans and energy development II.* Boston: Anthropology Resource Center and Seventh Generation Fund.

Jorgensen, J., S. Davis, R. Mathews. (1978). "Energy, Agriculture and Social Science in the American West," *Native Americans and energy development.* J. Jorgensen, et. al. Cambridge, Massachusetts: Anthropology Resource Centre, 3-16.

Kuznets, Simon. (1972). "Present Underdeveloped Countries and Part Growth Patterns," *Readings in economic development.* W. Johnson and D. Kamerschen, eds. Cincinnati: South-Western Publishing Co., 38-52.

Kyint, A. (1972). "The Demand Approach to Economic Development," *Readings in economic development.* W. Johnson and D. Kamerschen, eds. Cincinatti: South-Western Publishing Co., 218-229

Owen, N. (1978). *Can Tribes Control Energy Development, Native Americans and energy development.* J. Jorgensen, et. al. Cambridge, Massachusetts: Anthropology Resource Centre, 49-62.

Pendley, K. and C. Kolstad. (1980). "American Indians and National Energy Policy," *The journal of energy and development,* 5, 221-251.Robbins, L. (1984). *Energy Developments and the Navajo Nation, Native Americans and energy development II.* J. Jorgensen et. al. Boston: Anthropology Resource Centre and Seventh Generation Fund, 35-48.

Schultz, Theodore. (1972). "Investment in Human Capital in Poor Countries," *Readings in economic development.* W. Johnson and D. Kamerschen, eds. Cincinatti: South-Western Publishing Co., 298-307.

Waldram, J. (1985). "Hydroelectric Development and Dietary Delocalization in Northern Manitoba", Canada, *Human organization,* 44:41-49.

Whyte W. and L. Williams. (1968). *Toward an integrated theory of development.* New York State School of Industrial and Labour Relations. Ithaca: Cornell University.

Wilber, C. ed. (1977). *The political economy of development and underdevelopment.* New York: Random House.

Zakariya, H. (1976). "New Directions in the Search for and Development of Petroleum Resources in the Developing Countries," *Vanderbilt journal of transnational law,* 9, Summer, 545-577.

6
Native Land Claims

Joan Scott-Brown

Land is important to all people and it is no less important to the Aboriginal peoples of North America. Indians have always had a special affinity for the land; it is their identity and culture. The Department of Indian Affairs has recognized this fact and stated that Aboriginal people have always claimed a special relationship to the land as the basis for their cultural distinctiveness and legally designated status. Indians believe that they have the right to live on the land now called Canada because this right was given by the Great Spirit.

For the Native people, land is more than a piece of soil. Indian Elders have said that "from the time our ancestors came upon this land it was considered ours." They were the first settlers in North America following the Mastodon across the Bering Straits during the periods of glaciation. The various Indian groups established their own area for hunting and fishing and gathering such plants as blueberries, camus roots or wild rice, and growing crops such as corn or tobacco. These areas were respected by other groups. Indian people did not invade one another's area without first seeking permission. Of course there were skirmishes, but these were not often due to trespassing.

Historical Practice

The concept of the ownership of land was one of the main differences between the European settlers and the already present Aboriginal people. Land ownership, as the European understood it, was a "Fee Simple Title" to an area of land. "Fee Simple Absolute" is an estate limited absolutely to one man or his heirs and assigns forever without limitation or condition (Cumming and Mickenberg, 1972, p. 40). This is the highest form of title known in Common Law. This concept was unknown to the Indian who believed that land was there for all to use and to respect.

For the European settler, coming from a country in which a feudal system of land ownership and closure had been in effect for many hundreds of years, Canada seemed a wide open land. It was not farmed or enclosed, which meant it could not be owned by anyone and so the settler could claim it. The Indians did not enclose land because many tribes were nomadic, without a permanent settled habitation. One settler, John Winthrope, reasoned that the Native people had a "natural right to the land, and if the settler left enough land for the Natives to use, then he could use the rest, there being more than enough (land) for them and us" (Winthrope papers, 1931).

In international law there are three ways by which an exploring nation can acquire new land. These are: a) conquest, b) cession, and c) discovery. Possession of Canada was not obtained by conquest either by the European or the AmerIndian. The term "AmerIndian" is used to denote a wider North American context insofar as the issue of land claims is concerned. The AmerIndian came into the area when it was not inhabited. The Europeans, particularly the English, were granted a commission to discover countries then unknown and to take possession of them in the name of the Christian King of England. The European claim was based on the Right of Discovery. The Maritime powers of Europe, between about 1600-1650, were all on voyages of discovery at the same time, each going to many of the same areas of the globe. In order to avoid conflict, it was necessary to establish a principle that would enshrine the first explorer's rights to an area above all others. The principle chosen was the Right of Discovery. By this, the nation making the discovery had the sole right to acquire the land and make settlements on it. This was an exclusive principle which shut out the rights of competition among those who had agreed to it. It regulated the right given by discovery (Cumming and Mickenberg, 1972, p. 17).

The charter or grant given to European explorers stipulated that they only occupy land not previously occupied by a Christian prince. This was a claim under the provision of "Terra nullius," which meant that the land was not inhabited, or that the inhabitants did not have the same religious convictions as the discoverers. If the land was completely devoid of human habitation, however, the land title and political jurisdiction could be claimed on the grounds of "Vacuum domicilum" (Berkhofer 1978). The problem lay in the "degree" of occupancy, for what was seen as vacant by the European settler's concept of usage was in actual fact fully occupied and used by the nomadic North American Indians. The presence of the Aboriginal people, who were often hostile to the explorer, meant that the land could not be claimed under Vacuum domicilum and so, in order to justify their occupation, the European had to exercise the claim, "Terra nullius" and the lack of the Christian religion.

The explorers never actually considered the idea that the land was already owned by the original inhabitants. In 1532, a theologian, Francisco de Vitoria, (often called the Father of Aboriginal rights) delivered two lectures at the University of Salamancas on the rights of the

Aboriginal people of North America. He argued that the Indians were the true owners of the land and that their lack of belief in the Roman Catholic faith could have no effect. He suggested that the Indian was no less intelligent than some Spanish peasants and were equally fit to have legal rights. He further postulated that the Pope had no temporal power over Indian lands. Spain could have no claim to the land through Discovery because this only referred to unoccupied land. Pope Paul III obviously agreed and he issued a Papal Bull in 1537 stating that "Indians were truly men with the same rights as a Spanish peasant." This was supported by Spain's "Law of the Indies" in which the Indian was placed on an equal footing with Spaniards and a form of protection for Indian land was allowed (Cumming and Mickenberg, 1972).

The concept of the Indians being the true owners of the land was a problem considered by a Dominican priest, Bartolome de las Casas, in the 1600s when he argued the case before the Holy Roman Emperor, Charles V. Aboriginal ownership, however, was not countenanced by the Canadian government when incoming settlers moved along the Atlantic seaboard and encroached on Indian lands. Originally the British government wanted the Indian as an ally against the French in the struggle for North America. Two proclamations were issued, the first by the Privy Council in Great Britain in 1791 which forbade the various colonies from passing any grants on lands owned by Indians, and the other was the Royal Proclamation signed in 1763 by King George III.

The Royal Proclamation was a policy arrangement for the protection of Indian lands. The British government recognized that Indian title could only be extinguished by a bi-lateral agreement, so this became the model of signing treaties which eventually was the basis of the government's Indian policy. Treaties had already been signed between equal nations of the Aboriginal people and the Crown, but the Royal Proclamation implied that the Indian and Indian lands needed protection. One third of the Royal Proclamation was devoted to matters relating to Indians (Johnston, 1984, p. 4).

After the fur trade began to dwindle, the Indian-European relationship began to change. The Indian, once considered an equal and ally, was now considered to be a ward of the Crown in need of protection. The land that Indians had once owned, by right of possession, was now held in trust by the Crown. The Royal Proclamation created the boundaries for the establishment of Upper Canada, but more importantly it outlined the policy for dealing with Indian lands. Some observers suggest that the Royal Proclamation served to promote and clarify the pre-existing and conceded rights of Indian people.

Great Britain desired that Indian land be respected. This was noted in a report by the Secretary of Indian Affairs to Sir William Johnson in 1756, in which he noted that:

> the Indians by putting their land under the protection of the Crown understood that this was not a cession or surrender. . . . They intended to look upon it as reserving the Property and Possession of the Soil to themselves and their heirs (Cumming and Mickenberg, 1972).

This interpretation presupposes the understanding that the Indians were using the Crown to protect their land, not ceding it to the Crown. Although the Royal Proclamation has been called the "Charter of Indian Rights," it did not deal with Indian lands in the West. The Indians of the West were outside the area considered by the Royal Proclamation. The governmental policy of the time was to obtain land from the Aboriginal people by signing a treaty which contained some form of compensation. The English legal system (which also applied to the Colonies), stated that the citizens of a newly acquired dominion do not lose their property or civil rights (Asch, 1984). These rights remain unless the Sovereign passes a law which directly diminishes the rights of the original inhabitants. The only legislation in Canada to do this was the signing of a treaty. With the numbered treaties the Crown obtained land from the Aboriginal people in return for specific compensation and rights. The Indian people who did not sign a treaty did *not* relinquish the Aboriginal rights to their land.

Legalities

Today the government has a problem dealing with Aboriginal rights because these are title to the land based on the fact that the Native people of Canada were the original occupants of the land. Pierre Trudeau, in his 1969 statement on Aboriginal rights, stated that Aboriginal rights could not be restored, but he did say "We will be just in our time. This is all we can do."

The Royal Proclamation recognized that the original people *did* have title to the land, and while the treaties recognized these rights, they also restricted them. Land was ceded for cash payments and the promise of the continuance of unrestricted hunting and fishing on unoccupied Crown lands.

In British Columbia, where the signing of treaties was limited, the argument persists over the validity of Aboriginal rights. The B.C. government maintains that Aboriginal rights were extinguished by legislation of the *Colonial Acts and Ordinances* signed when British

Columbia entered Confederation in 1871. The terms of this union neglected any reference to Aboriginal rights or title.

The meaning of Aboriginal rights, although enshrined in the Canadian constitution, remains unclear. Three first minister's meetings called to define Aboriginal rights failed to do so. Cumming and Mickenberg define Aboriginal rights as "those property rights which inure to Native peoples by virtue of their occupation upon certain lands from time immemorial." This is a very restrictive view because Aboriginal rights extend far beyond only property rights. Exactly what is covered by the term "Aboriginal rights" has yet to be defined. The Canadian constitution, section 35 (1) recognizes "existing Aboriginal and Treaty of the Aboriginal peoples of Canada;" however these have not yet been fully delineated. For Native people, Aboriginal rights include the right to land as well the right to self-determination and self-government. What exactly property rights and ownership of the land mean, however, need to be clarified. Several court cases have attempted to do this.

Chief Justice Marshall in a a judgement handed down in the case of *Johnson and Graham's Lessee v. MacIntosh* (1823) stated that:

> the original inhabitants of the land were the rightful occupants of the soil with a legal and just claim to possession of it and to use it according to their own discretion, but their rights to complete sovereignty as independent nations, were naturally diminished, and their power to dispose of the soil at their own will to whomsoever they please was denied by the original fundamental principle that discovery gave exclusive title to those who made it (Cumming and Mickenberg, 1972, 17).

Justice Morrow in a Supreme Court case of the Northwest Territories in 1973 upon the application of the indigenous people of the N.W.T. asserting a claim to legal title of the land by virtue of their occupation prior to the entry of the Colonial government concluded:

> there are certain well established characteristics of legal title if the Indian or Aboriginees were in occupation of the land prior to Colonial entry. These are:
> a) possessory right, the right to use and exploit the land;
> b) a communal right;
> c) there is a Crown interest underlying this title, it being an estate held by the Crown; and
> d) the right is inalienable, it cannot be transferred and can only be terminated by reversion to the Crown.

Morrow concluded that in view of the facts, the Aboriginal people occupying the area covered by the proposed caveat came fully within this criteria and that in the terms of Hall in the Calder case were therefore the prima facie owners of the land. He therefore ruled that the Dene could file a claim to Aboriginal title in the land registry system in the N.W.T. (Sanders, 1983).

A court case in 1851 ruling on whether the Six Nations had a legal right to the reserve that had been established for them ruled that: "We cannot recognize any peculiar law of real property applying to the Indians — the common law is not part savage and part civilized" (Sanders, 1983).

The Nishga believe that the Nass Valley in British Columbia belongs to them because they have never sold or given away any part of it; neither have they signed a treaty. They challenged the belief of the British Columbia provincial government that their rights had been extinguished and thus took their case to court beginning in 1913. The case eventually reached the courts and became known as *Calder* (named after the then chief) *vs. the Queen*. The case was placed before the Supreme Court and in 1973 a decision was handed down. Three judges ruled that Aboriginal title continued to exist, three judges ruled that Aboriginal title did *not* exist and the seventh judge ruled against the Nishga on a technicality; they had not obtained the Crown's permission to proceed against them. Although the Nishga did not win the case, the ruling was not exactly a loss either; to date, however, the Nishga case remains unresolved.

In the case of the *St. Catherine's Milling and Lumber vs. the Queen* (1883) the Privy Council, in order to resolve the issue, had to address the nature of Indian title. This case was basically a fight between the federal government and the Province of Ontario over lands which the Indians had surrendered and in which the Indians were not directly involved. During this case, the court saw Native title as a "possessory right," the right to use and occupy the land similar to a "Usufructuary right." In 1888, the interpretation of this ruling was changed to a "personal usufructuary right dependent upon the goodwill of the Sovereign" (Frideres, 1988, p. 93).

"Usufruct" is a term derived from Roman Law. It has been defined as a "right of enjoying a thing, the property of which is vested in another, and to draw from the same all the profit, utility and advantage it may produce, provided it be without altering the substance of the thing" (*Black's Law Dictionary*). Usufruct terminated upon the death of the holder. Again this issue has not been satisfactorily settled. Cumming and Mickenberg state that in Canada there is no definite judicial statement on whether Aboriginal right is a usufructuary right to hunt, fish and farm on the land the Indian people hold. They do state, however, that this is a restricted view inconsistent with the legal precedents in the field. They view Indian title as having all the incidents of a "Fee simple estate." Fee simple absolute is "an estate limited absolutely to a man and his heirs and assigns forever without limitation or condition" (*Black's Law Dictionary*, 1951). It is the highest form of title known to Common Law (Cumming and Mickenberg, 1972).

It was the 1973 ruling in the Calder case that prompted the federal government, who until now had been dealing with claims based on failed treaty obligations, into realizing that they would have to deal with Native people who had not signed treaties. Prior to this, all land claims had been handled on an individual basis either by the Department of Indian Affairs or the Justice Department. In 1962, the government had attempted to set up an Indian Claims Commission, with a Claims Commissioner. This was later proposed in the White Paper of 1969 and rejected by the Indian people, who did not want a government-appointed and, therefore, biased commissioner. In spite of this objection, in 1974 the Office of Native Claims was created and an Indian Commissioner, Dr. Lloyd Barber, was appointed. His position was eventually dissolved in 1977. In 1981 the government published a booklet entitled, *In All Fairness*, which set forward the government's position on comprehensive claims. There are now two major categories of claims being processed. These are:

a) Comprehensive claims, a term used to describe claims based on Native occupancy and use of traditional areas. These are basically hunting and trapping rights and economic and social benefits. This policy asserted that a blanket extinguishment of Aboriginal rights should no longer be a precondition for settlement. Comprehensive claims are claims by Indian people who have *never* signed a treaty and whose rights have not been superseded by law. These types of claims occur more frequently in the northern areas of Canada. Frideres claims that a greater emphasis is placed on the cooperation between Native people and the government for extinguishment of Aboriginal title and for specific rights such as hunting and fishing (Frideres, 1988). Subsurface rights are now to be included, and settlement can be in the form of cash, government bonds etc. but they are specific and finite. The first comprehensive claim to be settled was with the James Bay Cree and the Inuit. This was after Mr. Justice Malouf of the Quebec Supreme Court had ruled that the James Bay hydro-electric project could not proceed until the rights of the Cree and Inuit of Northern Quebec had been dealt with, which cost the government of Quebec a million dollars a day (Sanders, 1983).

The other type of claim dealt with by governmental policy is:

b) a specific land claim. This refers to claims that are the fulfilment of treaties and governmental administration of Indian lands. These are claims entered by Indian people whose ancestors signed treaties and which are therefore based on broken treaty rights. The problem here is that the provinces under the 1930 Natural Resource Agreement administer all unoccupied Crown land, and only the provinces can return the land or make resource agreements. The federal government can make case compensation only. In western Canada, more than 70 bands have filed specific land claims. Many bands, especially in Manitoba, Saskatchewan and Alberta have launched claims saying that they have received less land than promised under the treaties. In many cases it is true that the government, by a stroke of the pen in Ottawa, eliminated much Native land. For example, after World War II, Indian land was given to returning war veterans, and the consent of the Indians involved was never obtained. The first of these "cut off" claims was settled with the Penticton band in 1982. About 35 of these claims have been settled so far. A claims advisory board has been established in northern Alberta to settle claims for Native groups who were overlooked during the signing of the treaties or who did not receive reserves. Just recently the Woodland Cree of northern Alberta have settled their land claims but the Lubicon Lake Cree are still waiting.

The tone of the document, *In All Fairness*, is tough. It talks about land claims, not Native claims, and rejects any suggestion of Aboriginal self-determination. The government is concerned about Native land claims because if Native people gained control of a sizable portion of land in the North they could block any further economic development and delay proposed megaprojects.

Ottawa offers two types of title to land:

a) land for exclusive use by Native people, with sub-surface rights, and
b) surface rights, including hunting and fishing, but open to non-renewable resource development.

Ottawa is willing to offer a Fee Simple Title, but this does not allow Native people the power to legislate over their land or prevent expropriation by the government. Ottawa sees Native land claims as real estate transactions involving property rather than an ongoing social contract between peoples. Government officials also want the settlements to be final to end any possibility of future claims.

New Policies

The federal government issued a second booklet in 1982, entitled *Outstanding Business*, which deals with other Indian claims and with Inuit claims. Many of the Indian and Inuit claims remain as unfinished business. In 1986, Bill McKnight, then Minister of Indian Affairs, issued an update to the comprehensive policy. The major changes are:

a) a streamlining of the process for acceptance or rejection of a comprehensive claim;

b) the presentation of options to achieve certainty of title, the blanket extinguishment policy no longer applies;

c) details are supplied on the negotiation of self-government, an area in which the government wants to show it is moving;

d) greater attention to third party interest and public concern; and

e) changes in the negotiating process.
    (Purich, 1986, p. 56)

The new policy on Native land claims was announced in 1973, and since that time Aboriginal rights have been entrenched in the Canadian Constitution. First ministers could not come to an agreement with the First Nations as to whether the right to self-government is an existing right, and the First Ministers' meetings of 1982-1987 would not even consider this possibility. It would seem that a ruling on this matter will have to come from the court.

There are still many cases awaiting a decision. Three comprehensive land claims have been settled since the policy was put in place: the James Bay agreement in 1975, the Northeastern Quebec agreement in 1978 and the Inuvialuit claim of the Mackenzie River Delta in 1984. There are at present 53 claims that have either been submitted or are waiting to be processed. George Erasmus recently stated that at the present rate of settlement it will take 160 years to settle these claims (Richardson, 1989).

The Teme-Augama Anishnabai claim by the people of Lake Tegami, Ontario, is an outstanding case and these people were omitted from the signing of the Robinson-Huron Treaty. In 1884, the government surveyed a 100-square mile reserve, but the Ontario government refused to transfer the land. In 1901, they established the Tegami Forest Reserve. The potential richness of the forest was an important factor in the refusal to relinquish the land to the Native people. In 1989, the Ontario government completed two logging roads in the disputed area. The Bear Island Indian band, who have been asking for a land settlement for the past

112 years, decided to block the roads until the Supreme Court hears the claim to 16 000 square kilometres in the area. This case is still pending.

The Lubicon Lake Indians did not sign Treaty Eight which was the treaty negotiated in their area. In 1939, the Department of Indian Affairs sent officials to survey an area for a reserve, which was approved in 1940; however, with the government's preoccupation with World War II little was done to establish a reserve. In 1942, an official in the government decided that many Lubicon band members were not really Indians and their names were omitted from the band list. The number of Lubicon Lake band members was contested when the area for a reserve was being negotiated during the 1980s. An all-weather road into the area, contested by the Lubicons, was completed in 1978, and oil companies began to move into the area, destroying much of the habitat and frightening away the game which the Lubicon subsisted on. Between 1979 and 1982, 400 oil wells had been established in Lubicon territory. The number of Moose obtained by the Lubicon had dropped from 200 in a year to less than 20. The Lubicon Lake people took their complaint to the United Nations Committee on Human Rights in 1985, stating that Canada was denying them the right of self-determination. Canada denied these allegations, stating that the Lubicon were not "a people" and were therefore not entitled to assert the right of self-determination (Richardson, 1989).

The Lubicon band has attempted to have their claim settled in the courts, but this move was quashed by a decision of the Supreme Court that has a rule against rehearing applications for leave to appeal. A renewed application by lawyers for the Lubicons to overturn the previous ruling which had decided against granting an injunction was refused. With this avenue blocked, the Lubicons resorted to other means. These included boycotting the "Spirit Sings" exhibit held during the Winter Olympics in Calgary in 1986, and in 1988 putting up road blocks to hinder access to local oil wells. The premier of Alberta, Don Getty, entered the picture, and began negotiations with the chief of the Lubicons, Bernard Ominayak.

The question of the size of the land settlement has now been settled, but the amount of compensation is still being debated. Until this problem has been resolved, the oil wells in the area are not operating, although the two oil companies involved in the dispute claim they have lost more than $500 000. In the meantime, another problem has arisen; the area adjacent to the Lubicon land has been leased to Daishowa Canada which is a large pulp mill conglomerate that intends to build a large pulp mill near Peace River. This would not only void Lubicon land of trees, it would also be a main source of pollution. This situation remains unresolved.

Elsewhere in Canada, two agreements-in-principle have been reached; one with the Yukon Indians, and another with the Inuit of the Tungavick Federation of Nunavat in the Central and Eastern Arctic. A third tentative agreement was made in April, 1990, between the government and the Dene and Metis. However, this was not accepted by all the chiefs of the five Native groups in the area. The main stumbling block was the government's policy requiring Indians to give up their Aboriginal rights. This agreement collapsed in November 1990. The negotiations for this agreement began over 20 years ago with the government of Pierre Trudeau.

According to the *Globe and Mail* (January 3, 1990), the focus on land claims negotiations will not be in British Columbia. In the Bitksan-Wet'suwet'en case, an injunction preventing Westar from logging in the Shedin watershed area was won in 1988, but a land claims case is yet to be tried. The Nishga Tribal Council, in talks with the federal government, reached a framework agreement that calls for a land claims agreement within three years *(Globe and Mail,* November, 1989).

The Ongoing Challenge

There has been a continual attempt by government to obtain land from the Aboriginal peoples of Canada and many of the promises made to achieve this have been reneged upon, leading to the necessity of the many pending land claims yet to be settled. A total of 578 specific land claims were submitted to the Department of Indian Affairs in 1990, and have yet to be considered. Many comprehensive claims have also been submitted.

The dispute at Oka during the summer of 1990 is one land claim issue that has been ignored. This is a dispute that has festered for more than a century. One hundred and three years ago, a dispute over land at Oka made the front pages of the newspapers of the day. At this time, the land dispute was between a Roman Catholic seminary and the Mohawk Nation. The seminary wanted 275 Protestant Mohawks to leave the area and relocate in the Muskoka region where a small band of Protestants had set up a reserve. Church officials proposed that the seminary and the government set up a fund to purchase "improved farm land" at $10 per acre. The seminary had intended to turn the land occupied by the Mohawk into a townsite for French settlers. The Indian Council rejected the offer *(Globe and Mail,* November 30, 1990).

In 1990, the land dispute was ignited by the expansion of a golf course onto Mohawk sacred land. On May 11, 1990, the Kahnesatke Mohawk set up a blockade to stop the town of Oka expanding a golf course onto land the Mohawk had laid claim to. This dispute was clouded by a gambling dispute on the reserve, which was an internal struggle for money and power, an argument over bingo halls, casinos and slot machines. This dispute erupted into violence and resulted in the death of two men. The St. Regis-Akwesasane Reserve straddles Ontario, Quebec and New York State. The reserve is 28 000 acres in size and is home to approximately 8 500 Akwesasane Mohawks; 4 500 live in the United States portion of the reserve and 4 000 live in Canada.

This reserve has several forms of jurisdiction: the governments of Canada via the Department of Indian Affairs; the government of the United States with the Bureau of Indian Affairs; the police forces of the R.C.M.P.; New York State; Ontario and the Surete du Quebec. On the reserve, the Mohawk have three governing bodies: the tribal council on the American side; the band council on the Canadian side (who are both elected), and the traditional council of chiefs, whose positions are inherited. The latter recognize the authority of the Long House and not that of the elected councils. There is also the militant Mohawk Sovereign Security Force, called the "Warriors;" these are a group of people formed as a means of security on the United States side of the reserve. These many forms of control do not favor cohesion or consensus on the reserve.

The Mohawks are part of the Six Nations Iroquois Confederacy which arose after the War of 1812, and the Canadian-U.S. border was redrawn which went right through the middle of the Akwesasane Reserve. Many of the Mohawk fought with both the English or French in the colonial wars.

On May 11, 1990, the Mohawks of Kanesatake set up barricades to bring attention to their land claim and the encroachment onto this land by the town of Oka. On July 11, a force of 100 men from the Surete Du Quebec attempted to dismantle this blockade and one policeman was killed. Also on July 11, the Mohawks from the Kahnawake Reserve, near Chateauguay, blocked the road leading to the Mercier Bridge linking the community to Montreal.

Negotiations were begun between the Government of Quebec and Mohawk leaders. The federal government announced that it did not wish to be involved, though they did attempt to buy the disputed land. The New York governor also distanced himself from the troubles on the reserve, suggesting that the violence was on the Canadian side.

The talks broke down and Premier Bourassa of Quebec sent in the army on August 27 to dismantle the barricades at both Oka and Kahnawake. This was an action using the *National Defence Act*, an act designed to settle local disturbances or riots. The Prime Minister, Mr. Mulroney, acknowledged that the standoff at Oka was a national emergency and a threat to national security, but he did not use the *Emergency*

Measures Act, which replaced the *War Measures Act,* because the use of this act requires a parliamentary debate. The government was on a summer recess at that time and would have had to be recalled.

The Mohawks helped the army to remove the barricades at Kahnawake, but the army and the Mohawks continued their standoff at Oka. This blockade continued until September 26, 1990, when the Mohawks left the detoxification centre where they had been cornered by the army for nearly a month. The Defence Department spent 60.6 million dollars to keep the army on standby at Oka for six weeks and the event marked a deteriorating point in the relationship between the government and the Indians of Canada. The government was shown in very poor light because they ignored the problem instead of trying to solve it.

George Erasmus has outlined several solutions to the problems facing Native people today, many of which hinge on the issue of land. He believes that negotiations on self-government must take place as part of the land-claims process and should be given constitutional protection. The land claims negotiations must extend to jurisdiction over that land. Land, and jurisdiction over land, go hand in hand. The First Nations believe that "their Aboriginal claims includes ownership and jurisdiction over all land and resources within their traditional areas, and the claims resolution is a process of determining what land, resources and jurisdiction will be shared with the governments of Canada. The process is not one of negotiating extinguishment of Aboriginal rights, but of arriving at an equitable agreement on sharing" (Richardson, 1989).

A second recommendation made by George Erasmus is to implement the study by the task force on the comprehensive claims policy and speed up the land claims process. The number of land claims being negotiated should also be increased, because at the present rate outstanding claims do not stand a chance of being resolved within this century.

Perhaps central to the issues of resolving the outstanding land claims is the concept of Indian sovereignty which is central to Aboriginal self-government. Land claims and self-government cannot be separated. This is a difficult concept for the government of Canada and the provinces to grapple with. It is imperative though that this issue be resolved. With an Aboriginal government in place the Aboriginal people themselves could deal with the many problems facing them and could set up their own judicial system. They could borrow money from off the reserves to fund projects to employ their own people and so raise the standard of living. The environment and natural resources could be greatly enhanced by the knowledge of Native Elders. But more importantly First Nations would be given the recognition and respect so long denied them, of being the First Nations equal to the founding French and English nations.

References

Asch, Michael. (1984). *Home and Native land. Aboriginal Rights and the Canadian Constitution.* Toronto: Methuen.

Berkhofer, Robert. (1979). *The whiteman's Indian: images of the American Indian from Columbus to the present.* New York: Vantage Books.

Black's Law Dictionary. (1951). 4th edition. St. Paul, Minn: West Publishing Co.

Cumming, Peter and Neil Mickenberg. (1972). *Native rights in Canada.* Don Mills: General Pub. Co.

Frideres, James. (1988). *Native peoples in Canada: contemporary conflicts.* 3rd edition. Scarborough: Prentice-Hall.

Johnston, Darlene. (1989). *The taking of Indian lands in Canada: consent or coercion?* Saskatoon: University of Saskatchewan Native Law Centre.

Purich, Donald. (1986). *Our land, Native rights in Canada.* Toronto: Lorimer.

Richardson, Boyce. (1989). *Drumbeat: anger and renewal in Indian country.* Toronto: Summerhill Press.

Sanders, Douglas. (1983). "Do the Courts Uphold Indian Rights," *Pemmican journal,* 4-6.

Winthrope, John. (1931). *Winthrope's papers.* Boston: Massachusetts Historical Society, Vol. 2, 141.

7

Metis[1] Land Claims in Manitoba

Thomas Flanagan

After persistent lobbying and some near failures,[2] Metis organizations were able to get the concept of Metis Aboriginal rights entrenched in the *Constitution Act* of 1982:

35. (1) The existing Aboriginal and treaty rights of the Aboriginal peoples of Canada are hereby recognized and affirmed.

(2) In this Act, 'Aboriginal peoples of Canada' includes the Indian, Inuit and Metis peoples of Canada.

Although the Metis of all three prairie provinces have advanced claims of various types, it has yet to be determined whether Metis Aboriginal rights are still "existing"; what their scope may be; and, in particular, whether they include any rights to land.[3]

This chapter will discuss the situation in Manitoba, where Metis land claims are the most sweeping and the most legally advanced. The case of *Dumont et al. v. Attorney General (Canada) and Attorney General (Manitoba)*,[4] sponsored by the Manitoba Metis Federation, is a major attempt to use the courts to establish Metis land rights. I will return to this case after describing the historical background out of which it has arisen.

Historical Background

Many writers have described how the Metis of the Red River settlement, led by the young Louis Riel, resisted Canada's acquisition of Rupert's Land. In the spring of 1870, Riel's provisional government sent three delegates to Ottawa to negotiate the conditions under which the Metis would agree to confederation with Canada. Of the three, the most influential was Father N.J. Ritchot, Riel's confessor. Ritchot persuaded Sir John A. Macdonald and Sir George-Etienne Cartier, who conducted the negotiations for Canada, to make several concessions, including immediate provincial status, responsible provincial government, official bilingualism, and denominational schools.[5] The concessions embodied in the *Manitoba Act* also extended to land rights:

30. All ungranted or waste lands in the Province shall be, from and after the date of the said transfer, vested in the Crown, and

administered by the Government of Canada for the purposes of the Dominion, subject to, and except and so far as the same may be affected by, the conditions and stipulations contained in the agreement for the surrender of Rupert's Land by the Hudson's Bay Company to Her Majesty.

31. And whereas, it is expedient, towards the extinguishment of the Indian Title to the lands in the Province, to appropriate a portion of such ungranted lands, to the extent of one million four hundred thousand acres thereof, for the benefit of the families of the half-breed residents, it is hereby enacted, that, under regulations to be from time to time made by the Governor General in Council, the Lieutenant-Governor shall select such lots or tracts in such parts of the Province as he may deem expedient, to the extent aforesaid, and divide the same among the children of the half-breed heads of families residing in the Province at the time of the said transfer to Canada, and the same shall be granted to the said children respectively, in such mode and on such conditions as to settlement and otherwise, as the Governor General in Council may from time to time determine.

32. For the quieting of titles, and assuring to the settlers in the province the peaceable possession of the lands now held by them, it is enacted as follows:

    1. All grants of land in freehold made by the Hudson's Bay Company up to the eighth day of March, in the year 1869, shall, if required by the owner, be confirmed by grant from the Crown.

    2. All grants of estates less than freehold in land made by the Hudson's Bay Company up to the eighth day of March aforesaid, shall, if required by the owner, be converted into an estate in freehold by grant from the Crown.

    3. All titles by occupancy with the sanction and under the license and authority of the Hudson's Bay Company up to the eighth day of March aforesaid, of land in that part of the Province in which the Indian Title has been extinguished, shall if required by the owner, be converted into an estate in freehold by grant from the Crown.

    4. All persons in peaceable possession of tracts of land at the time of the transfer to Canada, in those parts of the Province in which the Indian Title has not been extinguished, shall have the right of preemption of the same, on such terms and conditions as may be determined by the Governor in Council.

    5. The Lieutenant-Governor is hereby authorized, under regulations to be made from time to time by the Governor

General in Council, to make all such provisions for ascer-
taining and adjusting, on fair and equitable terms, the
rights of Common, and rights of cutting Hay held and
enjoyed by the settlers in the Province, and for the commutation of the same by grants of land from the Crown.

33. The Governor General in Council shall from time to time settle
and appoint the mode and form of Grants of Land from the
Crown, and any Order-in-Council for that purpose when published in the *Canada Gazette,* shall have the same force and
effect as if it were a portion of this Act.[6]

Section 30 gave the federal government control of the public lands of
Manitoba, thus putting the new province in a different category from
the four original partners in Confederation. Riel had wanted provincial
control of public lands in Manitoba, but the federal government was
unwilling to yield on this point, fearing that its plans for immigration,
settlement, and railway construction might be jeopardized if it did not
retain control of "Dominion Lands" in the West.

Section 31 provided for a land grant of 1.4 million acres to the
"children of the half-breed heads of families." Behind this provision was
the fear that aggressive newcomers might purchase or homestead all
the good land in Manitoba, leaving the younger generation of Metis a
landless minority in their own province. Section 31 put the implementation of the grant under the control of the federal cabinet, except for
advice from the Lieutenant Governor of Manitoba on the location of the
1.4 million acres. Ritchot had wanted the grant to be under the control
of the provincial legislature and thought he had achieved this at one
point in the negotiations.[7] Absence of local control over the land grant
would later become an important source of dissatisfaction.

Section 32 required the federal government to confirm existing land
titles in Manitoba, whether acquired by occupation or by explicit grant
from the Hudson's Bay Company. This section addressed the land rights
of all old settlers, not just the Metis; but since about 90 percent of the
residents of Manitoba in 1870 were of mixed blood, it had a great effect
on the Metis. The chief difficulty arising from this section was the
practical definition of the phrase "peaceable possession" in s.32(4).
There were many disputes in particular cases whether the degree of
occupancy of land prior to 1870 was sufficient to justify confirmation of
title under the heading of "peaceable possession."

Section 32(5) addressed the special issue of customary hay and pasture rights. Most of the Red River settlers lived on long, narrow river
lots fronting the Red and Assiniboine Rivers and a couple of their
tributaries. These lots were of variable width but usually about two
miles deep. Behind the "inner two miles," the settlers had been allowed

by the Hudson's Bay Company to cut hay and pasture their livestock on an additional "outer two miles." Many disputes arose out of the vague wording of s.32(5), which promised to commute these usufructuary rights with grants of land, but did not specify the precise nature of the rights nor the ratio of compensation.

Section 33 required the form of land grants to be approved by the federal cabinet. The effect of this provision was to ensure that Manitoba land matters were considered at the political level and not handled in a purely administrative way by the Department of the Interior, created in 1873.

There is a good deal of controversy over the implementation of the land provisions of the *Manitoba Act*, particularly ss.31 and 32, which were supposed to confer tangible benefits upon the Metis population considered both as old settlers (s.32) and as a special group of partly Indian ancestry (s.31). I will first try to establish a common ground by giving an outline, in as neutral and objective a way as possible, of the implementation of these land provisions.[8] I will then try to explain why the Manitoba Metis Federation today claims that the Metis received little or no benefit from the land provisions of the *Manitoba Act*, and that the implementation was unconstitutional.

When the federal government appointed A.G. Archibald as lieutenant governor of Manitoba, it requested him to offer advice on the implementation of s.31. That advice was substantially incorporated into an order-in-council of April 25, 1871, which established the first regime for Dominion lands.[9] The order provided that the Metis children's land grant would be carried out by means of a lottery to be conducted by the lieutenant governor. Following Archibald's advice, the wording of s.31 was interpreted loosely, allowing all Metis persons, whether children or adults, to participate in the lottery. That meant that individual allotments would be 140 acres, since there were about 10 000 Metis in the province.

A controversy arose in Manitoba in the summer of 1871 because the government did not want to choose the location of the 1.4 million acres before completion of the survey. The French Metis, wanting to ensure that the children's reserves would include certain well-wooded and watered lands, announced the boundaries they wanted and tried to keep white settlers out. Archibald restored an uneasy calm when he declared that he would try to honor the Metis preferences as much as possible when it came time to make the binding selection of the 1.4 million acres.[10]

By the summer of 1872, the Dominion lands survey was sufficiently advanced that the selection could begin. Consulting closely with the Metis parishes over a period of several months, the lieutenant governor and other federal officials chose blocks of townships totalling 1.4 million acres. These were located for the most part immediately behind the parishes among whose inhabitants they were to be distributed. Lieutenant Governor Alexander Morris, who had replaced Archibald, began drawing lots for 140-acre grants on February 22, 1873.[11]

This beginning, however proved unsatisfactory to the Metis, or at least to some of their leading spokesmen. It had become apparent that many Metis were making advance sales of their rights, and their children's rights, to participate in the lottery. Robert Cunningham, editor of the *Manitoban* and M.P. from Marquette, raised the matter in the House of Commons, urging the government to comply strictly with the wording of s.31 and restrict the grant only to "the children of the half-breed heads of families." Exclusion of the adults would presumably dampen speculative sales, since children would not receive their patents until they turned 18.[12] Sir John A. Macdonald quickly complied with the request and introduced the necessary legislation to restrict the grant.[13] This action received the approval of Archbishop Tache, Father Ritchot, and Louis Riel.[14]

Exclusion of the adults meant that the 1.4 million acres could be shared among fewer recipients, so the allotment size could be enlarged. Drawings for 190-acre allotments recommenced in August, 1873,[15] but complications continued to arise. There were many problems with the precise location of the 1.4 million acres, the most serious being an overlap with the "outer two miles" (discussed below). There was also uncertainty about how to verify applications for the land. The Dominion lands agent in Winnipeg advised that his small staff could not handle the approximately 7 000 applications expected.[16]

When the Liberals came into power after the Pacific Scandal led to the fall of Macdonald's government, David Laird became minister of the Interior. After making a first-hand investigation in Manitoba, he decided a fresh start was necessary. An order-in-council of April 26, 1875, provided that a special commission would receive applications to share in the lottery. The size of the allotments would be finally determined after the number of participants was fixed, and only then would the lottery be carried out.

The commission consisted of two lawyers, John Machar from Kingston and Matthew Ryan from Montreal. They toured Manitoba over the summer of 1875, approving 5 088 children's claims. Making an allowance for about 500 claims still to be received, the government set the allotment size at 240 acres,[17] and drawings began in the last week of October, 1876.[18] In the meantime, Matthew Ryan's commission had been extended to allow him to receive applications in the Northwest Territories from eligible recipients who had left Manitoba before 1876.[19]

For reasons that are not fully understood, the drawings, which were conducted parish by parish, were not completed until February 1880. Patents, however, were issued in batches as phases of the drawings were finished. The first batch arrived in Winnipeg on August 31, 1877,[20] while others were delivered at irregular intervals into the early 1880s. In the end, 6 034 patents for allotments of 240 acres were issued to Metis children, for a total of 1 448 160 acres.[21]

Unfortunately, officials had underestimated the number of late applications, so the reserved land was exhausted before all applicants could receive a share. Under an order-in-council of April 20, 1885, 993 latecomers were given scrip for $240, which they could use to purchase Dominion lands wherever they wished.[22]

Little of this land remained with the Metis for any length of time. It has already been recounted how speculative sales began even before the first drawings in February 1873, leading to the exclusion of the Metis adults from the grant. Another result at the same time was passage of the provincial *Half-Breed Land Grant Protection Act*, allowing Metis who had sold their claims to repudiate their bargains without penalty, as long as they repaid the purchase price.[23] The Manitoba legislature tried to weaken this protection in 1875, but the federal cabinet disallowed the amendment.[24] In 1877, however, the legislature removed the revocation provision prospectively for sales made after July 1, 1877; and this time the federal government did not intervene.[25] Subsequent provincial legislation allowed Metis children to sell their grants at age 18 if they had parental consent.[26] Provision was also made for judicially approved sales by children under 18 upon parental application to the Court of Queen's Bench.[27]

It is difficult to generalize about sales because they took place in many forms. Since the recipients had been by definition "children" as of July 15, 1870, many were over 21 by the time patents were issued in 1877 and afterwards. Some sales, therefore, were normal real-estate transactions between adults. In many cases, however, the land was sold before the patent was received or issued, or even before the lottery was conducted. Technically, vendors sold their right to the proceeds of the lottery. Federal regulations tried to ensure that the patent would be issued directly to the Metis child, but purchasers could circumvent this barrier by getting the seller to sign a power of attorney empowering the purchaser to pick up the patent at the Dominion lands office.

About 560 allotments were sold under judicial supervision because the sellers were under 18 at the time.[28] A provincial investigation of these sales in the fall of 1881 revealed many abuses, and judicial sales were discontinued.[29] But this was only a delay, since the children could sell with parental consent when they turned 18, or with no restriction when they turned 21.

Anecdotal evidence of extremely low prices in the range of $25 or $35 has been widely reported in the literature. To gather more systematic evidence, I drew a 1 percent sample (60 cases) of the 6 034 allotments. The average sale price for the 49 cases about which information could be found in the records of the Manitoba Land Titles Offices was $193.47. A few very low prices in the range of $40 were found for early sales, but these were exceptional cases, since the law permitted the repudiation of sales prior to July 1, 1877. In very broad terms, prices began at about $100 in 1877, increased to an average of over $250 during the land boom of the early 1880s, then fell back to slightly over $200 thereafter.

Whether these prices were high or low is ultimately a matter of opinion, but they must be seen in the context of contemporary prices. A basic workman's wage was about $1.25 a day in the early 1880s. Letter carriers in Winnipeg made $400 a year, prison guards $600.[30] A sale price of $200 was thus the equivalent of several months wages from a full-time job. It is not surprising that such prices led the Metis to sell; it was probably more cash than most of them were accustomed to see at one time.

The government made separate provision for the approximately 3 000 Metis heads of families who were removed from sharing in the 1.4 million acres after Cunningham's protest in the spring of 1873. Legislation passed the next year authorized grants of 160 acres, or $160 scrip redeemable in Dominion lands, to the heads of families.[31] The Machar/Ryan commission received their applications at the same time as it enumerated the children.

After the government opted for scrip rather than land, the first scrip note was signed on May 1, 1876.[32] In the end, 3 186 scrips were issued to Metis heads of families.[33] As with the children's land allotments, allowance was made for late applications from individuals who had left Manitoba.

There were fewer formalities attending scrip, so the Metis sold it even more quickly than they sold the land. As with the 240-acre allotments, much of it was sold before it was ever received. It is impossible to gather systematic data about prices because no legal sales records exist. However, there are many references to the price of scrip in the newspapers of the day and other contemporary documents. It appears that speculators were paying about $35 or $40 for claims to scrip before it was actually issued,[34] and not much more than that when the first flood of scrip was released in 1876. But prices seem to have gone up to about $80 in 1877 and about $100 in 1878, in correlation with the rising price of land in those years.[35]

In the view of the government, implementation of s.32 of the *Manitoba Act* had to wait until the Settlement Belt was resurveyed, so that land titles could be described in standardized terms. In the years 1871-74, more than 3 000 river lots conforming to existing patterns of settlement were surveyed along the Red and Assiniboine rivers; and almost 400 river lots were surveyed in settled areas along Lake Manitoba or on lesser rivers such as the Seine and Rat.[36] Many of these latter areas had no actual habitation but had been staked by old settlers wanting a continuation of the river lot system.

Claims under ss.32(1) and (2) were relatively straightforward because they were already listed in "Register B" of the Hudson's Bay Company.[37] Claims under ss.32(3) and (4) were more difficult to deal with because they had not been formally recognized by the HBC before the transfer to Canada on July 15, 1870. Through legislation passed in 1874 and amended in 1875, Parliament created a unified approach to the implementation of these two subsections:

Whereas it is expedient to afford facilities to parties claiming lands under the third and fourth sub-sections of the [Manitoba Act] to obtain Letters Patent for the same:

> Be it enacted that persons satisfactorily establishing undisturbed occupancy of any lands within the Province prior to, and being by themselves or their servants, tenants or agents, or those through whom they claim, in actual peaceable possession thereof, on the fifteenth day of July, [1870], shall be entitled to receive Letters Patent therefore, granting the same absolutely to them respectively in fee simple.[38]

The implementation of this legislation engendered many controversies over the precise meaning of "undisturbed occupancy" and "peaceable possession." There were many claims based on use of land prior to 1870 for purposes such as cutting hay or timber where the claimants had never actually resided on the lots. The most difficult cases were those known as "staked claims," in which the claimants had merely marked off the land and had not made much use of it. There had been something of a land rush in 1869-70 as old settlers, both Metis and white, had scurried to mark off river lots in anticipation of future demand by arriving immigrants.[39]

Conflicts arising over claims based on occupancy were arbitrated in several ways. There was at first a Commissioner of Conflicting Claims, then jurisdiction was transferred to the Dominion Land Board in 1882. There was also a special investigation by Justices Dubuc and Miller of the Manitoba Court of Queen's Bench, which led to some relaxation of the criteria for establishing occupancy.

The first two patents under s.32 were issued in 1874; 1 279 patents had been issued by 1880; 2 565 by 1886; and 2 750 by 1929 when the register for this category of patents was closed.[40] (The number of patents is less than the number of river lots because two or more contiguous lots were sometimes patented together when claimed by one owner).

The extreme slowness of the process was partly due to the rigourous standards demanded by the government for proving occupancy. In a discreditable episode in the early 1880s, a clerk in the Department of the Interior named Robert Lang took advantage of the slowness to set up an extortion racket. Using confederates in Manitoba, he offered to accelerate the issue of patents in return for payment of a bribe, usually a portion of the land patented.[41] The delays were also partly due to the fact that the initiative to apply lay on the parties. Patents had been unknown in Red River before 1870, and some owners felt no need to acquire them until they wished to sell their land.

As with s.31, it is clear that the government implemented s.32 in the sense that it issued patents. A large number of those patents, however, were not issued to Metis or other old settlers who had resided on or used the land prior to 1870. Many old settlers had claimed more land than they could use and were happy to sell part of it; others, especially French Metis, decided to leave Red River for frontier locations in the Northwest Territories or the United States. Many sales took place before the formal issue of patent, leaving the purchaser to obtain the patent by showing documented proof of the transaction.

Section 32(5), concerning the so-called "hay privilege," gave rise to difficulties of special complexity. The government initially located the 1.4 million acres of children's reserves in such a way that they included the "outer two miles" in the rear of the river lots, on which the old settlers had customarily cut hay and pastured livestock. Vehement protests and two official investigations led the government to offer full ownership of the "outer two miles" to owners of the adjacent "inner two miles." However, this could not be done in every case because of geographical problems (e.g., river junctions); fenced-off areas created by the old settlers themselves prior to 1870 ("park claims"); and homesteads claimed by immigrants in the years 1871-72, before federal officials had prohibited homesteading on the outer two miles. Wherever it was impossible to grant ownership of the full outer two miles, claimants would receive scrip in commutation, which they could use to purchase other lands.[42]

In the years 1874-76, the outer two miles were resurveyed into two-mile strips, making them in effect extensions of the river lots.[43] Applications for patent were accepted beginning August 15, 1877.[44] The government eventually made 1 250 grants of land in the outer two miles and an even larger number of grants of "hay scrip."[45] It also issued patents in the name of old settlers for about 130 "park claims" that were sprinkled throughout the outer two miles like raisins in a pudding.[46] As with claims under the first four subsections of s.32, much of the land and scrip granted under s.32(5) actually went to those who had purchased the rights from the original claimants.

Metis Contentions

In order to understand the legal basis of the Dumont case, it is necessary to bring in one more piece of history. When the *Manitoba Act* was debated in the House of Commons in May 1870, some members expressed doubts about its constitutionality. The problem was that s.146 of the *British North America Act*, 1867, allowed the Queen to admit new territory to Canada, but it did not empower the Parliament of Canada to create new provinces, endow them with constitutions, and provide them with representation in the Senate and House of Commons. Yet the *Manitoba Act* purported to do precisely these things.

Persistent doubts about the *Manitoba Act* led the Canadian government to seek imperial confirmation. The result was the *British North America Act*, 1871, which declared the *Manitoba Act* to be "valid and effectual for all purposes whatsoever" as of the date of royal assent (May 12, 1870).[47] Section 6 of the British legislation also set up barriers to amendments to the *Manitoba Act* by either the Parliament of Canada or the legislature of Manitoba:

> 6. Except as provided by the third section of this Act, it shall not be competent for the Parliament of Canada to alter the provisions of the [Manitoba Act] in so far as it relates to the Province of Manitoba, or of any other Act hereafter establishing new Provinces in the said Dominion, subject always to the right of the Legislature of the Province of Manitoba to alter from time to time the provisions of any law respecting the qualification of electors and members of the Legislative Assembly and to make laws respecting elections in the said province.[48]

The Manitoba Metis Federation contends that, in purporting to implement ss.31 and 32 of the *Manitoba Act*, Parliament passed statutes, and the cabinet approved orders-in-council, that conflicted with the *Manitoba Act* and were therefore *ultra vires*. They condemn the exclusion of the Metis adults from the 1.4 million acres, the conception of "undisturbed occupancy" formulated in the legislation of 1874-75, the decision to commute some of the hay privilege with scrip rather than land, and much more. In all, they question the constitutionality of eight federal statutes and ten federal orders-in-council, as well as of eight provincial statutes that regulated and facilitated the sale of the Metis children's allotments.[49]

The Metis will try to base themselves on the *Forest* case, in which the Supreme Court of Canada ruled that provincial legislation contrary to s.23 of the *Manitoba Act* was *ultra vires*.[50] But *Forest* concerned the *ongoing* matter of official bilingualism (s.23 requires acts of the Manitoba legislature to be printed in both English and French), as well as contrary *provincial* legislation. It is thus not a perfect precedent for *Dumont*, which concerns a *one-time* grant of land as well as *federal* legislation. There will be much legal debate over the interpretation of s.6 of the *Constitution Act* of 1871 and over the implications of *Forest*.

Against the provincial legislation regulating sales, the Metis may also use the secondary argument that they were considered Indians at that time, and that the 1.4 million acres reserved for their children were thus "lands reserved for Indians" in the sense of s.91(24) of the Constitution (B.N.A.) Act, 1867. Success in this argument might benefit the Metis by undermining the provincial legislation, but it would not challenge the federal enactments. It is also questionable whether the argument will work. The Supreme Court declared in 1939 that the Inuit were considered Indians at the time of Confederation,[51] but a recent discussion of the problem has argued that this is unlikely to extend to the Metis.[52]

The arguments described above do not directly involve Metis Aboriginal rights, but that question has been raised in a separate statement of claim filed in the Federal Court of Canada in 1986. The parties to *Dumont* are now proceeding only on the action originally commenced before the Manitoba Court of Queen's Bench; but if standing should ultimately be denied there, the case might reappear in the Federal Court of Canada. In that statement of claim, the Metis say that a "fiduciary relationship existed between the Crown and the Metis as an Aboriginal people," and that the *Manitoba Act* created a "trust relationship" between the Crown and the Metis regarding the lands mentioned in ss.31 and 32 of the Act. They contend that "the Crown was guilty of fraud or of fraudulent breach of trust or was privy thereto and was guilty of breach of fiduciary obligation" in implementing the *Manitoba Act*.[53]

The constitutional argument and the fiduciary argument seem to be two different ways of approaching the same evidence. The constitutional argument is more precise but also narrower. Rising or falling on standards of statutory construction with which the courts are familiar, it will chiefly involve the comparison of words in the *Manitoba Act* to words in other enactments. The fiduciary argument is vaguer but also wider. It makes greater demands for introducing evidence about the intentions of government officials and the effects of enactments, matters which are usually not relevant to statutory construction in the technical sense.

Historical Theories

The legal contentions of the Metis rest upon a large body of historical research. The first generation of studies carried out by employees of the Manitoba Metis Federation, or by those closely associated with it,[54] did not meet professional standards of accuracy and documentation and is not persuasive to readers outside the Metis political movement. However, a more serious body of work has been created by Professor D.N. Sprague of the Department of History at the University of Manitoba[55] and augmented by the efforts of several graduate students from the same institution.[56]

Sprague has harshly criticized every aspect of the federal government's implementation of the *Manitoba Act*'s land provisions.[57] Regarding s.31, he argues that the location of the 1.4 million acres should have been left under local control. The federal government situated the reserves in areas that were not favorable to Metis settlement, thus encouraging quick sales to speculators. The government was also negligent, or perhaps malicious, in allowing immigrants to interfere with the grant by homesteading in areas desired by the Metis for their children's reserves. Sprague also maintains that the Metis adults should not have been excluded from the grant, with the implication that the scrip they received was an illegal substitute for the land to which they were entitled.

He is critical of the administration of the grant on several grounds. The federal government did not set up effective safeguards against sales and speculation. Officials recognized powers of attorney to pick up patents without adequate checks into their validity. The federal government also violated the *Manitoba Act* by setting deadlines for applications, thus cutting off many valid entitlements to land. Even if these late applicants eventually got $240 scrip, that was still not in conformity with s.31 of the *Manitoba Act*.

The provincial government was equally at fault for not putting a stop to sales of the children's grants. The legislature quickly withdrew the benefit of its early attempt in this direction, the *Half-Breed Land Grant Protection Act*. Indeed, the legislature facilitated sales by allowing Metis youngsters of 18 to convey their allotments with parental consent, whereas the law did not allow white children to sell lands until they reached 21. The government and legislature tolerated corrupt practices in the Court of Queen's Bench for several years, allowing Metis parents to sell the allotments of children under 18.[58] Sprague calculates that, as a result of federal and provincial handling of the grant, about 80 percent of the allotments were quickly sold to purchasers.[59]

Simpler but equally detrimental problems surrounded the distribution of scrip to Metis heads of families. Deadlines frustrated legitimate applications, few safeguards were taken to ensure that the scrip was delivered to the proper recipients, and corrupt employees of the Department of the Interior appropriated scrip for themselves and their confederates. The underlying flaw in the scheme was that scrip was almost as liquid as money; it was a transferable note payable to bearer without identification. "As a result, virtually all of the money scrip which was supposed to have been awarded to half-breed heads of families never reached the claimants. As soon as it arrived at the Dominion lands office in 1876, assignees and attorneys picked it up instead."[60]

If anything, Sprague is even more critical of the implementation of s.32 of the *Manitoba Act*.[61] He holds that the Dominion lands surveyors systematically overlooked evidence of Metis occupation, thus making it impossible for many legitimate claimants to receive patents for their river lots.[62] Through legislation in 1874-75, the government illegally imposed residency requirements not contained in ss.32(3) and (4) of the *Manitoba Act*. Many Metis claimants to river lots decided to sell out and move on to the Northwest Territories when they realized they would never qualify for patents under the new legislation.[63]

The Commissioner of Conflicting Claims could hear and decide conflicts between local claimants, but he was not allowed to hear challenges against the illegal occupancy criteria imposed by the government. The Department of the Interior was also intolerably slow in issuing patents and negligent in the supervision of its employees, thus making it easy for Robert Lang to set up his extortion racket. Again Sprague has a statistical estimate of the damage done, suggesting that about 1 200 out of 2 000 Metis families were dispossessed by the cumulative effect of federal legislation, policy, and maladministration.[64]

Sprague is equally critical of the federal handling of the hay privilege.[65] The government reduced its value by allowing early immigrants to purchase land or homestead in the outer two miles before those lands were properly surveyed. Although the old settlers were ultimately compensated with scrip, this could not make up for loss of lands. Loss of hay and pasture land rendered many river lots uneconomic as farms, further encouraging Metis emigration from the province. "An appalling number of old settlers sold out and moved on."[66]

In alleging that many federal and provincial enactments were contrary to the *Manitoba Act*, Sprague reinforces the constitutional argument that the Metis want to make in *Dumont*. He also supports the fiduciary argument when he suggests that the federal government knew, or ought to have known, that its policies were driving the Metis off their land and out of Manitoba. It is difficult, however, to say precisely what Sprague thinks about the conscious intentions of federal policy-makers; the statements in his latest book are rather obscure on this point. Postulating the ongoing effect of "informal" discouragement to Metis settlers (the social pressure exerted by white immigrants) and of "formal" discouragement (government policies), he writes at the beginning of *Canada and the Metis:*

> Given the pressure from the informal side, opportunities for accommodation of the Metis were easily missed by all operators of the apparatus of formal control. Whether such moments passed by mere carelessness or by deliberate inaction cannot be known with certainty in every instance, but one overall conclusion is inescapably obvious: the Government of Canada conceded a legal framework for the permanence of the Red River Settlement as a province in response to force in 1870, and subsequently presided over the dissolution of the terms of the *Manitoba Act* with approximately the same regret as would be exhibited by an unwilling victim escaping from a sales contract negotiated under duress.[67]

The concluding sentence of his book is equally tortured:

> The presumption of benevolence is not appropriately replaced by one of consistent malevolence, but the exodus of the Metis from their original homeland and their difficulties in resettlement is more explicable by processes of formal and informal discouragement emanating from Canada than by the alleged preference of the Metis for the wandering life of homeless hunters.[68]

If one is arguing breach of fiduciary responsibility, it may not matter much whether the federal attitude was "consistent malevolence" or merely culpable negligence, but the difference is important from the standpoint of historical accuracy.

My own work has convinced me that Sprague's version of events is not reliable history, and that the problems within it are so deep-seated that it cannot be corrected with a few critical comments. What is required is a full and accurate account of the implementation of ss.31 and 32 of the *Manitoba Act*, written without an *a priori* assumption that the Metis were victimized by the government. Here I can only say that I have tried to write such an account and hope to publish it as a book.[69] When it is finally in print, scholars will have an alternative to the version of history that has been offered to support the Metis claims made in *Dumont*. The research community will have to ponder the validity of these different versions of history even as the judicial process will sort out their implications for Metis land claims.[70]

The Dumont Case

The Manitoba Metis Federation first filed their statement of claim with the Manitoba Court of Queen's Bench in April 1981, but they did not press for a trial date at that time. Their resort to the court was initially a symbolic gesture to put additional pressure on the federal and provincial governments, with whom they were engaged in desultory negotiations.

The Metis escalated the importance of their case in 1985 by retaining Thomas R. Berger as their chief counsel. Berger had extensive political experience as provincial leader of the New Democratic Party in British Columbia and as a Member of Parliament. He served more than a decade as a justice of the Supreme Court of British Columbia, resigning in 1983 amidst controversy over political statements that he had made during the constitutional patriation debate. He also has a long association with Native peoples and the cause of Aboriginal rights. He represented Indian clients in *Regina v. White and Bob,* which began the current cycle of Aboriginal rights litigation, as well as in *Calder v. Attorney General of British Columbia,* which is a major case on the meaning of Aboriginal rights. He also conducted the Mackenzie Valley Pipeline Inquiry, recommending in 1977 that a 10-year moratorium on development be imposed so that Native land claims could first be settled.[71]

Berger entered the fray energetically, writing to the Metis association in October 1985:

> In this case we will be putting the conventional view of Canadian history on trial . . . Some will say that the injustices the Metis allege in this case happened long ago, that their claims are specious and half-forgotten. We are a nation, however, that believes in the rule of law. Commitments were made, but were not kept. These commitments are not ancient history.[72]

His hand strengthened by the completion of a first draft of D.N. Sprague's book, which provided historical evidence to accompany his legal arguments, Berger began to press for a trial date.[73]

The Attorney General of Canada (i.e., the lawyers of the federal Department of Justice) responded with an application to strike the statement of claim. The federal government, in other words, asked the Manitoba Court of Queen's Bench to dismiss the Metis case on procedural grounds without hearing its merits. The two reasons given in support of this request were that the plaintiffs lacked standing to sue, and that the issue raised was non-justifiable.[74]

In layman's terms, "standing" is the right to sue. Complex rules arising from legislation, case law precedents, and judicial practice govern the question of who is entitled to commence litigation. Generally speaking, one must demonstrate that a legally recognized right has been injured or is threatened. Suppose, for example, that the nice old man who lives next door has been cheated by unscrupulous sellers of aluminum siding. No matter how outraged I may feel at this injustice, I cannot sue the sellers, because I have suffered no loss. My neighbor would have to sue on his own behalf, or perhaps the Crown could prosecute if evidence of a criminal violation existed.

Whereas standing refers to the status of the parties to a dispute, "justiciability" refers to the nature of the question raised by the dispute. Although the distinctions are not always clear, courts generally restrict themselves to deciding matters of law and do not attempt to decide matters of government policy. To make an extreme example, if Canada declared war on another country, it is unlikely that one could effectively challenge that decision in court. Lawyers for the Crown would contend that the declaration of war was a non-justiciable issue, and judges would almost certainly agree.

The Metis won the first round of the procedural fight. Justice Barkman of the Manitoba Court of Queen's Bench ruled in their favor with respect both to standing and to justiciability. On the first point, he noted the Metis claim that the *Manitoba Act* provided for a kind of "Metis Reserve," which, if it had become a reality, would have provided continuing benefits to the Metis people. Without having to decide whether this was the proper interpretation of the *Manitoba Act*, he held that the claim gave the plaintiffs standing because it asserted a tangible present interest on the part of the Metis.[75] On the second point, he rejected the Crown's assertion that the dispute was purely academic because the enactments whose constitutionality was impugned were "spent," that is, their operation had finished long ago and they had no present impact. Barkman noted that the Metis were simply asking for a "declaratory judgment," that is, a statement that their constitutional rights had been violated. "I am satisfied," he wrote,

> that the granting of a declaration, if the plaintiffs are successful, will have the practical effect of supporting the position of the plaintiffs in their negotiations with the federal government relating to the Metis land claims. I therefore conclude that this action is appropriate for declaratory relief.[76]

The crucial point for Barkman seemed to be that the existence of negotiations made the issue more than academic, and therefore justiciable.

The procedural victory won by the Metis in 1987 was overturned the next year when the federal government appealed to the Manitoba Court of Appeal. That court held by a margin of four to one that the issues in the case were non-justiciable. The majority did not agree with Justice Barkman's view that s.31 of the *Manitoba Act* had arguably created a collective and continuing interest in the form of a "Metis Reserve," deprivation of which would give the present generation of Metis standing in court. The Metis statement of claim itself had asserted that "approximately 85 percent of Metis persons" had been deprived of their land rights under the *Manitoba Act*, and this very assertion showed that the rights were individual in character.[77] Justice Twaddle wrote for the majority:

> What the court is being asked to consider in this case is the constitutional validity of spent legislation which does not affect anyone's current rights. The rights affected by the impugned legislation were the statutory rights of individuals who are now deceased. These rights are not being pursued individually by the legal representatives of the persons whose rights they were, but generally by descendants whose degree of relationship is not even stated.[78]

The court could still have provided a declaratory judgment of unconstitutionality if that had been "essential to the settlement of an extrajudicial claim."[79] The utility in this case would have been the furtherance of the Metis negotiations with Canada in pursuit of a contemporary land base and self-government. But the majority took the view that "the settlement of the Metis claim will not be promoted in any real sense by the making of the declaration sought by the plaintiffs."[80] The federal government had already expressed willingness to negotiate with the Metis, and it could consider the impact of past legislation without a judicial declaration about its constitutionality.

Berger applied for leave to appeal from the Supreme Court of Canada, and an oral hearing on that application was held on January 23, 1989, before a panel of five justices. The court has not yet delivered judgment at the time of writing. If leave to appeal is granted, a hearing on the issues of standing and justiciability before the Supreme Court probably cannot take place until 1990. The court may take up to a year to reach decisions, write opinions, and get them translated; so the procedural issues may not be definitely resolved until 1991.

If the Metis are successful in this appeal, there will then be a trial on the substance of the case before the Manitoba Court of Queen's Bench. The issues are of such magnitude that, no matter who wins at the trial level, the other side is almost certain to appeal, and the case is likely to wend its way upwards again to the Supreme Court of Canada. It is quite possible that, even if everything moves ahead in normal fashion, the judicial process will not render a final verdict until 1995 or later.

Such slowness is one factor that makes Aboriginal-rights litigation problematic for Native peoples. Another difficulty is that decisions sometimes turn on aspects of the law, such as standing and justiciability, that have nothing to do with Native rights. If the Supreme Court of Canada rules against the Metis on these issues, it is possible that they may be able to act upon their case in the Federal Court of Canada, or they may be able to repackage their claim in some way to get it back into the Manitoba courts. In either event, much time will have been lost.

But in the long run, how long the case takes, or even whether the Metis win or lose, may not matter as much as the fact that the case is heard; for the hearing and the appeals will provide weeks of free publicity to the Metis cause. *Dumont* is not only a lawsuit, it is a step in the political process by which the Metis hope to gather public support for their claim, thereby putting pressure on Manitoba and Canada to make concessions at the negotiating table. Even a clear-cut judicial victory in *Dumont* would probably be only a declaratory judgment without other remedy. The provincial and federal governments would be embarrassed by an adverse finding, but any solution would still have to be reached through negotiations.

In *Calder*, the Nishga Indians lost at every level of the judicial process, up to and including the Supreme Court of Canada. Yet the attention surrounding *Calder* played some role in influencing the government of Pierre Trudeau, which had announced that it would no longer negotiate claims based on Aboriginal rights claims, to change its position.[81] Judicial defeat helped to produce political victory. A similar interweaving of judicial and political events would not be surprising in *Dumont*. The Metis undoubtedly hope to win in court, but they may also believe that that even a setback in the judicial forum may contribute to ultimate success in the political arena.

Abbreviations used in Notes

AASB	Archives de l'Archeveche de Saint-Boniface
AO	Archives of Ontario
M.R.	Manitoba Reports
NAC	National Archives of Canada
PAM	Provincial Archives of Manitoba
S.C.	Statutes of Canada
S.C.R.	Supreme Court Reports
S.M.	Statutes of Manitoba

Notes

[1] Following Donald Purich, *The Metis* (Toronto: James Lorimer, 1988), p. 5, I prefer to spell the word "Metis" without an acute accent, thereby emphasizing that it has become an English word that embraces mixed-race persons of either French or English extraction. However, the accent will be found in many of the sources cited in this chapter.

[2] Purich, *The Metis*, pp. 172-177.

[3] For an earlier discussion, see Thomas Flanagan, "The Case Against Metis Aboriginal Rights," *Canadian Public Policy*, 9 (1983), pp. 314-325.

[4] 52 M.R. (2d) 291 (1988); 48 M.R. (2d) 4 (1988).

[5] The best account of the negotiations is Philippe Mailhot, *Ritchot's Resistance: Abbe Noel-Joseph Ritchot and the Creation and Transformation of Manitoba* (Ph.D. thesis, University of Manitoba, 1986).

[6] S.C., 1870, c.3., ss.30-33.

[7] G.F.G. Stanley, "Le Journal de l'abbe N.J. Ritchot," *Revue d'Histoire de l'-Amerique Francaise*, 17 (1964), p. 549, entry of May 2, 1870. N.J. Ritchot to G.E. Cartier, May 18, 1870, in Canada, House of Commons, "Report of the Select Committee on the Causes of the Difficulties in the Northwest Territory," *Journals of the House of Commons* (1874), Vol. 8, App. 6, p. 73.

[8] The most reliable published account is still Herbert Douglas Kemp, "Land Grants under the *Manitoba Act*," *Papers Read Before the Historical and Scientific Society of Manitoba*, Series III, no. 9 (1954), pp. 33-52. The various publications of Professor Sprague, as discussed below, contain a great deal of additional detail, but offer a highly partisan interpretation. D. Bruce Sealey, *Statutory Land Rights of the Manitoba Metis* (Winnipeg: Manitoba Metis Federation Press, 1975), is also partisan and erratic in judgment.

[9] A.G. Archibald to Joseph Howe, December 27, 1870; NAC, RG 15, vol. 236, file 7220. Order-in-council, April 25, 1871, confirmed by the *Dominion Lands Act*, S.C., 1872, c.23.

[10] Joseph Royal et al. to A.G. Archibald, May 24, 1871; *Manitoban*, June 17, 1871. A.G. Archibald to Joseph Royal et al., Jqune 9, 1871, ibid. A.G. Archibald to Joseph Howe, June 17, 1871; NAC, RG 15, vol. 230, file 167.

[11] *Manitoban*, March 1, 1873.

[12] House of Commons Debates, March 12 and March 24, 1873; NAC, RG 14 D 4, P-58, pp. 16, 35.

[13] Order-in-council, April 3, 1873. S.C., 1873, c.38.

[14] A.A. Taché to Robert Cunningham, March 28 and April 16, 1873; AO; MU 762. N.J. Ritchot to A.A. Tache, May 12, 1873; AASB, T 12072-75 (Ritchot went to Ottawa in the spring of 1873 to lobby for the same purpose as Cunningham). Andre Neault and Amable Gaudry to Robert Cunningham, July 23, 1873; AO, MU 762 (letter in Riel's hand). For drafts of this last item, see G.F.G. Stanley et al., *The Collected Writings of Louis Riel* (Edmonton: University of Alberta Press, 1985), items 1-169 to 1-172.

[15] *Le Metis*, August 16, 1873.

[16]Donald Codd to J.S. Dennis, February 8, 1874; NAC, RG 15, vol. 230, file 829.

[17]Order-in-council, September 7, 1876.

[18]*Manitoba Free Press*, October 24, 1876.

[19]Order-in-council, June 14, 1876.

[20]Donald Codd to J.S. Dennis, August 31, 1877; NAC, RG 15, vol. 238, file 9321.

[21]N.O. Cote, "Administration and Sale of Dominion Lands," NAC, RG 15, vol. 227.

[22]Ibid.

[23]S.M., 1873, c.44. Royal assent was reserved by the Lieutenant Governor, but the federal cabinet let the Act stand. A.A. Dorion, memo of February 21, 1874, in W.E. Hodgins, *Correspondence—Reports of the Ministers of Justice and Orders in Council upon the Subject of Dominion and Provincial Legislation, 1867-1895* (Ottawa: Government Printing Office, 1896), p. 779.

[24]S.M., 1875, c.37. Edward Blake to Privy Council, October 7, 1876, printed in Hodgins, *Correspondence*, pp. 804-805.

[25]S.M., 1877, c.5. A.A. Lash, memo of May 3, 1878, in Hodgins, *Correspondence*, pp. 821-822.

[26]S.M., 1878, c.20. Amended by S.M., 1979, c.11; S.M., 1883, c.29; and S.M., 1884, c.24.

[27]S.M., 1878, c.7.

[28]Entered in volumes labelled C, B, E, X, and Minute Book in PAM, GR 462. Complete records of each judicial sale are in PAM, GR 181, temporary boxes 104-107.

[29]The complete transcript of evidence heard by the inquiry is in PAM, RG 7 B 1. Gerhard Ens, "Metis Lands in Manitoba," *Manitoba History*, 5 (1983), pp.2-11, gives an account of these abuses based on the evidence of the inquiry. Ens, however, does not make it clear to the reader that judicial sales occurred in only a small minority (about 560 of 6034) of the Metis children's land grants.

[30]*Civil Service List*, 1882.

[31]S.C., 1874, c.20, 22.1-2.

[32]The cancelled scrip notes are stored in NAC, RG 15, vols. 1479-1484.

[33]N.O. Cote, "Administration and Sale of Dominion Lands," NAC, RG 15, vol. 227.

[34]E., g., an ad in the *Manitoba Free Press*, October 9, 1875, offering to sell claims at $40.

[35]Prices taken from various issues of *Le Metis* and the *Manitoba Free Press* in the years 1876-78.

[36]This account is slightly oversimplified. Some areas were at first surveyed on the rectangular principle, then resurveyed into river lots when it became clear that there were numerous claimants under s.32. Lorette, Oak Island, Rat River, and St. Malo were resurveyed in the years 1877-1884. For informa-

tion on surveys, see the parish maps in the PAM, plus the surveyors' field notes in PAM, RG 17 C 1.

[37]There are two copies of Register B that do not entirely agree: one in the Hudson's Bay Company Archives, PAM; one in NAC, RG 15, aperture card book 185.

[38]S.C., 1875, c.52, s.3. amending S.C., 1874, c.20, s.3.

[39]After returning from Ottawa in June 1870, Father Ritchot led a party of Metis to Rat River to stake claims and staked two for himself. NAC, RG 15, vol. 140, MA 79 (C-14902). As described in Mailhot, *Ritchot's Resistance*, Ritchot was an acute land speculator, although he used the proceeds for Church projects, not personal gain.

[40]The register is in NAC, RG 15, aperture card book 186. The totals given here come from *Canada Sessional Papers*, 1886, no. 8, p. xvii, and 1887, no.7, p.4.

[41]An extensive file on the Lang affair is in NAC, RG 15, vol. 232, file 2447.

[42]Order-in-council, April 17, 1874.

[43]Report of Inspector of Surveys in *Canada Sessional Papers*, no.9, p. 23, and 1877, no. 11, p. 31.

[44]Newspaper clipping in NAC, RG 15, vol. 232, file 2447, pasted to letter of Robert Lang to D.L. Macpherson, January 19, 1885.

[45]See NAC, RG 15, aperture card book 184, for the register of land grants in the OTM. Ibid., vol. 582, file 186711, contains a schedule of scrip grants through early 1889.

[46]Tabulated from Parish Settlement General Register, vol. I, PAM, RG 17 D 1.

[47]34-35 Victoria, c.28, s.5 (U.K.). See Paul Gerin-Lajoie, *Constitutional Amendment in Canada* (Toronto: University of Toronto Press, 1950), pp. 50-58.

[48]Ibid., s.6.

[49]Plaintiffs' statement of claim filed with the Manitoba Court of Queen's Bench, August 1986, ss.9, 9A, 10. This statement of claim amended the one originally submitted April 15, 1981, and its enumeration of unconstitutional enactments is slightly different.

[50]*Forest v. Attorney General of Manitoba*, [1979] 2 S.C.R. 1032.

[51]*Re Eskimo*, [1939] S.C.R. 104.

[52]Bryan Schwartz, *First Principles, Second Thoughts: Aboriginal Peoples, Constitutional Reform and Canadian Statecraft* (Montreal: Institute for Research on Public Policy, 1986), pp. 227-247.

[53]Plaintiffs' statement of claim filed with the Federal Court of Canada, May 20, 1986, ss.10-13.

[54]Emile Pelletier, *Exploitation of Metis Lands* (Winnipeg: Manitoba Metis Federation Press, 1979; 2nd ed.); D. Bruce Sealey, *Statutory Land Rights of the Manitoba Metis* (Winnipeg: Manitoba Metis Federation Press, 1975); Manitoba Metis Federation, *Riverlots and Scrip: Elements of Metis Aboriginal Rights* (Winnipeg, 1978).

[55]D.N. Sprague, "Government Lawlessness in the Administration of Manitoba Land Claims, 1870-1887," *Manitoba Law Journal*, 10 (1980), pp. 415-441; idem, "The Manitoba Land Question," *Journal of Canadian Studies*, 15 (1980), pp. 74-84; D.N. Sprague and R.P. Frye, *The Genealogy of the First Metis Nation* (Winnipeg: Pemmican Publications, 1983); P.R. Mailhot and D.N. Sprague, "Persistent Settlers: The Dispersal and Resettlement of the Red River Metis, 1870-85," *Canadian Ethnic Studies*, 17 (1985), pp. 1-30; D.N. Sprague, *Canada and the Metis, 1869-1885* (Waterloo: Wilfrid Laurier University Press, 1988).

[56]Gerhard Ens, "Metis Lands in Manitoba," *Manitoba History*, 5 (1983), pp. 2-11; Nicole J.M. St-Onge, "The Dissolution of a Metis Community: Pointe a Grouette, 1860-1885," *Studies in Political Economy*, 18 (1985), pp. 149-172. Sprague's collaborator P.R. Mailhot was also his Ph.D. student.

[57]Sprague, "The Manitoba Land Question," pp. 75-79; idem, "Government Lawlessness," pp. 416-422; idem, *Canada and the Metis*, pp. 90-113.

[58]On this point, see Ens, "Metis Lands in Manitoba."

[59]Sprague, "Government Lawlessness," pp. 421, 437.

[60]Sprague, "The Manitoba Land Question," p. 79.

[61]See in general Sprague, "Government Lawlessness," 422-423, 426-433; idem, "The Manitoba Land Question," pp. 79-83; idem, *Canada and the Metis*, pp. 113-139.

[62]Mailhot and Sprague, "Persistent Settlers," p. 5; Sprague and Frye, *Genealogy of the First Metis Nation*, Table 1.

[63]St-Onge, "Dissolution of a Metis Community." The author without further examination accepts the validity of Sprague's view of the 1874-75 legislation.

[64]Sprague, "The Manitoba Land Question," p. 81; idem, *Canada and the Metis*, p. 138.

[65]Sprague, "Government Lawlessness," pp. 424-426.

[66]Ibid., p. 426.

[67]Sprague, *Canada and the Metis*, p.x.

[68]Sprague, *Canada and the Metis*, p. 184.

[69]The author worked on the *Dumont* case as a historical consultant to the federal Department of Justice in the years 1986-88. The book mentioned above arises from that research.

[70]On the use of historical evidence in trials, see Donald J. Bourgeois, "The Role of the Historian in the Litigation Process," *Canadian Historical Review*, 47 (1986), pp. 195-205.

[71]For Berger's life, see Carolyn Swayze, *Hard Choices: A Life of Tom Berger* (Vancouver: Douglas & McIntyre, 1987). See also Berger's books *Fragile Freedoms: Human Rights and Dissent in Canada* (Toronto: Clarke Irwin, 1981), and *Village Journey: The Report of the Alaska Native Review Commission* (New York: Hill & Wang, 1985).

[72]Cited in Swayze, *Hard Choices*, p. 214.

[73]Berger contributed a "Foreward" to *Canada and the Metis*.

[74]*Dumont et al. v. Canada (Attorney General) and Manitoba (Attorney General)*, 48 M.R. (2d) 4 (1987), at 9.

[75]Ibid., at 10.

[76]Ibid.

[77]52 M.R. (2d) 291 (1988), at 295.

[78]Ibid., at 296.

[79]Ibid., at 297.

[80]Ibid.

[81]Jean Chretien, announcement of August 8, 1973, cited in Douglas Sanders, "The Nishga Case," *B.C. Studies*, 19 (1973), p. 19.

8

Understanding Aboriginal Rights and Indian Government

John D. Snow, Jr.

The literature detailing and analyzing the notions of Aboriginal rights and Indian government in Canada is prolific and one-sided. Few, if any, Indian writers have attempted to project the Indian viewpoint concerning these two concepts. In order to begin defining the concepts of Aboriginal rights or Indian government, an understanding and appreciation of Indian spirituality is paramount. After all, the foundation of Indian society is spiritual. From this foundation flow the concepts of Aboriginal rights and Indian government. A discussion of the Indian perspective of these concepts will illustrate why conflicts and discrepancies in the definitions between Indian and non-Indian are in conflict. These polar definitions each lead to solutions; however, it follows that these solutions create a dichotomy which reinstates the original conflict.

The following discussion of Indian spirituality will highlight ancient knowledge systems of the Indian people. A historical overview of the development of Aboriginal rights will follow, and will feature definitions of Aboriginal rights from an Indian perspective. Aboriginal rights determine the "end" of Indian wants and needs in Canada and Indian government is envisaged as the "means" by which to achieve Aboriginal rights. The conflicts that arise will be shown through a comparison based on philosophy, definitions, and solutions. The conclusion will offer a compromise between Indian and non-Indian views in Canada.

Indian Spirituality

Indian spirituality is difficult to define because it is both tangible and intangible. Spirituality is based on a knowledge system, the oral tradition, Indian language, and traditional teachings. The knowledge system of Indian philosophy is both simple and complex. The oral tradition is the unique communication system of this system. The languages of the Canadian Indian people are varied and are unique to this country. The teachings include ceremonies and rituals which are religious in context.

The knowledge system encompasses a tribal world-view of the cosmos. Indian philosophy on life and the surrounding environment complements the mind, body, and soul. This development of working in harmony with nature is one fundamental concept of Indian reality. In order to understand the intricate knowledge system, the oral tradition in practice, the importance of language and the teachings of Indian people, it is necessary to describe religion within an Indian setting. An event which illustrates this concept is the Ecumenical Conference held annually on the Stoney Indian Reserve at Morley, Alberta.

Indian Elders and clergymen gather round a sacred fire. The ground is covered with grass, small bushes and flowers. Poles face north to south to form a rectangular arbor. The roof of the arbor is made of poplar branches. Indian Elders, tribal leaders, young men, women, and children all gather at this spiritual meeting. All are listening to a speaker. All are thinking and speaking with their hearts to the Creation which surrounds them. Stories are told. Legends are recounted. Indian people from all over North America gather for this spiritual event every year. It is a time of renewal. It is a time to thank the Creator for all that exists. It is a time for prayer and contemplation.

Young people seek answers and ask questions. The Elders are vital in advising the youth. The Elders are respected because they continue to uphold the beauty and the force of the Indian religion. Elders do not teach to a classroom of students. Elders are also students, learning from the Great Spirit and in turn imparting their knowledge. The classroom is not a cold institutionalized center. The classroom is such as the outdoor setting detailed above. Lessons are not told directly but are understood through experiences, metaphors, and symbolism discussed in stories. It is through such Indian gatherings that the community spirituality of the Indian people is strengthened. This single example is only one in the continuous cycle of life for Indian people.

The knowledge system of the Indian people is spiritual in totality. However, several key concepts contribute to the end product of spirituality or Indian reality. One fundamental concept of Indian reality is the development of working in harmony with nature. Traditionally, the tribe worked in concert to provide a living for all members of its internal community. Although there were individuals with special gifts such as knowledge of hunting and gathering, worship and wisdom of warfare, the sum of the talents would be drawn on as required through a consensus of opinion by tribal members.

The oral history of the Redman in North America is intimately tied to the distinct knowledge systems of a tribe or nation of Indians. There are numerous instances in tribal histories of gifts bestowed to Indian people by the Great Spirit. It is from these gifts that life in the Indians' "Garden of Eden" became possible. Through the oral tradition, the Indian existence or world-view is dynamic.

Knowledge systems of Indian people are dynamic and fluid. The use of language is a central feature for creating Indian reality, and in reinforcing spirituality. Each tribe speaks a different language. However, within each language system there may be several dialects in existence. For instance, within the Sioux language system there exist the Dakota, Lakota, and Nakoda dialects. From each of these systems emanates a tribal world-view. These language systems still exist today. This is just one example of the complex nature comprising a tribal world-view.

Differences in language forms also exist amongst other tribes such as the Cree, Blackfoot, Saulteaux, Dene, Inuit, Aleutian, Ojibawa, and Iroquois. The list is endless, and contrary to popular belief there is no *one* individual encompassing language for all Indian tribes. As a result, tribes have distinct polities, many of which flourish even today.

Central to all Indian tribes are gifts and teachings endowed to us by the Great Spirit, the Creator. The teaching of Indian people is that we are our brother's keeper. Indian people are concerned for one another. Indian people help one another without expecting payment; they share what they have. This spirit of caring, looking out for the interest and consensus of a tribe reflects the democratic nature of Indian tribes. To illustrate the contrast between the Indian and non-Indian society, Julia Seton in *The Gospel of the Redman* writes,

> The culture and civilization of the whiteman are essentially material; his measure of success is how much property have I acquired for myself? The culture of the Redman is fundamentally spiritual; his measure of success is how much service have I rendered to my people . . . " (Seton, 1963).

From this quote we note that the Indian world-view is radically different from that of the non-Indian. In Indian spirituality there is also a special tie to the land. This is reflected in the numerous rites and ceremonies performed during the year in keeping with Indian custom. These extremes are difficult to reconcile.

The complexity of Indian spirituality is only touched upon in this discussion. It is paradoxical that the simple teachings and beliefs of the Indian people are so difficult to convey to non-Indian people who allegedly esteem intrigue. However, from this beginning point, it is possible to see why two competing views of history, definitions, and solutions exist. Spirituality creates a fundamental reality for the Indian people. Within this greater circle of religion are complex concepts which will enhance and direct the ensuing discussion of Aboriginal rights and Indian government.

A Brief History

The history of Indian people in North America, (known as a Great Island), is part of each separate trfbe's knowledge system. Knowledge concerning Indian existence has been handed down through the oral tradition for generations and this practice still continues today.

I attended an Indian spiritual conference for 15 years on the Stoney Indian Reserve in Morley, Alberta, Canada. I vividly recall taking part in a sunrise pipe ceremony with half a dozen Elders in the chief's teepee, nestled in the foothills. Prayers were offered in giving thanks for life and creation. The ceremony was not long but rich with ritual and meaning. Here, I felt whole and at peace with the cosmos. Later on in the day, a Cree Elder from the Poundmaker Indian Reserve in Saskatchewan offered a prayer and began to speak about the creation of the Indian people on this Great Island. He said that the Indian and the land are one. The Indian people sprang forth from the earth. The earth is our mother. We are her children. The earth breathes life into her children and provides for them. This is how the Indian came to be on this land.

This is just one illustration of an historical narrative given by an Elder to the people. Indian nations who inhabit the North American continent have a long history of rich oral traditions. The Indian existence does not begin with the execution of a written document or proclamation; it begins with the existence of the people and their interaction with and within the cosmos.

Indian oral history includes many teachings which bring purpose to Indian existence. The Indian people know they have been created for a special purpose. It is believed that there is a time coming in the future when Indian people will be needed in this land. Because of this need and the spiritual tie to the land the Indian people will continue to exist and will continue to struggle to survive. These teachings precede the written word of this land. The Indian people have been created as stewards of this land which is a role they will continue to uphold.

When the unfolding of the history of Canada is undertaken, the non-Indian will begin with definitions of legal documents or initial European accounts of "how the Indians were dealt with." The Indian people, however, began with a society that was born in Canada. The Indian people have a religion, a language, and a culture that originated in this land. The notion that history in Canada begins with European contact is demeaning for the Indian and very arrogant of the immigrant Europeans who came into Canada to claim. The Indian claim to special status in Canada is not so much a claim as it is fact. The non-Indian has reinforced this fact by acknowledging the rights of Indian nations in historical documents.

The unique nature of Aboriginals in Canada is clarified by the initial meeting of Indian and European nations. The first legal document that establishes a recognition of Indian tribes as separate nations in the eyes of the European is the Royal Proclamation of 1763. Jackie Henry, in *The Proclamation of 1763*, wrote "The Proclamation of 1763 was the Crown's first expression of good faith" (Henry, 1989, 10). Henry recognizes two flaws in the Proclamation: first, the Crown was best suited to alienate Indian lands, thus creating inequity for Indian people and resulting in a hierarchical relationship over the Indians. Secondly, Henry recognizes that there is uncertainty of the constitutional status of the Proclamation. Under the *Canada Act* of 1982, section 25(a), there is recognition of the Proclamation where it falls under the protection of the *Canadian Charter of Rights and Freedoms*. However, this protection extends only to existing Aboriginal rights and freedoms. Modification to any of the Indian treaties could result in the permanent loss of Indian rights (Jackie, 1989, 11).

Henry observes that an inequity exists in the Royal Proclamation's spelling out of the responsibility and control over Indian lands. He also notes that the constitutional status of the proclamation is uncertain.

The Royal Proclamation remains a critical document in understanding Indian-government relations. The resolution of its inherent inequity, however, requires Aboriginal participation in constitutional development. The uncertainty of the Proclamation's constitutional status requires Aboriginal people to formulate the political and legal positions regarding our place in the Canada Constitution.

Defining Aboriginal Rights

The term, "Aboriginal rights," is a relatively new concept which encompasses not only the Indian but also the Metis and Inuit people of Canada. In the past, prior to repatriation of the Constitution, Canada had unilaterally-defined Indian rights. The three areas of Canadian government, executive, bureaucratic, and judicial, have defined, derogated and abrogated Aboriginal rights in Canada. It is a modern challenge for Indian people to define their rights and therefore define their relationship with Canada.

When the "Indian" definition of Aboriginal rights begins, it must include the premise of Indian spirituality. From this premise flow notions of land, customs, philosophy, and solutions to reconciliation of the two definitions concerning Aboriginal rights. This term is not literal with specific prerequisites to give meaning but rather it is a general term to conceptualize the feelings that Indian people have regarding their rights.

Aboriginal rights concern rights to land. Land is not real estate to the Indian people. The ancient teaching that one must be part of the land is central to the teachings of most tribes in Canada. Indian stewardship extends to all of nature and to all of the adjoining processes. Medicine and herbs taken from the land must include prayer and a bestowal of gifts to the land to show gratitude for their privilege. In the case of my own tribe, the Stoneys, our people would gather special medicinal herbs and journey to the mountain hot springs. This was a natural retreat to the land. Many have still tried to maintain this tie to the land but unfortunately these places have become wilderness or protected areas.

By this means, the tribal rites and customs have been limited. These acts of gathering and using nature's gifts are part of the Indian philosophy which heals the body and soul of a people. Without knowing Indian religion, non-Indians declare sacred areas as sanctuaries to obtain the tourist dollar. Often the federal government has infringed on Indian religious freedoms, hunting and livelihood, and this conflicts with the Canadian *Charter of Rights and Freedoms*. Other ceremonies, including the Sundance, are held during the summer months. This ceremony is deeply religious and is held to ensure harmony with all of creation.

Through these ceremonies, the Indian plays a significant role in maintaining harmony with the land. Many of the ceremonies are intended to renew a deep spiritual tie to the cosmos. This wider universal view is used in recognizing the totality of Creation. The Indian sees all things as being related in the tangible as well as the intangible universe. Indian metaphysics views the cosmos as important in the lives of people, places and things. This wider view is constant within the Indian philosophy of land and nature.

It is against such a backdrop that it is helpful to study Indian development in Canada. It is no wonder there are few Indian scholars who are able to deal with the complex theoretical issues of Indian development regarding the definition of Aboriginal rights and their place in the Canadian Constitution.

The time has come to undertake a process of review. The European-based theories on the progress of scientific development seek to subdivide a problem into its component parts. This approach will not take into account the intricate nature of Indian thought. Indian thought or philosophy is not reduced into parts because the unity of Indian society based on religion is the unique trait that Indian people seek to maintain.

The inclusion of the Metis and the Inuit in the term "Aboriginal rights" is a further hindrance in compiling a definition. To reduce the Aboriginal people into one mass will only serve to compound the process of defining Aboriginal rights. The definition will now have three meanings for three distinct peoples, and may not necessarily lead to solutions. For the Indian people there is a need for great consideration to be given to the religion which is rooted in Indian knowledge systems.

Analysis of knowledge systems can come about through constructive dialogue between governments and Indian peoples, involving social, political, economic, and legal resource people. The crucial issue before Indian scholars is to convey the Indian reality through explanation, description, and interpretation of Indian knowledge systems as those systems relate to a particular tribe. In order to attain this end, quality education institutions must be developed which complement the needs of particular tribes. Quality education of the Indian must begin in the classroom from the grade school level to university. Indians and non-Indians must work jointly to address, resolve and implement solutions resulting in a win-win situation for Indian and non-Indian alike. More importantly, people from both sides must be committed to constructive change and continue a follow-up in order to meet the challenge of constitutional, political, legal, economic, and social reform. Clarification of the Indian-federal role must not be dictated through court rulings alone. Indian scholars and educators must seek out answers by questioning the status quo. For example, why are Indians in the predicament they are in? Resolutions to these questions will only be answered in a joint problem-solving scenario.

Indian Government

Indian tribes basically exercise their power of government through consensus in the oral tradition. In addition, each tribe has a language of its own. Indian knowledge systems derive from observing nature and the universe and comprise the Indian legal, political, economic, social and religious philosophy that existed long before the immigration of Europeans. Systems of Indian government such as the Iroquois example illustrate the complexity of such a system. For example, the idea of democratic government was in practice in North America prior to the drafting of written documents by the European. Numerous authors have observed that there is a need to redefine and negotiate the terms of Indian government. The lack of authoritative texts is an obstacle which may be overcome with discussions between Indian and non-Indian political participants.

It is through Indian knowledge systems that Indian people formulate concepts into policies, rules, and principles for government. In light of the complex nature of Indian tribes and their oral traditions, Aboriginal peoples must develop authoritative analyses regarding the development of Indian government.

Daughtery illustrates the complexity of Indian government by detailing the structure of the Iroquois Confederacy which is symbolized by the longhouse. The Seneca, Mohawk, Onandaga, Oneida, and Cayuga were members of the confederacy. The Seneca were the keepers of the western Door and the Mohawks, keepers of the eastern door. The Onandaga occupied the central position in the longhouse, on either side of the Onandaga, were the Oneida and Cayuga. From this structure formed in 1540, we note the beginnings of a division of power structure. In later years, Ben Franklin would use this concept to formulate structures in the American Constitution. Therefore the historical conceptualization of democratic government is truly a North American Indian idea.

When Indians speak of Indian government, non-Indian people get uncomfortable. Fundamental concepts of Indian government have been in existence for many years and now need only to be articulated and perhaps expanded. Hunter outlines a need to establish a definitional understanding when we are dealing with Indian government. He argues that bands are similar to municipalities but are different in that a fiduciary relationship is entailed in the band-government relationship. He argues that there is also a need to confirm the status of Indians in Canada. Fundamentally there must be a confirmation of the Indian right to Indian government. This will require a delineation of the jurisdictions of both Indian and federal governments (Hunter, 1978).

In an analyses of the judicial arm of governments in Canada today, there are no authoritative texts addressing the complex nature of Indian government. We as Indian people must co-ordinate tribal efforts by consulting with Elders and traditional leaders in developing *cultural authority* which reinforces the customs and traditions of each respective tribe. Indian theories regarding these issues have not been developed or encouraged in Canada. Why have Indian people been held back in this regard?

The Canadian government has rarely acted on behalf of the Indian people. They rarely secure Indian support for Indian-related policies. Only non-Indians with no background in Indian societies have decided our future. The Indians in Canada have suffered a subtle but very effective form of discrimination. Within the past 50 years, Indian people have endured practices which are unconstitutional today. By virtue of the *Indian Act*, Indians were required to carry pass-cards in order to leave and return to their reserves, so that their mobility was limited. The sad history of the mission school destroyed family units by taking away children and placing them in foreign environments. It was not until the 1960s that the Indians could even vote in this country. Some Aboriginals have even now never voted in a country which is called a democracy.

Such atrocities are commonplace for Indian people and the recognition of self-determination through Indian government will begin a productive place for Indian people in Canada today.

The oral tradition, the idea of consensus and democracy, the need for joint discussions and the publication of authoritative texts are constructive elements which can influence the development of Indian government. However, it is paramount that the question of Indian government be addressed by each respective tribe, and the knowledge systems of each tribe must be implemented into each Indian government form.

Conflict Resolution

History and social studies classes do not usually unearth the underlying controversies of the Indian treaties in the development of Canada as a nation-state. It is only recently that some Native studies programs have been developed in post-secondary institutions. There are voluminous studies looking at, counting, and analyzing Indian reserves and archaeological sites, but there is little literature written by Indian people exploring Indian knowledge systems and conveying their significance to non-Indians.

Resolutions of conflicts between Indian and non-Indian will only occur when an understanding of both cultures is ascertained by negotiators on both sides. Today there is still no acceptance or research into the philosophy of the Indian people. In addition, the definitions or solutions which Indian people articulate are varied due to the unique language or knowledge system of each tribe. Solutions can only begin when past grievances are replaced by future progress for both the Indian and non-Indians in Canadian society.

In order to demonstrate Indian philosophy I will recount elements of a speech given at a conference which I attended this year. It concerns the importance of Indian metaphysics as it relates to scientific analysis. I am currently a voting member of the American Indian Science and Engineering Society. The American Indian Science and Engineering Society is an organization which seeks to develop Indian professionals in the fields of science and engineering disciplines. In November of 1990, I attended their annual conference in New York. At the annual conference various multinationals and business corporations actively recruit Native professionals.

I attended one banquet at the Hyatt Regency where we were addressed by a Navajo, Fred Begay. This man had not undertaken a formal education until he was 22 years old. Mr. Begay stood before us as a scientist with Los Alamos Laboratories in Alberquerque, New Mexico. He currently holds a Ph.D. in mathematics and nuclear physics. He spoke about our need to know Indian language and customs. He explained how Indian philosophy can impact on the concepts of quantum physics and theories of causality. This was indeed a profound experience for myself and it demonstrated to me that Indian philosophy has something to offer society at large. Certainly the power of Indian logic is strong.

So when we deal with the issues of defining or examining Indian Aboriginal theory we must be mindful of the complex nature of the philosophy in which Indian theories are grounded. I am sure many concepts and theories have yet to be explained by Indian scholars but I have hope that this will occur in due course.

From this experience I believe it becomes important to nurture and tap the resources of concepts and theories which Indian tribes have to offer. Each tribe has its own special knowledge system and when we speak of Indian government all these topics become operative. So when the question is put in a political forum of what the Indians want or what they mean by self-government, there is a wide array of underlying assumptions which must be explained. These concepts and theories can impact on legal, socio-economic and even political view points.

Conclusion

A study of the phenomenon of Aboriginal rights and an analysis of Indian government are not simple undertakings. However, it is essential to note that in any discussion of Indian people the predominant factor to precede definitions and analyses is the understanding of Indian spirituality. With an understanding and appreciation of the unique spiritual view of the Indian people, each separate societal trait may be better understood.

The discussion of Indian spirituality is only one dimension of the magnitude of teachings which Indian people have to offer. Spirituality is essential in the understanding of the objectives of the Indian people. When such a study is undertaken, the traditional academic approach to Indian studies pales by comparison. Moreover, it offers a key to understanding Indian peoples and perhaps a bridge by which to join together what has been historically regarded as two distinct worlds.

The resolution of conflict between the Indian and non-Indian societies that exist in Canada today will only commence with the willingness of each side to understand and comprehend the values of the other. The Indian people have lost their homeland but they do not intend to lose their language, culture or society. The spiritual society of the Indian will continue and will positively flourish and enhance Canadian society. It is available for study and analysis and offers a rich untapped potential in helping to resolve current societal challenges.

References

Daughtery, Wayne. (1982). *A guide to Native political associates in Canada. Ottawa, Ontario: Treaty and Historical Research*, Research Branch, Corporate Policy, Indian and Northern Affairs.

Henry, Jackie. (1989). *The proclamation of 1763, the archivist. National Archives of Canada*. November - December, Vol. 16, No. 6.

Hunter, P. David and Associates. (1978). *The legal status of the band and band government*. Ottawa, Ontario: Treaties and Historical Research Branch. Indian and Northern Affairs.

Seton, Julia and Ernest Thompson Seton. (1963). *The gospel of the redman*. Sante Fe, New Mexico: Seton Village.

9

The Challenge of Cultural Destiny: The Role of Language

John W. Friesen

One of the chief concerns of ethnocultural communities in Canada is the maintenance of their cultural identity. Although the Native peoples can lay claim to being the original inhabitants of the land, thereby avoiding "immigrant" status, they too face the difficult challenge of retaining the traditional mode of their cultural configuration. Much of the pressure experienced by Native people emanates from the nation's implicit melting-pot orientation toward a kind of uniculture or, if the French have something to say about it, minimally a two-culture nation.

Recently an upsurge of interest in heritage languages has been evident, fuelled no doubt by a variety of motivations. On a formal level, it was the enhancement in language programing for official languages that sparked parallel interest on other fronts. Efforts to develop language programs have also been noticeable in many ethnocultural communities. For example, in Alberta, where the concept of the heritage language school was born in 1970, there are large enrollments, i.e., Ukrainian, 1 105 students; German, 953 students; Hebrew, 669 students; and Yiddish, 77 students. Native language programs also enroll large numbers of students.

Several other provinces have similar programs, although Ontario rejected the idea of offering basic school instruction in other than the two official languages, except on a temporary basis to help children acquire English skills. In 1977, that province instituted a heritage language program that provided funding for heritage language teaching up to two-and-one-half hours per week outside the regular five hours per school day. By 1982, there were over 80 000 students enrolled in these programs. (Martel, 1984).

Heritage language programs were not originated without resistance, for example, since assimilationists/nationalists have argued that these schools are a hindrance to the process. They argue that without a knowledge of either of the official languages immigrant children stand to lose out on gaining a proper place in mainstream society. If students have deficiencies in an offical language, it would be contrary to good pedagogy to give them instruction in another language. Bilingualism in any form is therefore viewed by this group as antithetical to a strong national identity. Opponents of second language instruction also take the position that a child's mind can absorb only so much information. Any time spent in other than "essential" instruction is time lost from important material (Ashworth,1988, 187).

Language learning is generally big business in Canada nowadays, and a large number of programs are readily available to any interested person. Many of these programs are advertised by community or commercial organizations, and touted as comprising an opportunity to advance economic possibilities, travel abroad, or to enhance personal enrichment. Some would even go so far as to suggest that national defence can be a language issue. The Chief of the Canadian Defence Staff is proud of the Armed Forces' official languages accomplishments and affirms the position that individuals should have the right to defend their country in their own language (Sloan, 1990, 6).

The Complexity of the Language Arena

A strong argument can be made that attention began to focus on the language phenomenon with the establishment of the two official languages and the related debate about having two official cultures as well. Alternately, Canada could have two official languages and a multiplicity of "official" cultures, i.e., multiculturalism. In Quebec, the word "multiculturalism" is avoided because policy-makers prefer to think in terms of only *two* official cultures as well as two official languages; thus the term, "intercultural" is substituted to denote the presence and activities of other cultures, albeit having a non-official status.

Ethnocultural communities in Canada who auger for additional recognition of languages other than English or French often encounter difficult road blocks. Other than token gestures, they are pretty well on their own in developing ways of teaching such languages. The road blocks may be evident in various ways — lack of appropriate funding, disinterest on the part of policy-makers who fail to find much political gain with such support, and perhaps even public dispproval.

In some provinces, a measure of financial support *is* available to finance heritage language schools, but such funding is limited. Generally, these schools cater to a very specific audience in that the students of any particular school are members of a specific ethnocultural group. German language schools enroll students from the German community; Ukrainian language schools enroll students of Ukrainian background, etc. Specifically, the major purpose of these schools is to foster cultural maintenance, mainly through language teaching, but efforts are sometimes made as well to teach a modest amount of ethnocultural history, values and/or religion. In some instances these schools also attempt to teach language arts in the first language of the student through the teaching of heritage language. As a general observation, however, the underlying objective of all such activity is to foster cultural maintenance and identity.

Some critics have pointed out that the aggrandizement of programs in French official language teaching has been encouraged by non-puristic motivations, economic factors, for example. The civil service is cited as a primary suspect; after all, a large percentage of Canadians are employed in the civil service at one level of government or another and this kind of employment requires facility in both official languages. As the federal policy becomes more entrenched as a Canadian value, such facility may eventually become manadatory, at least in government service. French critics have argued that the bilingual policy has played unfairly against their youth because they experience less need for facility in the English language than Anglophones do for French; hence, English is much less taught in their schools. Anglophones, on the other hand, outnumber the French in nine of ten provinces and thus realize much greater opportunity in learning the second official language. There appears to be a direct correlation between learning French as a second language and gaining employment in government. Most Francophones in Canada live and work in Quebec which is predominantly unilingual. Thus Quebec Francophones who learn English will have very little use of it since it is not even required in the Quebec government service.

The benefits of learning a second language are not limited to gaining civil service opportunities. A second language *does* provide personal enrichment, but its useage also functions as a corollary passport of sorts for travel, opening up new literary and cultural vistas to those who wish to make use of a new dimension in learning. More than that, however, language offers a glimpse into lifestyle and belief systems. It makes possible the appreciation of a different philosophy. It is for this reason that ethnocultural leaders are so concerned about the need for their youth to become familiar with their heritage language. Thus, they continue their campaigns for the inclusion of heritage language instruction at the various levels of schooling in Canada. Regardless of the merits of their concerns, however, it is doubtful that they will be fully realized in the near future. A similar situation exists with regard to the possibility of universal instruction of both official languages. High on the list of road blocks are such factors as funding, public conceptualizations and the struggle by government to work out equitable delivery systems.

The Function of Language

Many ethnocultural community leaders who are concerned about cultural survival argue that heritage language is the primary key to the survival of their particular lifestyle. These individuals take the position that the content of culture is contained in language and without its maintenance that culture will deteriorate. Thus, to know the language is to be a part of a given culture. An opposing view, somewhat softened, is that due to a variety of forces and influences, cultures change over time. The composition of culture at any given time is therefore different from that of any previous generation. However, that composition is as valid a form of culture as that of any previous generation because it reflects the active lifestyle of a particular generation. When new words are introduced into language useage the concommitant culture changes. Even then it is *still* a valid culture, and it is as meaningful to the generation which employs the resultant language as any can be. The counter argument is that conceptual changes in language result in cultural losses that can never be recaptured. It is therefore important to retain the linguistic and conceptual content of culture as long as possible.

Gordon's oft-cited model for evaluating minority acquiesence to cultural assimilation makes no mention of language loss as a factor in the process, perhaps because its research base is distinctly American. Gordon identifies such factors as: changes in cultural practices, adopting dominant group relationships, intermarriage, gaining a sense of peoplehood with the dominant group, absence of discrimination on the part of the group being assimilated, and arriving at the position that there are no particular issues of concern to minority members pertaining to their loss of identity (Gordon, 1964, 70). The forgoing does not mean that language is unimportant to cultural maintenance, but it *does* raise questions about its rank of importance among related factors. It is possible, after all, to maintain a strong cultural identity without specific language useage, but this does not mean that cultural *content* can necessarily be preserved without language specificity. Research also suggests that where language maintenance is desired, the best agency to accomplish this goal is the home. Other institutions can, at best, play a supplemental role (Hayden, et. al., 1977).

In contrast to other factors which figure in the quest to maintain culture, language is often conceptualized as the most significant. This may be true in certain instances, but evidence suggests that some ethnocultural groups have also done well while utilizing other means of reaching their goal (Backeland and Frideres, 1977; Anderson and Frideres, 1981; Breton, 1979). One of the preferred ways has been geographic isolation, a pattern of living that has worked to some degree for many groups. The Anabaptist groups which originated in the 16th-century Reformation, i.e., Amish, Hutterites and Mennonites have managed to keep a physical distance between themselves and mainline society, which has also helped them to keep psychologically and sociologically apart from the mainstream of society. Similarly, Indian reserves function as distinct and separate communities in many ways, governed as they are by their own laws and decision-making bodies. Another more recent and less tenable example originated in the 1960s with the "back-to-the-landers" movement in British Columbia. This phenomenon featured a migration of young people in their 20s and 30s to the isolated areas of the British Columbia Interior in search of "inner peace." Claiming weariness from the rat-race promoted by the conformist middle-class social climbers of urban living, the back-to-the-landers regaled against many modern conveniences including electricity and plumbing. After a generation of trying to eke out a living through part-time employment at semi-skilled jobs, a series of gradual changes became evident and the movement dwindled.

To a certain extent, a design which fostered geographic isolation was built into the prairie settlement plan for immigrant groups who chose to move to Canada at the turn of this century. The plan was supported by both government policy makers as well as immigrants. The bloc-type of communities that originated across the West acknowledged that ethnocultural groups preferred to live among their own kind. Thus each settlement became more or less socially and psychologically complete, and each separate community followed a similar format for living; they built sod huts and schools and churches and worried about who their children would marry. Their anxieties were articulated in their individual native languages, but still their concerns conveyed a common agenda — how to survive culturally in a pluralistic nation.

Another form of isolation preferred by ethnocultural groups with a penchant for exclusivity is the practice of endogamy. By ensuring that their youth select marriage partners only from within their ranks it is commonly believed that the essence of a given culture will be maintained.

Operant social forces which reinforce bonds and deter marrying outside are community solidarity and sectarianism (Palmer, 1985). Trends are, however, that intermarriage among many immigrant groups is on the increase, tending to blur formerly distinct ethnocultural lines. Even close-knit groups like the Amish of Lancaster County, Pennsylvania (or Waterloo County in Ontario), lose upwards of 30 percent of their youth membership through intermarriage. Generally those involved in relationships with individuals outside their ingroup find fellowship with other conservative religious groups such as Mennonites, because they are formally restricted from mingling with their heritage group. Thus, their actions force them to become victims of the isolating practices of their own heritage group.

In analyzing the phenomenon of lingusitic content related to ethnic endogamy, Stevens and Swicegood concluded two things: first, persons with a non-official first language are more likely to marry endogamously, and second, beyond the preferences related to individuals' characteristics, features of the linguistic context, specifically the relative size of the minority-language subgroup and the rate of linguistic assimilation, also generate variation among ethnic group levels of endogamy. Linguistic assimilation precedes the overall assimilation of an ethnocultural group through widespread ethinc intermarriage, thus making the case that while language is not an exclusive guarantree for cultural maintenance, it *is* a very signifcant factor (Stevens and Swiceghood, 1987).

Further excluding dimensions of close-knit minorities are demonstrable through institutional efforts such as schooling. By establishing private schools, clubs and other organizations that function as socializing agents for their young, it is believed that interaction with outsiders will be minimized. In a Winnipeg, Manitoba, study it was shown that Canadian Francophones have successfully maintained a stong sense of identity among their young through institutional completeness. This means that the basic social needs of the group's youth were met through forms of social structure engineered and controlled by the leadership of the group in question (Comeau and Driedger), 1978). The Francophone success has come despite restrictive experiences in the language sector in Manitoba.

Despite admirable success in maintaining cultural identity through other means, Manitoba Francophones also regard language as a vital component of their cultural identity. Efforts to curtail French language rights have been a perpetual struggle since the beginning of this century when the government of Prime Minister Wilfred Laurier refused to protect the French language. In 1915, one-sixth of Manitoba's schools were bilingual but many of the schools had teachers who were ill-qualified to teach in both English and French. While this situation did little to promote the French identity in the West, they still persevered. Undoubtedly, their ability to mobilize their cultural forces on other fronts paid off and was probably even aided by the opposition they encountered. In the meantime, the push for assimilation that swept the West during the period of high immigration from 1890-1914, was targetted at the French, as well as at other groups, despite their status as a founding nation and the possession of rights pertaining thereto. It was only in the 1960s that the strongly assimilative bent of the school systems was partially rectified when the Manitoba government finally passed legislation that allowed for the teaching of either official language in the province's schools. While the Province of Manitoba is often cast in a villainous role with regard to French language rights, it is well to recall that similar developments transpired in other regions of the West. The attack on Saskatchewan separate schools which began in 1913, for example, culiminated in a heated election issue in 1917 featuring incalculatable repercussions. Space does not permit an elaboration of the details of the Saskatchewan experience, but the unhappy memories of it linger in the French community (Le Blanc, 1990).

The Survival of Native Languages

The justification of the foregoing prelude is that most language research in Canada has thus far eluded the Native community. This phenomenon is changing, however, because many Indian leaders believe that language is the primary key to Indian cultural survival, and there can be no substitute. History shows that Indian language rights have largely been ignored by government. During the decades in which residential schools provided for Native education, no provisions were made for language training. Instead, Native languages were regarded as contrary to assimilative educational objectives. Native languages that *did* persist were retained through "underground" methods, under the care of secret societies and informal teaching procedures in the homes. Only recently, with the closing of residential boarding schools, and their takeover by educators hired by government, have language programs been installed in schools. Since 1970, a variety of language instruction courses have been established in Indian communities across the nation. These programs were first established on a bilingual model using the Native language as a basis. The methodology included a transitory process to English so that the procedure would not strip children of their own language. Students received 100 percent instruction in the Native language in kindergarten, 80 percent in grade one, 60 percent in grade two, 50 percent in grade three, etc. By junior high school, all instruction was in English.

The 1980s witnessed an intense effort on the part of Native leaders to increase opportunities for instruction in Native languages. The universities were a favored target including a campaign to develop teacher training courses for language instruction. Today the University of Manitoba offers an undergraduate degree program in Native languages in conjunction with the Manitoba Association for Native Languages (Norton, 1989; Manitoba Association for Native Languages, 1986).

By 1986, in the public school sector, 14 607 students were enrolled in courses offering Native language as a subject, and 25 443 were involved in classes where a Native language is used as the language of instruction (Commissioner of Official Languages, 1986, 204). At first glance these numbers appear impressive, but these programs often provide little more than peripheral knowledge of the language in question. Essentially, language familiarity may be evaluated by the number of speakers who utilize a language in their daily ongoings. The normal place for this to occur is the home and to a lesser extent, the community. Initially then, it is logical to conclude that a revival of Indian languages would need to target on the home.

One of the most taken-for-granted facts about Indian languages is the complexity of their identification. Authorities estimate that there are 11 Indian language families which make up for 50-58 languages, and they vary greatly in relative size. The startling reality of the impending decrease in useage of most Indian languages has reached dramatic proportions. Only three of the languages, Inupik, Cree and Ojibway, have more than 5 000 speakers. Thirteen languages have between 100-500 speakers, and five extremely endangered languages have between 10-100 speakers. Eight languages have fewer than 10 speakers (Morrison and Wilson, 1986, 24-25). Another factor in the process, albeit less significant, is intermarriage between members of different Native communities resulting in English being used as the principal home language. Against this background it is easy to appreciate why Indian leaders are concerned about language and cultural loss.

There are many reasons for the loss of Native languages, including deliberate policies inaugerated by government, educational agencies and sometimes by religious and missionary groups. Many such efforts are still underway even today. Administrators of these institutions have often perceived that mainline societal enculturation is hindered by the maintenance of Indian languages and so they have forcefully forbidden their use.

In Canada, the financing and promotion of the official languages has similarly taken its toll on the Native sector because of the underlying philosophy that a thorough knowledge of an official language is a more important than the linguistic objectives of any specific ethnocultural community. In the United States a campaign is underway to make only English the official language of many states as well as amend the U.S. Constitution to prohibit the use of other languages (Brandt and Ayoungman, 1989). Against this campaign, through legally-supported channels, the handwriting is on the wall in terms of predicting the uphill battle for Native languages in the days ahead.

The 1984 First Minister's Aboriginal Constitutional Conference was made aware of the crisis proportions of Native language status in Canada. After the hearing, research was commissioned by the Department of Secretary of State to assess the number of speakers in each Native language group in Canada. Based on the preliminary results of the research, which showed a continually diminishing number of speakers for Native language groups, a First National Aboriginal Language Policy Conference was announced to discuss and perhaps develop a national Native language policy for Canada. Soon after, the federal government set up a commission to study the feasibility of a national Aboriginal language institute (Norton, 1989).

In the meantime, Native leaders have continued their efforts to develop language retention programs which take into account the principles which make for effective use of the language. A brief elucidation of a few such examples will illustrate the complexity and magnitude of such efforts.

Language Preserving Projects

The approaches taken by various tribes to preserve Native languages vary somewhat, but an underlying commonality of concern exists. These efforts comprise quite diverse facets including the establishment of language composition and parameters, development of written materials, training of instructors, and the execution of appropriate programing.

Perhaps the first step in developing a language program is to make certain that the language in question has sufficient acceptability in the community in which it is to be promoted. The experiences of the Dene Nation of northern Canada (Northwest Territories) illustrate the intensity of the background work essential to building a language program. In 1985, the Dene Nation began to investigate the feasibility of attempting to standardize a Dene writing system. This was to be undertaken within a 10-year period (Biscaye and Pepper, 1990). Part of the difficulty of the project stemmed from the fact that there are five Dene languages spoken in the N.W.T. This gave added challenge to the project and the linguists had to decide between varying systems for each dialect. A further challenge was to make sure that the systems had symbols for all of the sounds which were recognized as distinct sounds by speakers of that language. Third was the challenge of choosing alphabets and writing conventions for each language which would conform to a standard across the five languages.

Preparing a language form includes a myriad of responsibilities not readily appreciated by non-linguists. These include dealing with alternate pronunciations, alphabet symbols, word divisions and punctuation. Extralinguistic issues include literacy training, publication of reference materials, second language teaching, linguistic research, place names, and promotion of Dene literature. The Dene project was carefully subdivided into five distinct phases to incorporate the above objectives. The second phase, consisting of soliciting feedback and support from local interest groups was completed by 1990. The third phase has been initiated, and comprises the selection of a committee to make decisions about a writing system. The fourth phase will involve the preparation and publication of reference and teaching materials, and the final phase will concentrate on literacy campaign and promotion of public awareness.

Another example of establishing language composition and acceptability was undertaken by the Mi'kmawey School in Nova Scotia. The project operates on a bilingual basis, and was begun in response to the realization that the provincial system could not provide adequate training in Native content, including language, and thus an alternative program was developed. Specifically, it was discovered that Native students who spoke their own language were being victimized by being assessed as having learning disorders. Initiatives for a band-controlled school seemed the best action that could be taken (Battiste, 1987).

A first step in the Mi'kmaq language project was to determine a proper form for the language itself. It was soon discovered that both the forms and functions of the Mi'kmaq language are governed by the contexts of society. Mi'kmaq literacy is consistent with the thesis that oral cultures whose tradition retained the knowledge and history of the people had many inherent meanings that served different functions for different groups of people at different times (Whiteman and Hall, 1981). Historically, social change in Mi'kmaq has been preceded by a change in literacy form. For example, the early missionaries and explorers sought the development of Mi'kmaq orthographies for their own purposes. Later, when the Mi'kmaqs developed their own written language forms, they relied on additional sources of input for cultural information that went beyond the social and political paradigms usually employed. This reliance on the spirit world added a cultural dimension which was overlooked by linguist experts outside the Mi'kmaq culture.

Upgrading and refining written forms of the Mi'kmaq language has been a continual process for 20 years. The first renovation essentialy modified the traditional Pacifique writing system. The authors eliminated many diacritical marks from the system and added long and short vowel distinctions by using an apostrophe position after the vowel to indicate length. By 1977, it would have been improper to describe the Mi'kmaq written language form as Pacifique since it was basically new in every way. Still, use of the older form persisted because Elders continued to use it in religious functions. However, in 1980 the Grand Council of the Mi'kmaqs formally adopted the new script system for writing their language. The action put an end to controversial arguments over the two forms and the campaign to promote Mi'kmaq cultural knowledge and tradition through a consistent language form took on more unified proportions. Tribal Elders endorsed the action, realizing that a unified approach would be the best way to guarantee the transmission of Mi'kmaq language, culture and religion (Batiste, 1987). Their endorsation reveals how serious the Elders were in wanting to protect the integrity of their cultural heritage.

A language program demonstrating the dimension of content formation emanates from the Stoney tribe located some 56 kilometres west of Calgary, Alberta. In l965 the Stoney Tribal Council developed a writing system for their language following the Roman orthography tradition. Three years later, when the tribe opted for self-government and suddenly found itself with responsibility for all branches of cultural development, a concern was voiced about cultural transmission. One of the programs quickly initiated was an oral history program developed by the newly-formed Stoney Cultural Education Program. Using tape recorders, program workers interviewed tribal Elders for information pertaining to Stoney history and legend content. This information was later transformed into a series of curriculum books for the local school.

Framers of the plan envisaged that the gathered content would be taught to Stoney pupils by Stoney teachers but several shortcomings were quickly realized. Very few Stoney youth actually undergo the necessary training to teach the language, and financial cut-backs forced the limitation of necessary publications (Friesen, et al. 1990). In l988, an attempt to revive the Stoney Cultural Program was undertaken which resulted in the completion of eight legend books as curriculum content. Two local Stoney teachers piloted the program using legends as the primary content for language teaching. Unfortunately, one of the teachers fell ill and died prematurely, but his efforts continue in the spirit of the program.

The Stoney experiment teaches a number of lessons about using legends as teaching content. Space permits only a few observations. In the first instance, legends are usually related only by Elders, that is, people deemed worthy to dispense such teachings. In the Stoney tradition there are at least three kinds of legends: first, those repeated primarily for amusement, i.e., stories about the Trickster (îktomni), second, those employed for moral or purposive teaching, and third, those which have spiritual meaning and which may be related only by a respected Elder. Essentially, legends belong to the storyteller in question, and although the content of a story may vary from one storyteller to another, each version belongs to the original teller.

The complexity of dealing with different versions of legends is parallelled by the nature of the Stoney language. For example, the Stoney tribe has three subdivisons or bands and each band may have variances in language usage. In addition, the tribe is situated on three geographically separate reserves which makes communication difficult and which may result in other language differences. Finally, as with other tribes, a distinction may be observed with regard to traditional versus more modern orientations with regard to language useage which breaks down further to include family differences in speech practice. In the Stoney project these complexities gave rise to many earnest and detailed discussions. Undoubtedly, these intense moments contributed a sense of urgency to the project.

Possibly the best known Indian education program in North America is managed by the Navajo tribe in Arizona. The approach to language teaching at the Rock Point Community School, for example, started in 1967, and is bilingual. With most other facets of the program provided for, the Navajo local school board has more recently concentrated on procuring teachers for the Navajo language component (Reyhner, 1990). Initially, most of the teachers who were hired were without college degrees, but an on-site program brought the possibility of college graduation to many of them. Community leaders concluded that the only way an isolated Navajo community would get a stable and qualified teaching staff would be to train local people. Thus by combining higher education opportunities for individuals who possessed language knowledge, the community accomplished two purposes. The plan also provided stability to the program. By 1989, 21 teachers of a staff of 50 had worked 10 years or more at Rock Point, and only one non-Navajo teacher was employed in the elementary school.

The Rock Point community is fortunate to be a part of a much larger effort to develop appropriate curriculum materials for language instruction. The campaign to undertake the provision of curriculum began in 1973 with ample funding through the Navajo Reading Studies Project. Through the intervening years funding has become sparodic and reduced and students have been engaged to provide supplementary materials through writing newspapers and longer booklets. In keeping with the times, the Navajo bilingual program utilizes the same contemporary teaching channels for both English and Navajo instruction. This includes regular techniques such as use of video equipment, drama and speech practice. In addition, hands-on instructional approaches are employed for certain subjects following the "realia" approach outlined by Hoffman (1988), and the "context" idea promoted by Cummins (1989).

Concerns about the effects of bilingual education have been expressed by the Rock Point project leaders from the beginning. Consistent testing with the California Test of Basic Skills has shown that Rock Point students do equally well as other Navaho students at almost all grade levels in reading, language arts and math, while maintaining their skills in Navajo language development. Additional evaluation is undertaken through periodic testing by a Navajo language evaluator and an English language evaluator who are employed for that purpose.

Toward a Conclusion

Without trying to engage in the debate as to the significance of language in assuring cultural maintenance, it should be pointed out that the campaign to teach and preserve Native heritage languages is fraught with many complexities. In the first instance, the integrity and parameters of language itself needs to be established, both from the perspective of community approval as well as from the standpoint of linguistic integrity. In the past, many well-meaning linguists erroneously concluded that cultures relying on the oral tradition were at best only partially literate. This assumption was based on the observation that since there was little or no written communication among the tribes, they must be only partially literate. No one made much effort to understand the symbolic literacy of Native cultures, the invaders did their best to erradicate it on the basis that it was a threat to their own literacies or a hindrance to a quick Native understanding of the Christian Scriptures (Battiste, 1986).

In building a language program, its framers need to struggle with the challenge of deciding on format and content without yielding to the subtle assimilative forces inherent in the modern language preservation process. After all, since the structures of language preservation today are essentially non-Native, arising as they do from non-Native, academic sources, it stands to reason that some outside influences regarding content, etc., will be manifest. Although no one can be sure to what extent these forces are active in any given language-preserving program, the cause is still greater than the concern.

The more "standard" complexities of language program development, including curriculum building, teacher selection and training, evaluation, etc., will no doubt continue to challenge linguists and leaders for some years. More recently, the preference for bilingual education has manifest itself, and although not all of the evidence is in as yet, language promoters will need to watch the barometer to determine the efficacy and/or possible side effects of this kind of training (Kalantzis, et.al., 1989).

In the final analysis, the persistence of Native languages will rest on two main elements, one of which is the will of the Native people themselves. The second is the entrenchment of language rights in appropriate legislation by the nation's governments. Both elements have a somewhat unpredictable and emotional side to them, the former originating in the heart of the Native community in the interests of cultural persistence, and the latter from within the hearts of Canadians in the interests of national pluralism. When these two concerns mesh, Native language maintenance will be assured.

References

Anderson, Alan B. and James S. Frideres. (1981). *Ethnicity in Canada: theoretical perspectives*. Toronto: Butterworth.

Ashworth, Mary. (1988). *Blessed with bilingual brains: education of immigrant children with English as a second language*. Vancouver: Pacific Educational Press.

Backeland, Lucille and J.S. Frideres. (1977). "French Canadians in Manitoba: Elites and Ideologies," in *Immigrant groups*. Jean Leonard Elliott, ed. Scarborough, Ont.: Prentice-Hall.

Battiste, Marie. (1986). "Micmac Literacy and Cognitive Assimilation," in *Indian education in Canada, volume I: the legacy*. Jean Barman, et. al., eds. Vancouver: University of British Columbia Press, 23-44.

Battiste, Marie. (1987). "Mi'kmaq Linguistic Integrity: A Case Study of Mi'kmawey School," in *Indian education in Canada: volume. 2: the challenge*. Jean Barman, et. al., eds. Vancouver: University of British Columbia Press, 107-125.

Biscaye, Elizabeth and Mary Pepper. (1990). "The Dene Standardization Project," in *Effective language and education practices & Native language survival*. Jon Reyhner, ed. Choctaw, Oklahoma: Proceedings of the Ninth Annual International Native American Language Ussues (NALI) Institute, 23-29.

Brandt, Elizabeth A. and Vivian Ayoungman. (1989). "Language Renewal and Language Maintenance," *Canadian journal of Native education*, Vol.16, No. 2, 42-77.

Breton, Raymond. (1979). "From a Different Perspective: French Canada and the Issue of Immigration and Multiculturalism," *TESL talk*, Vol. 10, 45-56.

Burnaby, Barbara J. (1984). *Aboriginal languages in Ontario*. Toronto: Minister of Education and Ontario Ministry of Colleges and Universities.

Comeau, Larry R. and Leo Driedger. (1978). "Ethnic Opening and Closing in an Open System," *Social forces*, Vol. 57, No. 2, 600-620.

Commissioner of Official Languages. (1986). *Youth, languages and education*. *Annual Report*, Part V, Ottawa: Ministry of Supply and Services.

Cummins, Jim. (1989). *Empowering minority students*. Sacramento, CA.: California Association for Bilingual Education.

Friesen, John W. (1985). "Language and Cultural Maintenance: Not a Simple Matter," *Contact*, Vol. 4, No. 4, 11-16.

Friesen, John W., Clarice Kootenay and Duane Mark. (1990). "The Stoney Indian Language Project," in *Effective language education practices & Native Languge survival*. Jon Reyhner, ed. Choctaw, Oklahoma: Proceedings of the Ninth Annual International Native American Language Issues (NALI) Institute, 30-38.

Gordon, Milton. (1964). *Assimilation in American life*. New York: Oxford University Press.

Hayden, R.G., Lucille Backeland and James Frideres. (1977). "Some Community Dynamics of Language Maintenance," quoted in "Franco-Manitobans and Cultural Loss: A Fourth Generation," *Prairie forum*, Vol. 2, No. 1, 1-18.

Hoffman, Edwina. (1988). "Practical Suggestions for Oral Language Development," in *Teaching the Indian child: a bilingual multicultural approach*. J. Reyhner, ed. 2nd Edition. Billings, Montana: Eastern Montana College, 86-96.

Kalantzis, Mary, Bill Cope and Diana Slade. (1989). *Minority languages & dominant culture: issues of education, assessement and social equity*. London: The Falmer Press, 29-50.

Le Blanc. (1990). "Minority Language Education after the Supreme Court Decision," *Language and society*, No. 32, Fall, 31-35.

Manitoba Association for Native Languages. (1986). *Report of the Native education concerns group on the Native language enrichment project*. Winnipeg: M. A. N. L., Annual Report, April, 1985- March 1986.

Martel, Angeline. (1984). "Minority-Majority Relations in Second Language Education and the New Canadian Charter of Rights and Freedoms," *Educational research quarterly*, Vol. 8, No. 7, 113-121.

Morrison, R. Bruce and C. Roderick Wilson, eds. (1986). *Native peoples: the Canadian experience*. Toronto: McClelland and Stewart.

Norton, Ruth W. (1989). "Recent Developments in Manitoba Native Languages." Unpublished paper, University of Calgary, 23pp.

Norton, Ruth W. (1989). "Analysis of Policy on Native Languages: a Comparison of Government Policy and Native Preferences of a Native Language Policy." Unpublished paper, University of Calgary, 35pp.

Palmer, Howard and Tamara Palmer. (1985). *Peoples of Alberta*. Saskatoon: Western Producer Books.

Reyhner, Jon. (1990). "A Description of the Rock Point Community School Bilingual Education Program," in *Effective language education practices & Native language survival*. Jon Reyhner, ed. Choctaw, Oklahoma: Proceedings of the Ninth Annual International Native American Language Issues, 95-106.

Sloan, Tom. (1990). "National Defence: Defending One's Country in One's Own Language," *Language and society*, No. 30, Spring, 6-7.

Stevens, Gillian and Gary Swicegood. (1987). "The Linguistic Context of Ethnic Endogamy," *American sociological review*, Vol. 52, No. 1, February, 73-82.

Whiteman, Marcia Farr and William S. Hall. (1981). "Introduction," in *Writing: the nature, development and teaching of written communication, vol. I, variation in writing: functional and linguistic-cultural differences*. Marcia Farr Whiteman, ed. Hillsdale, N.J.: Lawrence Erlbaum.

10

The Persistence of Native Education Policy in Canada

Sonia Brookes

A formal plan for the education of Canada's Indian people has existed since the Europeans first settled in this country. The purpose of such education was the same for both Indians and non-Indians, namely to prepare them to make choices and meet the challenges of the future. In essence, however, the underlying theme of education, especially that of the Indian, was one of assimilation. If the Indian people were going to cope in a European-designed Canada, they would have to learn new skills and conceptualize different values. These the school would teach.

Early Missionary Schools (1600-1750)

Missionary-operated schools in New France originated in the early 17th century (Patterson, et. al., 1974). Both the French government and the Gallican Church encouraged these schools as a viable means of building a French Christian colony without depopulating the mother country. This was to be achieved by assimilating the Indians into the newly-established communities. As preparation for joining the new society, orders were issued to the clergy in New France to instruct Indians in both the Roman Catholic religion and French culture.

As early as 1615, the Hurons of Georgian Bay were being educated by the Recollets. A school for the Micmac in Acadia was opened by the Capauchins in 1632, and by 1635 Father Paul LeJeune had opened a school for both French and Indian children at Quebec. These early mission schools were unsuccessful, however, because the missionaries found it difficult to teach Catholicism to nomadic tribes, and the classical languages aspect of the curriculum proved to be most unsuitable to Indian needs.

Shortly thereafter, another approach to Indian education was incepted whereby young Indian boys and girls were sent to France to be baptized and to attend boarding schools. The goal was for the educated Indians to return to their tribes and teach their people the French way of life. This approach also proved futile because more often than not the Indians would return as misfits — unable to function in either society

(Jaenen, 1986). By 1639, the practice was ended when it was recognized that this was not a feasible method of accomplishing francisation.

About 1667, the Jesuits began day schools on reserves. These reserves, also known as "reductions," were permanent Indian settlements. Their purpose was to attract Indian people into the French tract of settlement with a view to francising them and holding them to the Catholic religion and French allegiance (Jaenen, 1986). The reserves were close to, but separate from, the French settlements in an effort to shelter the Indians from the corrupting influences of alcohol, syphilis, and smallpox. Each reserve contained both a mission house and a church which were administered by missionaries. The educational program consisted of religious studies, agriculture and manual trades. Manual labor was considered to be essential to the curriculum, as laziness in children was believed to be the cause of most adult traits of weakness. King Louis XIV, in fact, heard that AmerIndian men were particularly lazy and he believed that schooling could avert this tendency. (Public Archives of Canada, 1665)

The success of the reserve program in acculturating Indians was limited. Although the children *did* adapt to the French diet and manner of dress, no other aspects of French culture were absorbed; nor were the students successful in agriculture or manual trades (Jaenen, 1986). Reserve schools were abandoned and the Jesuits began concentrating their efforts on "seminaries" or boarding schools. However, these schools also failed. The curriculum consisted of catechism, reading and writing, and proved to be impractical for Indian children. As well, the discipline of studies and loneliness resulting from the separation from their families was too difficult for them to bear. It was also very difficult to attain sufficient enrollment for the seminaries because mothers were reluctant to part with their children. In addition, Indian leaders were generally opposed to the schools because they wanted their children to remain at home in order to learn the ancestral beliefs and values of their culture, and take up their responsibilities to their kinsmen and tribe (Jaenen, 1986).

By 1750, the Roman Catholic Church was widely involved in educating Indians. Decisions regarding policy were made in France and usually on the basis of what would be most advantageous to the colonists. The sole purpose of schooling was the pursuit of francisation. As might be expected, the curriculum focused on religion, agriculture and apprenticeship in various trades. Formal instruction was given in both French and Indian languages. The structure of the program was based on the *Ratio Studiorum*, its principal aim being the spiritual welfare of the students. Teaching methodology focused on training the memory and the powers of concentration through the use of repetition, recitation, and examinations. Other characteristics of the plan included free tuition, scheduled holidays and public ceremonies for the bestowal of awards (Chalmers,1972).

Despite many efforts, the Indian education of this period met with little success. The missionaries found that assimilation was difficult to accomplish because the Indians were proud of their culture and heritage and not anxious to give it up. Not only were their traditional beliefs well-rooted, but the environment favored many Indian customs and practices (Chalmers, 1972). Thus, Indian leaders did not place a high priority on French-inspired, government-style education. True, the Indians did acknowledge French superiority in technical advances, but they were not impressed with European concepts of authority, morality, property, and work (Jaenen, 1986). The education goals favored the colonists, not the Indians, and therefore the programs did not accomplish their objectives.

The Press for Assimilation

By 1763, New France was absorbed into the British Empire and the control and administration of Indian affairs was taken over by the British Imperial government. Until 1830, this responsibility fell under the jurisdiction of the military whose prime concern was to maintain peace in Indian communities and to preserve their assistance as allies (Scott, 1914). This shift in focus created a void in Indian education, allowing the churches and their affiliate organizations to become involved (Chalmers, 1972).

One such organization was the New England Company, a philanthropic organization that strove to improve the condition of Indian peoples in the New England states. Following the American Revolution, the company moved to New Brunswick. Its objective was to civilize Indians by educating them in the English language, training them in a practical vocation and Christianizing them in the Protestant faith (Fingard, 1972). Although colonial boards, consisting of prominant Anglican clergymen, government leaders, members of the judiciary, wealthy merchants, and other solid citizens were established to oversee the educational program, policy and funding were controlled by trustees who were in England (Chalmers, 1972).

To encourage school attendance, the company allowed Indian parents to squat on company land near the school. Parents were also given provisions of food and clothing. Classes were made up of both Indians and non-Indians so that the Indian children would not feel picked on. However, these arrangements did not ensure success for the schools. A major obstacle was strong parental resistance to the use of any type of discipline with their children. A last attempt by the company was to introduce an apprenticeship (indenture) program whereby Indian children would be sent to live with select families and learn a trade. At certain times during the program they would be sent to a central school to be instructed by the company's schoolmaster (Hamilton, 1986). The difficulties encountered by this program emerged when they experienced rejection by their own people on returning home. Conversely, they were also not accepted by the white community (Hamilton, 1986). After 15 years of attempts, and what were deemed to be exhorbitant annual expenditures, not *one* Indian child had been apprenticed or received any degree of education profitable to himself or society (Chalmers, 1972).

The use of Indian languages remained a prominant feature during this period. Delaware, Chippewa, Cree and Micmac were languages used in the various schools. Grammars were developed and books were published in Native languages. In 1836, Reverend James Evans developed a Cree Syllabic orthography which is still being used today. Although Indians enjoyed learning in their own languages, by the end of this period the language of instruction became an issue. Enthusiastic Mohawk Indians of Tyendinga had requested of Bishop Strachan (1843) to be allowed to have a school where the Indian language would be used, as well as a second one in English. They even offered to pay for the cost of printing Indian books to be used in the school. However, they encountered difficulty with both the clergy and the government. The Superintendent of Indian Affairs, Captain Anderson, disapproved of the use of Indian books because he perceived the future of the Indians to be more entrenched with whites and therefore felt that teaching in Indian languages would be "time and effort lost" (Anderson, 1863).

The Industrial Schools

In 1830, the administration of Indian Affairs was transferred from the military to civil authority. The government felt that its new role with respect to Indians was to aid in their civilization. Education was to be the vehicle through which Indians were to be taken "from a state of barbarism" and introduced to the "industrious and peaceful habits of civilized life" (Scott, 1914).

The Indian Department intended to promote civilization through religious instruction, basic literacy training, and elementary training pursuant to settling the Indians on farms. The schools established during this period of time were identified by a variety of different titles, i.e., schools of industry, manual schools and industrial schools. The prime objective of the industrial schools was to teach the boys useful trades such as, shoemaking, carpentry, blacksmithing and tailoring. Girls were taught sewing, knitting, washing and cooking.

The lack of observable success of these educational endeavors caused growing concern within the church community as well as within government circles as to the Indians' future. The decline in the fur trade and the growing white population were factors that were interpreted as having a negative impact on the traditional Indian way of life. This motivated leaders in both camps to intensify their campaign for assimilation (Anderson, 1863). To prevent Indian people from facing "destruction and ruin" church policy makers suggested that Indians be taught to hold and respect the same values as dominant society (Cornish,1881). Government officials promoted a similar philosophy. Superintendent Anderson emphasized that the rationale for establishing schools of industry was to enable Indian children to "forget their Indian habits" (Wilson, 1986). Commissioner Perley of the Maritimes concurred, and emphasized the growing trend toward assimilation when he stated that industrial schools would ". . . lead to the perfect civilization of the rising generations of Indians . . ." thus eliminating all distinctions of the different races (Hamilton, 1986). The role of the church in "civilizing" the Indians was supported by government officials such as Major General Darling, a superintendent of Indian Affairs, who stated that Indians must ". . . embrace Christianity and civilization."

As to the success of these schools, a report of the Special Commissioner in 1858 concluded that the schools were to a great extent a failure. The commissioners saw little evidence that the pupils were applying the skills acquired in school after they returned home. The report did not blame the church societies which managed the schools, but *did* identify a series of impediments. These included: enrollment of pupils at a late age and consequently, short attendance; parental prejudice against the schools (they feared that the schools were intent on seducing their children from their traditional Native culture and traditional way of life); and lack of funds to establish the "school leavers" on the land. Despite the report, industrial schools became the norm in western Canada well into the next century. The promoters of this system believed that the schools had to be effective in obtaining the "desired result," that being, "the emancipation [of the Indians] from tribal government, and . . . final absorption into the general community" (Dennis, 1885).

Segregated Education — "Paternalism" (1860-1950)

Immigration and the increased demand for agricultural land impoverished traditional hunting grounds, thus depriving Indians of their livelihood. As assimilation had not yet been achieved, government officials introduced the reserve system with the intent of "protecting [Indians] from the encroachment of the whites" (Sir Francis Bond Head, cited in Morris, 1880). The creation of reserves resulted in segregated schooling. Because Section 91 of the *B.N.A. Act* assigned "Indians and Lands reserved for Indians" to the federal government, Indian education became centralized in Ottawa. In 1868, Indian education came under the jurisdiction of the Secretary of State, under the Department of the Interior in 1873, and under a separate Department of Indian Affairs in 1880. However, the actual schooling of the 1800s continued to be dominated by the various Christian churches as part of their missionary work. Both the churches' approach and legislation demonstrated paternalism which characterized the federal government's attempts to provide educational benefits to Indians (Davey, 1965).

With the passing of the *British North America Act* in 1867, the government's involvement with Indian education was increased. It was entrusted with the administration of previously concluded treaties, and the policy of making treaties was continued. By such treaties, Indians surrendered their exclusive interest in the land to the Crown, and in return the latter set aside a part of this territory for their use and provided them with additional benefits such as cash payments, annuities and educational facilities. References to education were stated in general terms whereby "Her Majesty agrees to maintain schools for instruction in such reserves" (Morris, 1880).

Although Indian education became the federal government's responsibilty, politicians and officials acted "on the assumption that Native cultures were themselves unworthy of perpetuation" (Hamilton, 1986). The Honourable Hector Langevin, a high-ranking government official, favored education for Indians because it would enable them to "share in the blessings of civilization" (Hamilton, 1986).

Because Canada's westward growth and the disappearance of the buffalo were impacting on the Indians' traditional lifestyle, the government felt pressured to pursue its campaign of assimilation. Nicholas Davin was commissioned to report on the American policy of segregated Indian residential industrial schools. Davin was impressed with the American results in terms of assimilation and was led to believe that the key in achieving success was to separate Indian children from their parents. Davin's recommendations included utilizing mission schools, both on the grounds of efficiency and economy. He also suggested future compulsory education so that Indians could be trained as department clerks and teachers. These considerations led the government to embark on a policy of the residential education for Indian children. Government leaders saw their responsibilty as having to emancipate Indian children from "ignorance and superstitious blindness" and to convert them into "useful members of society" (Hamilton, 1986). Between 1867 and 1950, the majority of Indian children received their education in residential schools on reserve lands.

Indian response to residential industrial schools was not favorable. Parents disliked the conversion and "civilization" of their children in distant schools, the stress on English (use of Indian languages was forbidden), and the teaching of women's chores to young men. Not many students attended these schools for longer than three or four years and very few attended any form of secondary education. Parents also objected to the work aspect of the schools; they preferred their children to learn to read and write.

By the 1940s, the "Indian problem" was becoming evident to both government and the general public. Indian education stressed agriculture and manual labor but did not enourage economic and social development. Instead of assimilation becoming the norm, a widening gap was occurring between Indians and non-Indians. Once again, education was viewed as a solution to a deplorable situation. Hence, a change in government policy to one of integration was seen as attaining the objective of raising the educational standards of Indians so that they could "participate in urban life" (Hawthorn, 1967).

Integrated Education (1960-1972)

The events of the second world war resulted in an international awareness of the need for improved race relations. In Canada, the situation of the Indian people was acknowledged and addressed in hearings by the Special Joint Committee of the Senate and the House of Commons (1946-48). The hearings were unique in that the committee requested briefs from Indian bands and organizations. The findings indicated that education played an important part in improving the circumstances of the Indian. The committee learned that federally-sponsored vocational education did not prepare Indians for pursuing higher levels of education, which in turn prevented them from seeking careers in industry and/or the professions. The end result was that Indian education in this form was hindering assimilation.

To facilitate the process of integrating Indian children into the Canadian mainstream, the committee recommended that "Indian children be educated in association with other children" (*Annual Report*,

1950). This and other recommendations were incorporated in Section 113 of the new *Indian Act* and authorized the government to enter into agreements with provincial governments (public or separate school boards), territorial commissioners and religious or charitable organizations on behalf of Indians for the purpose of education. These agreements became known as "joint agreements" and became the foundation of the integration policy. Although integration was promoted, the Act continued the established system of Indian day schools operated under joint departmental and religious auspices.

By 1964, 26 000 Indian children, or 45 percent of the Indian school population, were enrolled in about 950 provincial schools. Within federally-controlled schools some changes in policy were made so as to facilitate the enrollment of Indian children in provincial schools. First of all, Indian schools were to follow the curriculum of the province in which the school was located. This was to enable students to attend provincial high schools. As well, academic studies were stressed in Indian schools to at least the grade 10 level. This arrangement was motivated by consultations with prospective employers who insisted on hiring personnel with at least a grade 10 education (Simpson, 1972).

The concept of integrated education was envisaged as providing a long-term solution to end the relief-and-welfare economy found on most reserves (Hawthorn, 1967). By 1960, however, problems were becoming evident, and Indian students were not achieving the expected results. In a dramatic evaluative effort, a standardized achievement test covering reading, comprehension, and arithmetic was administered to grade four students across the country. Except in Quebec and southern Ontario, all the Indian students were at least ten months behind their non-Indian classmates of the same chronological age. Those in central Canada were anywhere between 16 and 19 months behind. The total retardation average (retardation on chronological age plus retardation on actual grade placement) was one grade and six months (Hawthorn, 1967). On the basis of this evidence, predictions were made that 80 percent of Indian children would not profit from the education system and would thus be unable to support themselves (Senate Committee, 1961).

Although government officials were adamant that integration should not be confused with assimilation (Daniels, 1967), some educators insisted that there was no difference. They emphasized that the educational system existed to mold Indian students to conform to dominant white society. In reality, integrated education was being forced upon Indian students as simply another method of assimilation (Cardinal, 1969). An example pertained to the matter of the clothing allowance that was given to those Indians who attended public schools. At first there was concern that the Indian children's traditional way of dress stood out from their non-Indian counterparts, and they felt ill at ease about it. Appearing different affected attendance, social status and psychological outlook; thus a clothing allowance was instituted for them (Hawthorn, 1967). Indian people, however, perceived the allowance as an "enticing pressure tactic" towards integrated education since those students who attended the reserve school did not receive such an allowance (Snow, 1977).

Although the Department of Indian Affairs tended to be positive in its outlook toward integrated education, teachers and parents questioned the policy. In trying to accommodate Indian students, officials established remedial classes for Indian children; at this point teachers began to question whether integration was meant to "... move Indians into the white man's school but teach them separately" (Miller, 1969). The Indian community was given to believe that by gaining educational parity with non-Indian students, their children would subsequently gain economic parity as well. Instead, a very high drop-out rate, up to 90 percent, persisted for Indian students (Hawthorn, 1967). The cause was attributed to a curriculum reflecting the attitudes and value system of a white middle-class society.

The policy of integration continued into the 1960s when Indian education was once again examined and the findings were published in the *Hawthorn Report* of 1966-67. The report viewed the success or failure of Indian education in terms of how well the system managed to encourage Indians to engage fully in economic competition as the "social equals of other Canadians" (Hawthorn, 1967). The findings of the report indicated that the economic status of Indians was poor in comparison with the rest of the Canadian population, with many households dependent on welfare. The report identified inadequate education and inadequate job training as important factors contributing to the economic backwardness of the Indian people. The report's analysis of education revealed that only 12 percent of Indian students were in their proper age-grade, with the average Indian child being 2.5 years behind the average non-Indian student. It also confirmed a 94 percent drop-out rate for Indian students.

Despite the failure of integrated education, the *Hawthorn Report* supported integrated education and claimed that it was the most feasible educational alternative. Shortcomings of the program were recognized, the major one being that the needs of Indian students were neglected within an integrated school setting. The report targetted pre-school education, pointing out that such experiences were very different for Indian and non-Indian students. For example, differences existed between the two groups in teacher attitudes toward the child, parental interest in learning, verbal practice and development, discipline, and sanctions and routines for learning. Indian children were encouraged to be independent sooner than their non-Indian counterparts, they had limited conversations with adults, and were permitted to do things motivated soley by personal interest. They rarely suffered from parental punishment and were exposed to flexible or almost non-existent routines. The non-Indian child's growth and development was controlled and monitored; he was urged to try things regardless of interest, taught skills thought to be useful in school, exposed to rigid routines and experienced punishment when he did not comply with adult demands.

The *Hawthorn Report* concluded that the middle-class milieu fostered nurturing conditions for educational growth and development compared with the reserve milieu. This meant that the cultural milieu of Indian children contributed more to school failure than success. Because of this discrepancy, the report made several recommendations focusing on the special needs of Indian students. These included suggestions that remedial language courses be provided to compensate for language deficiencies and kindergartens and nursery schools be established by the Indian Affairs Branch. These arrangements were meant to ease the cultural shock experienced by the Indian child in making the transition between home and school. According to the report, cultural differences were not to be tolerated but rather, eradicated. Although the writer of the report may have been well-intentioned in making these recommendations, they inadvertently encouraged the cultural assimilation of Indian children into dominant society. Indian culture did not appear to be recognized as being valuable to the dominant society's way of life and was not incorporated as a vital component of the educational program. The report even went so far as to suggest that through education, Indians would free themselves of cultural exclusion.

Indian Policy Statement, 1969: The White Paper

The findings of the *Hawthorn Report* served as the basis for the federal government policy statement also known as the "White Paper" (Government of Canada, 1969). The theme of the policy revolved around a familiar concept; Indians were no longer to be shut out of Canadian life because the time had come for them to share equally with other Canadians in all available opportunities.

In pursuit of the goal of equality, the government proposed to repeal the *Indian Act*, dissolve the Department of Indian Affairs, and henceforth provide Indians with the same services, through the same agencies, as were provided for all other Canadian citizens. Since education was a provincial responsibility, Indian education was to become a provincial matter. Hence, integrated education, as was recommended by the *Hawthorn Report*, was to become policy.

Although the White Paper, for the first time, recognized the validity of Indian culture and identified steps to promote its future, the feasibility of accomplishing this through the school system was not really addressed. Government education officials insisted that the aim of education was to develop "admirable Indian qualities" to the fullest, and to assist Indians to take advantage of all the opportunities that are available to all Canadians. However, in reality provincial schools were under the impression that it was their responsibility to assimilate Indian children. Very little was done to accommodate Indian cultural differences in the integrated schools, although some schools did recognize Indian culture and encouraged their pupils to relate legends of their tribes and perform songs and dances. Despite this, Indian children were still discouraged from speaking their mother tongue on the playground because this was considered to be discourteous behavior when in the company of those who did not understand.

Teachers were somewhat frustrated with integrated education because they tried to ignore cultural differences and keep to the established pedagogy. It was known that Indians traditionally learn better in groups and in informal settings with a non-competitive atmosphere, but the habits of dominant society prevailed. Even though it was clear that Indian students were differently motivated than non-Indians, they were still placed in large classes and subjected to the same teaching methodology and curriculum. Discipline was also considered to be a problem. It was recognized that the type of discipline which was effective with white children was not always effective with Indian children. Moreover, many teachers were not sufficiently familiar with Indian culture and traditions to discipline children in a meaningful way (Denhoff,1968).

By the end of the 1960s, integrated education was still not producing the desired results. Across Canada, 80 percent of Indian students were repeating grade one due to cultural shock. Indian Affairs Minister Jean Chretien's answer was to encourage the establishment of special courses to help Indians adjust to non-Indian school environments.

Indian Response

The Indian response to the White Paper and integrated education was one of fear — fear of losing their culture and identity. Harold Cardinal, president of the Alberta Indian Association, regarded the new proposed policy as a pathway to "cultural genocide" by means of assimilation (Cardinal, 1969). Indians were in agreement with the government that their economic situation and social situation were in need of improvement. They also recognized that revitalization of the community was their own responsibility. They viewed the role of the dominant society as irrelevant to Indians determining their own future (Cardinal, 1969).

The "Indian problem," as viewed by Indians, was one of gaining respect from their Canadian counterparts so that their way of life would be respected as a viable cultural entity in Canada's cultural mosaic. No longer was it believed that equality could be legislated. Rather, it was viewed as coming from economic strength, political power, good organization and through the pride and confidence of a people. To achieve this equality, the Indian people recognized the importance of education. However, they also realized that the education system had thus far failed to bring about equality. Dominant society's form of education was regarded as an alien cultural phenomenon for Native people, and its purpose perceived as "creating little brown men" (Cardinal, 1969).

In 1970, the formal Indian response was presented to the government by the Alberta Indian Association in a document entitled *Citizens Plus*, also known as the "Red Paper" (Indian Chiefs of Alberta, 1970). The focus of the paper was on preserving Indian identity. The Red Paper rejected the then current trend towards integrated education for a number of reasons. Concern was expressed that provincial schools were geared towards the fulfillment of the goals of dominant society. Curriculum, language and cultural differences perpetuated by the school would alienate Indian students. These factors were perceived to contribute to the feelings of inferiority and the high drop-out rate among Indian students.

Six months following the presentation of the Red Paper, the Union of British Columbia Indian Chiefs submitted their formal response to the White Paper. It was entitled "A Declaration of Indian Rights — The British Columbia Indian Position Paper" and became known as the "Brown Paper." It, too, interpreted the White Paper to be a policy towards assimilation and, in an attempt to avert the process, recommended that a provincial Indian School Trustee Association be established. The association was to ensure that the provincial education system would recognize the Indian contribution to the development of Canada and ensure that educational programs would encourage Indians to participate in their own social, economic and political advancement. Through this association, British Columbia Indians hoped to remain a functional culturally ethnic group while still participating in the provincial education system.

Indian Control of Indian Education

Both the Red Paper and the Brown Paper were influential in determining the future direction of Indian education in Canada. The ideas presented in those papers became the basis of the National Indian Brotherhood's (NIB) education policy in 1972, entitled "Indian Control of Indian Education." It was based on two principles, parental responsibility and local control, and applied to both reserve schools and integrated schools. The goals of the policy were to prepare Indian children for total living with the freedom of choice of where to live and work, and to enable Indians to participate fully in their own social, economic, political and educational advancement. A major concern was that these goals could be achieved without resorting to assimilation.

To ensure that the Indian child's socialization process in school was a continuation of the education received at home in the early years, and not an interruption as outlined in the *Hawthorn Report*, the NIB policy paper cited four areas in need of attention and improvement. These were: responsibility, programs, teachers, and facilities and services. Whether students attended federal or provincial schools, the NIB advocated that parental responsibilty be respected, the premise being that parents have a right to direct their children's education and that only they are qualified to decide whether actions taken will or will not lead towards assimilation.

With regards to federal schools, the concept of local control was recommended. The establishment of band education authorities, whose responsibilities would include not only budgeting, determining facilities and administering the physical plant, but also hiring of staff, cultural curriculum development, negotiating agreements with school jurisdictions, evaluating programs, and providing counselling services was recommended.

With regards to integrated education, the NIB did not support across-the-board termination of the arrangement. Rather, since 60 percent of Indian children were enrolled in provincial schools, it proposed changes to the structure of the joint agreements. The NIB's dissatisfaction with past joint agreements was based on the fact that they were made between the federal and provincial governments. Indian involvement was minimal and although they were to be consulted prior to the signing, they wanted to have representation on provincial school boards to ensure parental participation.

By recommending these changes, the NIB intended to reverse the trend toward assimilation. It was hoped that parents, through local control, would increase their participation at both the school board level and at joint agreement discussions. These actions would enhance their opportunities to influence their children's educational programs in the areas of cultural development, curriculum development, vocational guidance, counselling, and inservice training of teachers. This would minimize alienation and reduce the factors causing the conflict of values which had been identified as causes for Indians' failure in school.

The NIB proposed changes to curriculum as a means of reducing the cultural alienation that Indian children had been experiencing. To establish a more relevant system, the NIB recommended that school curricula in federal and provincial schools should recognize Indian culture, values, customs, languages and the Indian contribution to Canadian development. These changes, as well as the introduction of courses in Indian history and culture, were expected to promote a sense of cultural pride in Indian students. Recommendations were also made that funds be available for Indian people to work with professional curriculum planners in order to supervise the development of Indian-based curriculum.

Language was also targeted by the NIB They perceived it as a powerful tool in maintaining one's identity to be given top priority. Among the pertinent recommendations was the concept that primary instruction be given in Native languages, that teacher aides specialize in Indian languages, and that teaching requirements be waived to enable Indian people fluent in their mother tongue to become full-fledged teachers.

Further on the subject of personnel, the NIB suggested that to satisfy the perceived urgent demand for Indian teachers, training centres be established that would offer programs for those Indians who were interested and talented but who lacked academic qualifications to enter standard teacher training programs. Non-Indian teachers charged with teaching Indians were to undertake compulsory courses in intercultural education, Native languages, teaching English as a second language and Indian history and culture. These recommendations were regarded by the NIB as a means of improving the qualifications of teaching personnel.

It was recognized that Indian children would still have to encounter and cope with the influences of dominant culture in a school setting. To do so without losing one's identity, the NIB recommended that Indian counsellors and Indian teacher aides be employed in all school systems. Their role was to be one of helping students adjust to culturally unfamiliar school experiences.

One of the major changes recommended for Indian education was to establish day schools on the reserves. Not only were these schools to provide the necessary skills to cope with modern life, but they were to foster an environment where Indian identity and culture could flourish.

Recent Developments

The National Indian Brotherhood's policy goals were accepted in principle by the Minister in 1973 and were to be the basis for future development in Indian education (Indian Affairs Bulletin, 1982). According to the government, its current policy would emphasize a gradual assignment of control of education to Indians; they have also gone on record as supporting Indian people in ensuring their cultural continuity and development. However, an analysis of the policy suggests that it does not reflect the wishes of the Indian people. Local control, whether it pertains to a band-controlled school or a joint agreement with a provincial school, is somewhat misleading and is, at best, an ambiguous term.

Principal elements of the government's policy refer to management of educational services by a band authority, and the delegated authority is responsible not only to band members, but also to the Minister of Indian Affairs. As to future developments in Indian education, band councils and Indian organizations were to be "consulted to the extent reasonable." Because funding is delivered by the department, and the department held accountable to Parliament, it is the department that establishes standards and conditions for monetary use. This arrangement renders the possibility that programs desired by Indian people, perhaps for cultural maintenance purposes, could be disallowed in favor of government programs which may have a more assimiliating effect.

Examination of a currently used (1989) Alberta Education Agreement (an agreement providing for the transfer of education funds to a band), reveals that the band's responsibilities include planning, estimating and negotiating processes for the educational needs of students serviced under the band's jurisdiction. The inclusion of such a condition could be interpreted as allowing a band to exercise its judgement when assessing its needs. However, it is also stipulated that programs of study are to be provincially-accredited, and that any approved plans be on file with the provincial Department of Education and available for inspection by Department of Indian Affairs personnel at the beginning of the school year.

In essence, band control of Indian education is limited to the assessment of needs in accordance with existing programs available through Alberta Education. This creates a problem for the bands because numerous Alberta Education studies and task forces have indicated that there is much room for meeting the educational needs of Indian people. The Indian community has requested independent control of its education so that the needs of their students will be met. Under the federal government's terms of local control, they are required to pursue a provincial program which by its own admission does not serve the needs of Indian people (Alberta Region, 1989). It is also stipulated that the Minister of Indian Affairs will maintain his responsibility for Indian education programs and may take whatever action necessary to carry out that responsibility. It would appear that ultimate control for Indian education rests with the government and it is the government which decides what is appropriate programing for Indian people.

Local control, as presently structured, does not appear to have the impetus to avert assimilation. Because funding is dependent upon bands following provincial and federal government-approved programs, local control, as defined by the NIB, is lacking. The Assembly of First Nations' (AFN) recent review of First Nations' education indicates that First Nations believe schooling to be a focal point of cultural, social and educational activites in their communities and mainstream educational programs are often irrelevant to the values, needs and philosophy of their people.

Since 1973, 243 of the 384 on-reserve schools have undergone some form of local control which has increased Indian involvement in education. The process has not resulted in "control" insofar as decision-making power is concerned. This deficiency is of concern to Indian people and is considered to be contrary to policy proposed by the National Indian Brotherhood. Indian leaders believe that the current policy is also directly responsible for the school-related problems of Indian students.

Jurisdiction also remains a concern where Indian children attend off-reserve schools. For example, in Alberta in 1989, 51 percent of Indian students attended provincial schools. Because the *Indian Act* authorizes the Minister of Indian Affairs to enter into agreements with provincial governments for education services, it is the province which exercises jurisdiction and thereby controls all aspects of education. British Columbia, Manitoba, Saskatchewan, Ontario and New Brunswick have legislation which recognizes Indian representatives on provincial school boards, but this apparently has little impact on adequate representation (Assembly of First Nations, 1988). Poor school board representation results in limited influence over the programs, which in turn can lead to assimilation and be destructive to the Indian way of life.

It is only recently, in the 1988-89 school year, that new tripartite tuition agreements (joint agreements) between bands, governments and provincial school boards have been made in Alberta. It has taken 15 years since the NIB first made this recommendation. Although the government appears willing to include Indians in the negotiations and generally supports their demands for involvement in areas of classroom inspections, teaching methods, personnel matters and curriculum development, it is the individual school boards that determine the extent of Indian involvement. Hence, real control rests with school boards and not with Indian people. Once again (or still), Indian education is at the mercy of outside powers.

In terms of assimilation, the situation is grave. Because educational matters are subjected to government restrictions, and because the Minister is the ultimate authority, any innovation proposed by Indian people may be judged inappropriate and therefore vetoed. Provisions have not been made to ensure cultural maintenance. Without such provisions, and because schooling is such a powerful socializing agent, its inherent assimilative forces may triumph. This would almost certainly assure the demise of Indian culture and identity. Indian leaders are not necessarily pessimistic, however, because they know that Native cultures are dynamic, adaptive and adapting, and not limited to the past. As history has shown, they can invent structural forms and institutions as needed to survive and to strengthen group/individual survival (Couture, 1985).

References

Alberta Region. (1989). *General tuition agreement.* Edmonton: Department of Indian Affairs and Northern Development, Alberta Region.

Anderson, T. G. (1863). S.I.A. Manitowaning, to Col. S. P. Jarvis, C.S.I.A., Kingston, March 4, Strachan papers.

Annual Report. (1950). Bureau of Indian Affairs, Ottawa: Government of Canada.

Assembly of First Nations. (1988). *Tradition and education: towards a vision of our future,* Vol. 1. Ottawa: National Indian Brotherhood, 57.

Cardinal, Harold. (1969). *The unjust society.* Edmonton: Hurtig.

Chalmers, John W. (1972). *Education behind the buckskin curtain.* Edmonton: University of Alberta Press.

Cornish, George H. (1881). *Encyclopaedia of methodism in Canada.* Toronto: Methodist Book & Pub. House.

Couture, Joseph E. (1985). "Traditional Native Thinking, Feeling, and Learning," *Multicultural education journal,* Vol. 3, No. 2, 4-16.

Daniels, E. R. (1967). "A.S.T.A. Studies Possible Integration of Indian Students in Top Provincial Systems," *Alberta school trustee,* Vol. 27, No. 23, May, 28.

Davey, R. F. (1965). "The Establishment of Growth of Indian School Administration," *The education of Indian children in Canada.* Toronto: Ryerson Press.

Denhoff, P. (1968). "Integration in The Eye of The Storm," Arbos, Vol. 4, 19.

Dennis, Hon. Col. (1885). "Papers and Correspondence in Connection with Half-breed Claims and Other Matters Relating to the Northwest Territories," Canada: sessional papers, CSF, No. 116f, 4.

Fingard, Judith. (1972). "The New England Company and the New Brunswick Indians, 1786-1826: A Comment on Colonial Perversion of British Benevolence," *Acadiennes*, Vol. 1, No. 2, Spring, 30.

Government of Canada. (1969). *Statement of the government of Canada on Indian policy*. Ottawa: Published under the authority of the Hon. Jean Chretien, PC, MP, Minister of Indian Affairs and Northern Development. Also known as the White paper.

Hamilton, W. D. (1986). *The federal day schools of the Maritimes*. Fredericton: University of New Brunsick.

Hawthorn, H. B. (1967). *Survey of contemporary Indians of Canada*. Vol. 2, Ottawa: Indian Affairs Branch, 1967.

Indian Affairs Bulletin. (1982). *Indian education paper: phase I*. Ottawa: Department of Indian Affairs and Northern Development, Annex B, 8.

Indian Chiefs of Alberta. (1970). *Citizens plus. Ottawa: A presentation by the Indian Chiefs of Alberta to the Right Hon. Pierre Elliot Trudeau, Prime Minister, and the Government of Canada*. Also known as the Red paper.

Jaenen, Cornelius. (1986). "Education for Francization: The Case of New France in the Seventeenth Century," in *Indian education in Canada, vol. 1: the legacy*. Jean Barman, et.al., ed. Vancouver: University of British Columbia Press, 45-63.

Miller, E. (1969). "Integration?" *Northian newsletter*. No. 9, 3.

Morris, Alexander. (1880). *Treaties of Canada with the Indians of Manitoba and the Northwest Territories*. Toronto: Belfords, Clarke & Co.

Patterson, Robert S., John W. Chalmers and John W. Friesen. (1974). *Profiles of Canadian educators*. Toronto: D.C. Heath.

Public Archives of Canada. (1665). *Instructions to Talon*, 27 March, MG1, Series B. I.

Scott, Duncan C. (1914). "Indian Affairs," *Canada and its provinces*, Vol. 4, in Shortt and Doughy. Toronto: Brook and Co., 714-15.

Simpson, D. W. (1972). "Together or Apart — Today's Dilemma in Indian Education," *Indian education*, No. 2, 3-4.

Senate Committee. (1961). *Final report: education and development of human resources*. Ottawa: Joint Committee of the Senate and the House of Commons on Indian Affairs, 610-11.

Snow, Chief John. (1977). *These mountains are our sacred places*. Toronto: Samuel Stevens.

Wilson, J. Donald. (1986). "No Blanket to be Worn in School: The Education of Indians in Nineteenth Century Ontario," in *Indian education in Canada, vol. 1: the legacy*. Jean Barman, et. al., ed. Vancouver: University of British Columbia Press, 64-87.

11

Community Educational Control Issues and the Experience of Alexander's Kipohtakaw Education Centre

Joann Sebastian Morris
Richard T. Price

Indian control of Indian education has been an important theme in Canadian Indian educational circles since the early 1970s. With the adoption by the federal government of the National Indian Brotherhood's policy proposal for Indian control of Indian education, there was much optimism and many high expectations generated in Indian country. However, the new policy was not without its problems. Therefore, this paper includes a critique, especially that sufficient resources, a legislative mandate and a clear plan of implementation were not included in federal policy articulation. This inadequacy of federal policy/implementation led to the initiative being thrown to Indian communities, which assumed control over the schools on their reserves, under very difficult circumstances.

For First Nations' community schools to succeed, extraordinary efforts and learning through experience were required. The focus for this paper is therefore twofold: to describe the emerging concerns re community educational control issues after almost two decades of experience, and to note the concrete lessons learned through Alexander's Kipohtakaw Education Centrr. It is clear that important lessons have been learned by the First Nations educators, (including those at Alexander) and these lessons ought to be shared for at least the sake of current and future generations of Indian children.

Some Indian community schools are clear success stories and deserve acknowledgement. One such school is northwest of Edmonton, Alberta, namely the Alexander First Nation's Kipohtakaw Education Centre. Alexander demonstrated that a community can succeed at the task of Indian control of Indian education in spite of, rather than because of, government policies. Alexander's inspired Indian educators, with the support of the community and a vision of value-based quality education, have achieved a remarkable degree of success. The Alexander experience does have several distinctive features, including international recognition and a leadership role in the National Indian Education Forum, which make it quite unique and worthy of broader interest.

Nevertheless, the accomplishments of Alexander's school (and similar schools elsewhere) often remain fragile, and require ongoing elements of renewal.

The Effect of Policy

The Indian control of Indian Education policy which was adopted at the request of the National Indian Brotherhood by the federal government in 1973, has recently been the subject of several thoughtful reviews by Verna Kirkness and Dianne Longboat.[1] Kirkness identifies two major problems: "The first is the *definition of control,* the second is the *absence of a clear implementation plan.*[2] Kirkness goes on to point out that control still ultimately rests with the Department of Indian Affairs, not the local Indian community. Moreover, Kirkness outlines three problems of implementation, namely: inadequate funding, the absence of enabling legislation to free Indian communities from the restrictions of the *Indian Act,* and the difficulties of scale (and therefore cost) that would be faced by a local school board as compared to the range of services and resources that a more centralized administration of a government department could assemble. It is true that a few Indian schools in Canada have recently operated with their own legislative mandate, free from restrictive shackles of the *Indian Act* legislation, namely the James Bay Cree (*Cree Naskapi Act,* 1984) and the Sechelt Band (the *Sechelt Act,* 1986) but these are the exceptions rather than the rule.[3]

Longboat outlines in a similar fashion the institutional impediments to Indian control, including the political environment, the lack of legislative basis and various difficulties linked to policies and structures of the Department of Indian Affairs.[4] She also identifies an additional problem which the Minister of Indian Affairs, John Munro, acknowledged in a 1984 letter to the President of the Treasury Board:

> The major contentious issue is that education of Indians in federal and band operated schools is funded at a level below that of Indians attending provincial schools . . . Indian education authorities have become very frustrated. They are now operating in a much more challenging environment with fewer human and financial resources than their provincial counterparts.[5]

This department analysis of funding disparities flowed from its own internal policy reviews.[6] The 1983 all-party parliamentary committee review of Indian self-government and other analyses have confirmed the importance of the issue of control with regards to Indian education; in the words of the parliamentarians: "Indian people want real power to make their own decisions and carry out their own plans for Indian education."[7] In any event, by the fall of 1990, 300 First Nation communities have taken over their schools, and there remain in existence only 79 schools still operated by the Department of Indian Affairs across Canada.[8]

The conclusion that can be drawn from these various perspectives is that Indian control of Indian education policy suffered from major impediments revolving around issues of control, inadequate resources and no real plan for implementation. Given the absence of effective federal policy implementation and resources, it follows that the major share of responsibility for effectively initiating and implementing the local control policy fell to the Indian communities themselves. In the context of the constraints mentioned above, the question can be posed — how can Indian communities, which do not have a legislative or constitutional basis for control, (i.e., an externally recognized form of legal jurisdiction), actually achieve a degree of community control that is satisfactory from their perspective? This question is implicitly posed in the Alexander study and the overview of issues.

The case study of the Alexander Band's school and the overview of issues identified by Alexander and other Indian communities running their schools (after taking over from the federal government) are of vital importance to understand the reality of local education experiences in Indian country. However, most Indian schools have operated in a situation where resource constraints and the struggle for quality and control are daily realities. The following account of the Alexander experience can thus be viewed in the context of case studies of similar situations elsewhere in Canada.[9]

It is a testament to the dedication and determination of First Nation communities that so many have taken on the awesome responsibility of establishing and maintaining their own school systems. It was no small matter to accept responsibility and accountability for the education of their children.

Community Control Issues

Most reserves in Canada are small in size and population. The amount of funding a First Nation receives to administer a locally controlled school is allotted according to a government formula, based on the size of the student body. Hence, the smaller (or larger) the school population, the smaller (or larger) the budget. Operating with a budget that leaves little room for special programing, a school newly under band administration still must provide the full array of educational services.

While provincial and private school districts have separate funds for an administrative infrastructure, such is not the case for band-controlled schools. Whether one analyzes a provincial or separate school district, one sees an infrastructure that includes numerous divisions and branches, such as: office of the superintendent, staff to the school board, a personnel office, instructional planning, curriculum development, language(s) branch, career and continuing education, counselling unit(s), staff development, office of public affairs, security office, and maintenance and transportation.

The foregoing list is by no means exhaustive, yet it serves to illustrate the range of tasks that must be assumed by a First Nation community upon agreeing to administer education for their children. All is to be accomplished with a limited budget. It is well recognized by First Nation educators that staff at band-controlled schools must regularly fill no less than three of four roles, while being paid for only one. This is the problem of scale noted by Kirkness in her analysis.

Transitional Steps

The resumption of local control could be an easy transition if all that was required was exchanging one administrative body (the federal Department of Indian Affairs) for another (the local First Nation government). But that implies no further change would be needed. However, the local takeover of education generally occurs because parents want change in the present system. They want a new philosophy of education, new teachers, revised policies, a culturally relevant instructional program, and/or a true opportunity for parental involvement and input. So the resumption of control over education requires rethinking the entire education system to arrive at one that is more compatible with community-held values and aspirations.

Based on experiences with First Nation educators from across Canada, it is generally agreed that the planning phase, the rethinking of the inherited educational system, requires the greatest amount of time and the broadest community input before one can resume educational jurisdiction. It is a critical first step to call all segments of a community together and, over the course of months of meetings, to arrive at a *vision* of the type of educational system the community desires.

First Nations educators and communities have grown enormously in knowledge and experience since 1972. Their skills at implementing local school systems serve as an example of and resource to other community development efforts.

In particular, the well-recognized need for careful planning and wide community involvement was echoed in one of the recommendations resulting from the four-year National Review of First Nations Education conducted by the Assembly of First Nations. The recommendation stated:

> The federal government must designate sufficient financial resources to assist individual First Nations with a preliminary community needs assessment, with formulating a long-term education plan; establishing an education authority with equivalent powers and resources of public school education authorities, and obtaining training for jurisdiction over education. In a planned and measured fashion, First Nations will assume jurisdiction over all education programs from pre-school to post-secondary and adult education.[10]

First Nation parents, Elders, and other community members must ask themselves a series of critical questions, a sampling of which follows. What is our philosophy of education? What do we want our children equipped for upon graduation from the school system? In what specific ways do we want our school(s) to be unique? How will our culture and values permeate the entire school system?

These are not questions that can be answered lightly or in one meeting. Moreover, the answers from one community are not immediately transferrable to another. Each First Nation that has acquired legislative jurisdiction over education and each one that is currently in various stages of educational control must go through an intense period of self-examination and eventually come together as one mind, as a united community, on what they propose to create for their children, i.e., the development of a sustaining vision.

First Nations that are seeking educational control and jurisdiction in the 1990s are in a more enviable position than were the early communities which made a transition to local control in the 1970s and early 1980s. Nowadays, there are a variety of educational options that one may witness within First Nation communities. Those pioneers in the years immediately following the official acceptance of the Indian control of Indian education policy had to investigate non-Native educational models and/or forged new ground by developing unique Indian models of education. Whatever the source of the options, it remains a critical early step in the takeover process to offer a community the opportunity to make choices from a range of educational models.

Value-Based Education

Based on the community assessment of its situation, it has now come to be recognized by most First Nation communities and school systems that they must undergo a thorough review and analysis of their values. The prime source of information about traditional Indian values is local community Elders. The writings of contemporary Native authors are also useful to gather information about commonly held values from more than one First Nation. Traditional Indian values frequently include, but are not limited to, the following: cooperation, honesty, sharing, kindness, group identity, non-punitive child-rearing, respect for the elderly, extended family relationships, emphasis on non-verbal skills, respect for nature, cultural pluralism, and acknowledging one's place in the universal scheme of things.

On the other hand, mainstream culture and society often promotes competition, saving, materialism, individualism, emphasis on youth, nuclear family relationships, verbosity, dominion over nature, assimilation, and accepting mankind as being at the centre of the universe, among other values.

Since most educators, Indian and non-Indian alike, are by-products of the dominant society's post-secondary educational system, the values of that society are learned, consciously or not. Thus, educators at First Nation schools, all of whom are educated in the dominant society's post-secondary educational institutions, may inadvertently be promoting a value system that is contrary to many of the traditional values adhered to by the community itself. It takes an ongoing and concerted effort to implement and maintain an alternative system of values.

When resuming control over education, First Nation communities must give careful consideration to what policies and practices should be put in place to ensure that communally-held, traditional values, not those of mainstream society, are the ones transmitted. For example, they must ask: What teaching techniques can promote cooperative learning? How can classroom resources be more readily shared among students? How can a positive community identity be fostered? What discipline policies should be implemented such that honesty and kindness are rewarded, and their opposites go unrewarded? How can Elders be brought in regularly? How can parent-teacher interviews or home visits be expanded to incorporate extended family members? How can the instructional program place equal emphasis on observational and listening skills as well as verbal skills? What instructional or counselling techniques can be used to reinforce the student's important place in the universe?

These questions are but the beginning of a lengthy list that must be reviewed by community members when determining what will make their school truly an Indian school. Indian control of Indian education has meant in some instances, the mere replacement of Euro-Canadian administrators' by local First Nation educators. The real possibility of the Indian control policy is that it serves as an opportunity to create unique school systems that mirror the culture of the Indian population they serve, and yet are not unmindful of the requirements of the mainstream's educational system.

In a broader context, the need for value-based education was clearly indicated in one of the recommendations resulting from a recent two-year Indian education study in the United States. It reads as follows:

> Dialogue participants affirmed a holistic approach to education. Elementary, secondary and university programs for Indian students should be guided by the spirituality that is immanent in tribal communities. Education cannot be treated as an institution separate from communities. It is part of us, just as the sun, moon, stars, rain, snow, and wind affect us as we walk on Mother Earth.[11]

Curriculum Considerations

Among First Nation educators it is well recognized that the curriculum offered in a locally-controlled school is also critical to its success. In both the developmental and implementation phases of First Nation control over education, community members, First Nation educators and non-Native staff must reach agreement on the extent to which the provincial curriculum guidelines will be implemented.

Will parents worry that theirs is not a "real" school if the identical curriculum is not followed? What aspects of the provincial curriculum need embellishment? Which of the provincial curricular guidelines are culturally inappropriate? How much process curriculum (how children learn, i.e., hands-on activities) will be implemented? Will Native culture, language and history be taught as separate subjects or integrated throughout all subject fields, or will a combination of both approaches be used?

It is generally agreed among First Nation directors of education that the curriculum must be unique, thereby requiring it to be redesigned entirely and infused with Native content and values throughout. The importance of a value-based instructional program is paramount.

Changing School and Community Environments

In First Nations all across Canada, change is constant, particularly in terms of local leadership. On most reserves, the term of office for a chief and council is two, perhaps three, years. The same is true at most tribal councils. The terms of office for school board/parent committees members is likewise 2-3 years. In some communities, educational staff tenures are not much longer than 2-3 years. One begins to see the pattern of constant shifts in leadership and in staff responsibilities.

In such an environment, it is critical to engage in continuous in-service training of staff, school board members, chief and council, and the community as a whole. This is doubly important when one is implementing a new system, an innovative approach, an alternative and improved way of educating children. Against the backdrop of an ever-changing political and social environment, a one-shot fix-it does not suffice. Having achieved a new school system, does not guarantee that it will survive without constant training and re-training, and planning and re-planning. Developing a model school system is indeed an achievement, and one that requires constant attention and care to ensure its long-term survival.

Alexander's Kipohtakaw Education Centre

The schools operated by the Kipohtakaw Education Centre on the Alexander Reserve in Alberta are a prime example of community development and value-based education. Local control over the education system was formalized in 1982 at Alexander, a Cree community of 909, located approximately 40 kilometres northwest of Edmonton. Much work and planning preceded that takeover.

Education for Alexander residents had long been under federal jurisdiction. Federal responsibility has been exercised under section 91(24) of the *B.N.A. Act* and is linked to Treaty No. 6, which was signed in 1876 by Cree Indians and representatives of Queen Victoria and the federal government. As recent research attests, federal responsibility for Indian schools has not been a proud chapter in Canadian history.[12]

In 1964, Alexander's first education committee was established. Efforts were made to have greater input into and impact on the federal school in the community. In 1973, the school committee redoubled their efforts and sought to participate in decision making in not only the federal school but also at the provincial schools, where some Alexander students attended.

Three options seemed available to them. The first was to turn the school over from the Department of Indian Affairs to the Province of Alberta. The second alternative was to assume control for all students up to grade nine. Historically, high school students always attended off-reserve schools. The third option, and the one eventually selected, was to commence local control over the education system on a smaller scale, beginning with grades K-4.

In 1978, the school committee reviewed local statistics and noted that between 1968-1978 there were no high school graduates from their community. The school committee began looking at alternatives. At the same time as community members were expressing doubts about the federal control over education at Alexander, and were becoming more vocal about needed reforms in the provincial schools serving them, nearby provincial schools voiced alarm over the growing numbers of Alexander students who were attending their schools. Displeasure with the federal education system coupled with the province's resistance to accepting additional Alexander students, compelled the community to action.

In the fall of 1981, the band council and the school committee accepted in principle the concept of a five-year educational development plan which would commence September 1, 1981. According to that plan, 1981-82 would be a year of research and development; 1982-84 would be the build-up phase during which human and financial resources would be assembled and the program implemented; and 1984-86 would be the consolidation phase, when the school would be operational, with revisions taking place as necessitated by experience.

The active school committee eventually became an appointed school board. The first seven-member board consisted of two band councillors and five community members. On April 20, 1982, the chief and council signed a band council resolution giving full authority to the new school board to oversee all operations of the school. With time, community-wide elections for school board members replaced the appointment process. The first school board chairperson; George Arcand, Jr., said: "We decided to take control because we felt that the Department of Indian and Northern Affairs Canada and the provincial schools were not doing a proper job. We felt that by taking control, we could not do any worse, and we believed we could do much better."

Local control over education at Alexander went into effect July 15, 1982, and resulted in the September, 1982, opening of the Kipohtakaw Education Centre. Kipohtakaw is the traditional Cree name for the community and means enclosed or protected by trees. Nearly 100 children in nursery school, kindergarten and grades one to four enrolled that first year. They were served by a staff of 13: the administrator, secretary/bookkeeper, student counsellor, principal, five teachers, Cree language instructor, teacher assistant, maintenance and janitor.

The community set and followed their own pace, and in 1983-84 added grades five and six, and each year thereafter added another grade level until the 1989-90 school year when grade 12 students were enrolled. Three of these students graduated at year's end, the first graduating class of seniors ever at Alexander.

The process of planning was an arduous one and countless community meetings were held. As early as October, 1981, workshops were held covering topics such as: how children learn, the development of an educational philosophy, policy development, and financial management. In the 11 months preceding takeover, a total of 31 education consultants and trainers came to Alexander to share their expertise, and suggest educational models. In recent years, other band-controlled schools have recommended that the resumption of control over education must begin with active parental participation and an awareness of community attitudes and feelings about education. Such were the beginnings at Alexander.

Three years after assumption of local control, Kipohtakaw Education Centre received an international community development award and represented the Government of Canada and Alberta Education at the World Exposition on Rural Development in India in 1985.

The educational philosophy and practice at Alexander have brought the community ongoing recognition; both are deeply value-based. Early writings distributed by the Education Centre quote Robert Hutchins who said: "If the object of education is the improvement of humankind, then any system of education that is without values is a contradiction in terms."

During their research phase, school committee members and other concerned parents looked at a variety of educational models. They visited the ANISA program and the Lozanov Language Institute in San Diego, and Indian-controlled schools in Arizona, North Dakota, Manitoba, and British Columbia. They heard presentations on the Waldorf Program and the Montessori method. The system that best matched community values was the ANISA model of education developed by Dr. Daniel Jordan of the United States.

In brief, the ANISA model is a holistic one. It conveys the relatedness of all things in the universe and focuses on the important role an individual plays in relating to the whole. This concept is closely aligned with teachings of Cree, and other Native Elders.

In daily practice, the model also emphasizes teaching students how to learn, not just what to learn; how to see and listen, not just what to see or hear; how to think, not just what to think; how to feel, not what to feel; and how to strive, not solely what to strive for. In the words of Adele Arcand, a driving force behind the development of the Kipohtakaw Education Centre and its first executive director, "We don't want to graduate people who get all A's and flunk life."

Educational research and experience indicates that First Nation students are kinaesthetic learners, learning best when process curriculum is incorporated, not relying solely on content curriculum. Thus, the ANISA model was compatible with the cultural learning styles of the students at Alexander.

With time, greater emphasis was placed on incorporating Native content and practices into the school system, and an Alexander model of education evolved. That model builds upon the teachings of the Medicine Wheel, a concept relevant to many First Nations.

The four directions represented on the Medicine Wheel include at a minimum: the four seasons; the four races of humankind, each represented by a sacred color — red, yellow, black, and white — each of whom has a special gift to share with the world; the four elements of earth, air, fire and water; the four principles of caring (represented by sweetgrass), sharing (represented by animals), honesty (represented by trees), and faith (represented by mountains); and the four aspects of each human: physical, mental, emotional, and spiritual natures.

The Alexander model of education is holistic and steeped in the cultural values of the community. Arriving at a community philosophy of education, and developing an education system around that philosophy are extremely time-consuming activities and ones that don't end with the enunciation of that philosophy and educational model. Implementing them daily is the next challenge.

The following are but a few examples of practices implemented at Alexander. Management is done by the team approach through weekly meetings of the executive director, program directors and principals. Staff input is obtained at bimonthly staff meetings. There is a high level of inter-agency networking, particularly with the health and social services departments. Family case consultations are overseen by an inter-agency committee of which the education program is an active member.

There is a strong focus on healing Alexander as a community. Similar to other First Nations, Alexander has felt the negative effects of substance abuse, low employment rates, poverty, depression, and other social problems. Education is seen as a pivotal means to address these concerns, and it is important to implement a positive approach, starting with the children and the staff who work with them. To that end, the school board has implemented a policy requiring staff to remain alcohol and drug free as a condition of employment. Any staff member with a substance abuse problem is referred for treatment and therapy.

The Kipohtakaw Education Centre employs a wellness approach, looking after the mental, physical, emotional and spiritual needs of their students and staff. In contrast, most provincial school systems focus primarily on the mental (academic) needs of their students with minimal focus on their physical needs as well.

The curriculum at Alexander is modelled after the Alberta curriculum but does not follow it explicitly. To the content curriculum (what students learn), recommended by the province, have been added process curriculum (how students learn) and Native content. Curriculum committees work year-round to expand and enrich the mandated, provincial curriculum. Because it is as important to meet students' physical needs as it is to meet their mental, emotional, and spiritual needs, physical education classes are required through high school. A donation from the community allowed the purchase of work-out equipment including weights, stationary bicycles, and rowing machines, which are available to students and staff alike.

The environment in the classrooms is important to learning. The schools at Alexander maintain a low student to teacher ratio, averaging 10:1. In the elementary grades, this is maintained through the addition of at least one teacher assistant in each grade, all of whom are from the local community. The use of color has been researched and is effectively implemented in the current buildings, and has been taken into consideration when planning the color schemes for a new school slated to open in 1991.

Counselling is one of the most important services offered by the schools. One-on-one and group counselling are done. Weekly student support groups for students experiencing the affects of substance abuse in the home or personally are held. Specific training has been received by the two counsellors and all other staff, some of whom also co-facilitate the weekly talking circles for students.

The emotional needs of staff also are considered. To bring the staff together as a cohesive whole, two retreats a year are held, one in August and one in mid-winter. Bi-monthly staff support groups meet after school hours. A variety of in-service training opportunities are provided as a means to care for the teachers and support staff at the school on topics such as substance abuse, children of alcoholics, co-dependency, grief and meditation. Staff are encouraged to engage in personal growth and development workshops. Time for therapist appointments is granted. It is well-recognized that individuals can only help others to the extent they have grown themselves, so all staff — including clerical and janitorial staff — are encouraged to develop all aspects of themselves.

To address the spiritual needs of students and staff, daily ceremonies are held using sweetgrass, sage or tree fungus to begin the day. School board, administration, curriculum and other meetings also begin with this ritual. Prayers and greetings (handshakes or hugs) follow. On certain occasions, the pipe is brought in by Elders and an address is also given the students.

The Elders have been instrumental in giving direction to the Native studies curriculum committee, advising what should and should not be covered in the classroom. A Native studies scope and sequence chart has been developed with input from community Elders. The chart focuses on Alexander in the elementary grades, expands to other First

Nations in Alberta and western Canada, eventually studying First Nations from all across Canada, then American Indians, and finally other indigenous peoples around the world at the junior and high school level.

Cree language is taught daily. The amount of time is limited, however, and frustrates some community members who would prefer a full bilingual or immersion approach. Nonetheless, the commitment is strong to continue to offer Cree in order to keep this cultural tie with the Elders and a traditional world-view alive.

The Kipohtakaw Education Centre has chartered new ground, yet it must be ever alert to ensure its foundation, the community, is strongly supporting its efforts. Over the last eight years, it has gone through times of vigorous activity, of quiet maintenance, with intense community support, and reduced support. Yet through it all, the commitment to producing an educational system that is unique and that matches the culture and values of the students and community has remained paramount.

The National Leadership Role

The Alexander Tribal Government and the Kipohtakaw Education Centre took a bold step onto the national stage by issuing an invitation to Indian educators across Canada to attend a National Education Symposium on August 17-19, 1987, at Alexander. The symposium invitation included the following issues as agenda items:

-Quality Indian education;

-Formula funding; and

-Indian post-secondary education

The response from the grassroots was overwhelming as over 500 Indian educators and leaders held an intensive series of workshops and general assemblies to discuss these issues. One underlying theme was that education was too important to be left to the Indian politicians, who for years had concentrated on constitutional issues at First Ministers Conferences (which concluded in the spring of 1987). Indian educators themselves were determined to keep the priority of quality education (and the accompanying need for adequate resources) before the Canadian public and the federal government. However, this new thrust for direct involvement of Indian educators to become more pro-active in research, and consciousness-raising activities within Indian communities, as well as direct lobbying with government, was not perceived by the symposium delegates as a threat to Indian politicians. Rather, it was believed to be a complementary research and educational activity in relation to Indian political organizations (like the Assembly of First Nations) and Indian band councils.

More importantly, however, Indian educators were determined to form a new national educational organization and to pursue the goal of quality Indian education. In the words of the communique sent conference delegates as a follow-up:

> The National Indian Education Symposium has met and the people have gone home and many people in the Government and the Department of Indian Affairs will believe that the symposium is over and finished. They think that the symposium was just another meeting, another Indian gripe session. Only we who attended the forum know that it is not over and it is not finished. Those same people will be surprised to learn that we did not come together to gripe but to plan and do. For the first time in many years the united will and determination of Indian parents, grandparents, leaders and grassroots Indian people will be brought to bear upon government and people of Canada.[14]

Adele Arcand, executive director of Alexander's Kipohtakaw Education Centre, was appointed to the first board of the new National Indian Education Forum. Arcand and many other educational leaders then worked tirelessly for many months to give birth to a new organization which would embody their goals for Indian education.

The sustaining vision and goal of the new organization was quality education. This primary theme of the August symposium was defined in the conference summary:

> Effective quality education must be integrated into the life of the individual and the community. It must be responsive to the cultural, economic, political and social conditions in which individuals and families exist and it must engage the heart, imagination, intellect and body of the individual. Most of all the education must be based on the spiritual and cultural traditions of the people.[15]

The emphases of the linkage between education and culture has local, national and international roots. For example, the international indigenous peoples education conference co-hosted by Verna Kirkness of the University of British Columbia in June of 1987 had a conference theme "Education into culture, not culture into education." In other words, the centrality of Indian culture (instead of token deference to Indian culture) has strong support among the leadership of Indian and indigenous community schools in Canada and abroad.

Alexander's educational and political leadership under Chief Allan Paul was coupled with the talents of other strong political leaders and educators from every region and province in Canada. Annual educational symposiums were organized, (Symposium II at Kahnawake,

1988, and Symposium III at Kamloops, B.C., in 1990). By 1989, the status and credibility of this new organization became recognized by the federal government and Indian educators alike.

In the spring of 1989, a fast by university students to protest post-secondary education cuts by the Department of Indian Affairs took place in Ottawa. In the aftermath of this protest, Minister Pierre Cadieux awarded contracts to National Indian Education Forum (NIEF) and other Indian organizations such as the Federation of Saskatchewan Indians, to research and present alternative policy and policy process recommendations. The national leadership role of Indian educators in NIEF was clearly viewed as part of the mainstream of future-oriented efforts to improve post-secondary education. The reason for NIEF's credibility was in part due to the solid contingent of university students in its membership.

A series of workshops in various parts of Canada was held by NIEF in the summer and fall of 1989 to develop alternatives to federal policy. These workshops involved Indian educators, Elders, and leaders as well as a few consultants. An intensive national survey was completed to ascertain the views of local Indian communities. In September, 1989, NIEF participated in discussions with Minister Cadieux's representative, (along with other Indian organizations) and certain policy/procedural changes were made.

The culmination of the National Indian Education Forum's work was the systematic and far-reaching publication titled *Expanding Horizons*.[15] This report was co-sponsored by the Alexander School Board and key members of the Alexander team — Adele Arcand and Joann Morris shared the project coordinator responsibilities.

While the report's recommendations dealt with a range of matters including jurisdiction, resources and management, some of the key recommendations for quality education were:

> First Nations must have the opportunity to acquire quality education at all levels.

> The goal of education is to provide and enhance the relevant knowledge and skills that will assist First Nation people to achieve meaningful participation in our own communities and/or in the national community.

> First Nation children have the right to learn to speak, read, and write in their indigenous language or in the Aboriginal language most commonly used by the indigenous group to which they belong.

> First Nation educators have the right and must be given the opportunity to develop culturally-relevant curricula, textbooks, and other

instructional materials, incorporating specific knowledge required of our citizens.

First Nations students must learn about other Aboriginal people around the world: a global consciousness must be established.[16]

As we draw to a close the Alexander Kipohtakaw case study, it is necessary to bring together and integrate our main conclusions.

Conclusion

First Nation educators and communities have grown enormously in knowledge and experience since the early 1970s. Indian educators have developed skills at implementing local school systems, which serve as an example to, and a resource for, other community development efforts, such as the quest to become self-determining in other program areas and ultimately in overall self-government.

As these experiences have evolved, Indian school boards and Indian educators have gathered sources of power from within their communities and themselves, i.e., they have become empowered as they struggled with the adversity of their situations, which included the scarcity of resources and the enormous ground-breaking efforts to develop new educational models. In such situations, visionary leadership is of paramount importance and Alexander was fortunate to have a number of people in key positions both on their board and on staff. Indeed, the question of leadership is crucial in terms of the long-term viability of schools like Kipohtakaw.

At the same time, leaders cannot function effectively without community support. At the Alexander Reserve, the unifying theme, for both the community and the leading educators, was value-based education. This became the sustaining vision which nourished and empowered educators, students and community members. Another source of nourishment was the emphasis on healing within the school and in the wider community itself. These factors led to a real degree of achievement of community control. Thus, Alexander's Kipohtakaw Education Centre has all the crucial ingredients of a success story and therefore serves as an educational model for other communities. Yet, the basis of this success remains fragile and each new step in this educational journey requires a sustained effort.

It is important to remind others and ourselves of the nature of First Nation communities, namely that change is constant. With changes in political leadership, school board membership and education staff occurring with great regularity every 2-3 years, new and innovative programs must ensure that new players receive training and become involved and committed as early as possible. The sharing and nurturing of the community vision for the children's education is a key to turning an educational dream into an ongoing reality.

Notes

[1]Longboat, Dianne. (1987). "First Nations Control of Education: The Path of our Survival as Nations," in *Indian education in Canada, volume 2: the challenge*. Jean Barman, et. al., eds. Vancouver: University of British Columbia Press, 22-42. Verna Kirkness. (1984). "Indian Control of Indian Education: Over a Decade Later," *Mokakit*, Indian Education Research Association. Selected papers from the First Mokakit Conference, July 25 - 27.

[2]Kirkness, Ibid, p. 76, emphasis in the original.

[3]Cassidy, Frank and R.L. Bish. (1989). *Indian government: its meaning in practise*. Vancouver: Oolichan Books and the Institute for research on Public Policy.

[4]Longboat, Ibid, p. 26-39.

[5]Longboat, Ibid, p. 42.

[6]Government of Canada, "Indian Education Paper, Phase I." Ottawa: Queen's Printer, p. 12.

[7]See Government of Canada. (1983). "Indian Self-Government in Canada," *Report of the Special Committee*, p. 31, and the analysis of Deirdre F. Jordan. (1986). "Education and Reclaiming Identity: Rights and Claims of Canadian Indians, Norwegian Sami and Australian Aborigines," *Arduous journey*. J.R. Pointing, ed. Toronto: McClelland and Stewart.

[8]Department of Indian Affairs & Northern Development. (1990). Telephone conversation between Joann Morris and official from the department quoting figures for the 1989-90 school year. November.

[9]Gardner, Ethel. (1986). "Unique Features of a Band Controlled School: The Seabird Island Community School," *Canadian journal of Native education*, Vol. 13, No. 1., pp. 15-32.

[10]Assembly of First Nations. (1988). *Tradition and education: towards a vision of our future*, volume 2. Ottawa: Assembly of First Nations.

[11](1989). *Our voices, our vision: American Indians speak out for educational excellence*. New York: The College Board and American Indian Sciences and Engineering Society.

[12]Miller, J.R. (1989). *Skyscrapers hide the heavens: a history of Indian white relations in Canada*. Toronto: University of Toronto Press, chapters six and eleven.

[13](1985). *Alexander theory of teaching follow-up: philosophical foundations of the Alexander education program*. Edmonton: Kipohtakaw Education Centre.

[14](1987). The People of Alexander, Symposium Communication addressed to "Respected Friends and Relatives," p. 1, (September).

[15]Ibid, p. 1-2.

[16](1989). National Indian Education Forum and the Alexander School Board. *Expanding our educational horizons. The final report of the post-secondary research*

co-ordination project. (December) (available from the Alexander School Board, P.O. Box 1440, Morinville, Alberta, T0G 1P0).

Future Perspectives

12

The Role of Native Elders:
Emergent Issues

Joseph E. Couture[1]

Shorn of the various surface features from different cultures, Coyote and his kin represent the sheerly spontaneous in life, the pure creative spark that is our birthright as human beings and that defies fixed roles or behavior. He not only represents some primordial creativity from our earlier days, but he reminds us that such celebration of life goes on today, and he calls us to join him in the frenzy. In an ordered world of objects and labels, he represents the potency of nothingness of chaos, of freedom — a nothingness that makes something of itself.[2]

In discussing the relationship of humankind to the Earth, we must understand the basic difference between the Navajo view of Mother Earth, and what the Western European or contemporary American mind means when it tosses around poetic metaphors like "mother nature," or "mother earth."

The contemporary American means that the earth and all of nature is like his natural mother. But the Navajo (and other American Indians) means that his natural mother is the closest thing he will ever know that is like his real mother — The Earth.[3]

There are those who say that the Native Way holds a key, if not *the* key, to the future survival of mankind. They say that it is in the nature of the Native's relationship to the cosmos, the land, to all life-forms, to himself, manifest in ritual and ceremony. They say that to learn the "how and why" of the traditional Native stance is to find the key, to discover a "saving grace" of insights and a creative power beyond any rationality, all crucial to human continuance.[4] If that is so, as I know it to be, then, central to this discovery, and primary to the Native existiential positioning, is the presence and function of Elders. this paper is dedicated as a tribute to their contemporary emergence.

To that end, comments to situate somewhat my experience with Elders and some of the difficulties in writing about them are presented, some events are highlighted and interpreted, the importance of a number of Elder teachings are underscored, and the relevance of Elder inner and outer behaviors is set forth. A discussion of several other Elder-related issues leads to a conclusion to this paper.

Introductory Remarks

I agree with Brumble who says that Elders have become the focus of a "cultural dialectic."[5] Involved are Elders in treaty and non-treaty communities, as well as Natives and non-Natives. Included are social scientists of all stripes pushing to observe and analyze, striving for their syntheses, as well as increasing numbers of Natives engaged in a return to their roots. Both tend to look indiscriminately to Elders, wherever they can be found, for insights and guidance.[6] Both experience difficulties in this endeavor, the former hardly aware that what they expect to observe is restricted by the conditions necessary for their presence as observers[7] and the latter confused by the rarity of top or true Elders and by the relative immaturity and unsteadiness of younger spiritual teachers and ceremonialists.

It is true, in my view, that Elders themselves, of whatever type and development, form an unusual phenomenon. Like all other Natives, they too have been influenced by the forces and consequences of "Contact." Early on, they were, so to speak, hammered back into the woodwork. Long proscribed and banned by governments and churches, now barely emerged from decades of withdrawn, underground activity, they are perceived, not as harbingers of a lost Eden, but as the oral historians, guardians of the Secrets, as interpreters of the Life of the People, as unusual teachers and way showers to the People.

In the late 1960s, triggered by a sudden, strong wave of seekers, Elders, although flattered and grateful, were initially flustered and were forced initially to rethink and redefine themselves and their roles. They were faced with dire and unsettling questions about identity and survival, and with the basic paradoxes regarding the nature of the Native world and the fundamental issues about the world in which humans live.

My views on Elders derive in general from experiences with a number of true Elders over the years since 1971, and particularly from apprenticeship with several Medicine Elders initiated that same year.

Use of the term "Native" herein connotes inclusivity. It refers to all Original Peoples in Canada. In the context of this kind of discussion, by choice I favor this broad connotation since Elders themselves of all Tribes stress Native identity as being a state of mind, as it were, centered in the heart. The late Abe Burnstick's frequent reply to "Who is an Indian" was to exclaim, with finger stabbing his heart area, "An Indeeyin is Indeeyin rawt heah!"[8]

A difficulty confronting Native writers is to write for print-literate readers, especially of social science and professional education perspectives, as though these readers will somehow respond as to an oral literature.

To so write, for one thing, requires keeping in hand an immense oral "reference bibliography," i.e., the stories, legends, prophecies, ceremonies, songs, dance, language and customs of the People. To so write also requires that the qualitative dimensions of these sources be expressed and conveyed with integrity, e.g.,the non-verbal of the storyteller and the ceremonialist — and that is virtually impossible. And, although Elders have declared that the " . . . time has come to share the secrets . . . ." its achievement remains most awkward, if not painful.

Nonetheless, in my view and that of Brumble, the task of written sharing and communication, at this time in our history, however, must resolutely begin.[9] There is a need in the contemporary Native world to articulate traditional views, and to transmit with discernment and discretion to the extent possible, something of the fullness of the Traditional Experience and Story — as embodied in the highest, most evolved Elders — in its intricacies, beauties and ineffabilities. Further, in the view of Berry and others, there is a worldwide human need to survive to which Native North Americans have something significant to contribute.[10]

There is therefore a challenge, and the tentative solution followed here is to write as a storyteller as much as possible, from a general, social science perspective. In others words, as I now proceed, the best I can, with the expression and sharing of my thoughts and feelings regarding my experience with Elders, my endeavor attempts to circumscribe that experience and amplify it to some extent by deliberate association with Western social science and education constructs.[11]

In so doing, the hope is to avoid what someone has called the "barbarism of reflection," i.e., the over-refinement which is unable to sustain the poetic wisdom and imagination that establishes and sustains true Elders, and better yet, to suggest something of how normal and natural it is for Elders to think and behave a certain way.

My proposition assumes that traditional values are dynamic,[12] and can be and are being re-expressed in new forms, and that such, as it so behooves, is being brought about by Elders now at grips with an ever-increasing flow of Natives and non-Natives seeking advice and counsel, healing and inspiration, interpretation of the past and present, in their apprehension and concern over future survival.

Some History

The late 1960s and early 1970s witnessed the political emergence of Native organizations in Alberta. The opening round of activity by both political and service leaders and organizers, initially enthusiastic, climaxed in early 1969 in much discouragement and deep, angry frustration. Both deliberate and unwitting obstacles to program development were formidable. In negotiations, mutual distrust predominated. Confrontation was required and frequently resorted to, and conflict became a working condition in the drive to break open bureaucratic and political doors. It was a time also when programs were exceedingly difficult to start and maintain, largely for lack of adequate core and development monies, and partly for lack of skill and insight on both sides. In the midst of this period of dismaying hurt and resentment, a major shift in consciousness, nonetheless, slowly dawned. It started that same year with Native leaders seeking out Elders, and continued subsequently when others also began the trek back to the Elders of their Tribes.

Amazingly, and concurrently, and virtually everywhere in North America, signs of revitalization appeared. However, because past and current efforts to resolve the enormous cultural, socio-economic and political difficulties were stark, they were unsettling failures.

So began a period of intense introspection, induced by a sharp perception of disheartening results, and encouraged by an intuitive sense that Natives, through a return to cultural origins, might alloy their profound consternation and anger, and find answers to the basic question of "How can we change the direction of the destructive currents. The white man hasn't got any answers. What can we do for our children and our children's children? Maybe, if we talked to some old people..." That incipient awareness became the theme of the beginning struggles, a theme soon variously played across the country.

A second event, paralleled also subsequently in other areas of the continent, such as the Smallboy and Mackinaw camps in the Alberta Rockies, the Rolling Thunder camp in Nevada, etc., occurred in the fall of 1972. It is most noteworthy for it presents clear, milestone evidence of ominous stirrings within Native consciousness.

Elders from six different tribes in Alberta gathered for 12 days on the West Coast of Vancouver Island under the leadership of the Indian Association of Alberta. After two days of discussion on education-related issues, in substance, the following was declared:

> In order to survive in the 20th century, we must really come to grips with the White man's culture and with White ways. We must stop lamenting the past. The White man has many good things. Borrow.

Master and use his technology. Discover and define the harmonies between the two general Cultures, between the basic values of the Indian Way and those of Western civilization — and thereby forge a new and stronger sense of identity. For, to be fully Indian today, we must become bilingual and bicultural. We have never had to do this before. In so doing we will survive as Indians, true to our past. We have always survived. Our history tells us so.[13]

In discussion of that statement, the following comment was made by an Elder:

On a given day, if you ask me where you might go to find a moose, I will say "If you go that way you won't find a moose. But, if you go that way, you will." So now, you younger ones, think about all that. Come back once in a while and show us what you've got. And, we'll tell you if what you think you have found is a moose.[14]

Because of its obvious, singular importance, one particular event has been underscored. However, and once again, that one incident is to be understood within a continental context of similar contemporaneous events throughout "Indian Country." Since that era, and understandably, attention to Elders continues to accrue, especially to both their role and function, and to the relevance of their teachings to contemporary Native identity and survival.

Some Teachings

A few recurring sayings reveal characteristic simplicity, range and richness. For example:

"Don't worry. Take it easy. Do your best. It will all work out. Respect life. Respect your Elders. It's up to you. You have all the answers within you."

"Listen to what Mother Earth tells you. Speak with her. She will speak to you."

"What is Life but a journey into the Light? At the center of Life is the Light."

"Soon I will cross the River, go up the Mountain, into the Light."

These typical sentences set forth a deep, strong, moral and spiritual vision and understanding. These inter-related principles are corollaries or facets of an unitary, primary traditional insight that is variously stated. For example:

The centered and quartered Circle is the sign of wholeness, of inclusiveness of all reality, of life, of balance and harmony between man and culture (Traditional saying).

There are only two things you have to know about being Indian. One is that everything is alive, and two is that we're all related. (Anonymous Indian)

Comment

One sees here the classical themes of holism and personalism, of relationality, of an environment and cosmos which are alive. A broad characteristic goal of traditional education has always been that the whole person in the whole of his/her life be addressed. In the traditional setting, one effectively learns how to become and be a unique expression of human potential. These same traditional processes, in the context of extended family and community Elders, describe a strong sense of responsibility both towards self and towards the community.

Such statements also, in my view, provide reference points to the seeker in his/her journey "back," and suggest something of the richness of the spirit of Tradition, and provide as well "memory-bank data," as it were, for Elder reinterpretations, of which the 1972 Declaration is a prime example.

The 1972 statement is several-fold in its importance. For example, for the first time since the signing of the western treaties, top Elders responded in assembly as the historians of their tribes, as philosophers and teachers of Tradition. They expressed anew for the people the meaning of their history, in light of present conditions, and pointed out a saving and safe direction to pursue so that the People's History be sustained and forwarded.

Crucial also is that to describe the behavior needed, Elders focused on needed connections between the two general cultures, urging discerning openness and selectivity over distrusting and closed defensiveness. A further declaration emphasis is the redefinition of Native identity — a landmark moment — for, to become bicultural is designated as being a positive, warranted, existential act. At that meeting, it was clearly understood that to be bilingual would always be "better" and "richer," but what the Elders affirmed is that bilingualism is not essential for a core-sense of self as Native, keeping open thereby the possibility of authentic Nativeness to those large numbers of Natives who, for whatever reason, do not speak a Native language.

Thus, criteria were defined whereby the survival movement could judge whether or not it has found a "moose." That day Elder mediation, empowered, sanctioned and formalized, redirected the struggling emergence of the People.

Grown men cried that day . . . .

Traditional Native holism and personalism as a culturally shaped human process of being/becoming, is rooted in a relationship with Father Sky, the cosmos, and with Mother Earth, the land — a characteristic which has lead comparative religionists to rank Native American religion as a fifth classical world religion. These experts point to the centrality of land in Native spiritual and religious experience as its distinctive dimension.[15] This relationship with the land/cosmos is personalized and personal, and marked by a trust and a respect which stems from a direct and sustained experience of the oneness of all reality, of the livingness of the land.

The richness of this holism and personalism extends further. When one looks beyond or behind the externals of local and regional custom, language and history, more of the core dynamic of the Native Way of life is revealed. In the West, classical existentialism stresses the utter validity of subjectivity, i.e., of the feeling, reflective subject who has the freedom to make choices, and to determine thus his/her life. Therefore, what one does is of keystone importance. The doing that characterizes the Native Way is a doing that concerns itself with being and becoming an unique person, one fully responsible for one's own life and actions within family and community. Finding one's path and following it is a characteristic Native enterprise which leads to or makes for the attainment of inner and outer balance. This is in marked contrast with general Western doing which tends and strains towards having, objectifying, manipulating, "thingifying" every one and every thing it touches.[16]

Behavioral Features

The exemplars of such a way of living, relating and perceiving, of course, are the most evolved, or "true" Elders. The preceding references to typical sayings may now be usefully supplemented by a description of a number of Elders' behaviors.

It is no simple matter to describe Elder behavior, because of the deep inter-connectedness of all facets of their behavior. The observations which follow are not rigorously organized in pyramidal fashion, but rather as one link leading to the next, in cyclical fashion up and around a same conceptual axis — Elders.

Comment

I am of the opinion that true Elders are superb embodiments of highly developed human potential. They exemplify the kind of person which a traditional, culturally-based learning environment can and does form and mold. Elders also are evidence that Natives know a way to high human development, to a degree greater than generally suspected. Their qualities of mind (intuition, intellect, memory, imagination) and emotion, their profound and refined moral sense manifest in an exquisite sense of humor, in a sense of caring and communication finesse in teaching and counseling, together with a high level of spiritual and psychic attainment, are perceived as clear behavioral indicators, deserving careful attention, if not compelling emulation.

To relate to Elders, to observe and listen carefully, and to come to understand the what, why, and how of such behaviors, grounds, or enroots one, so to speak, in the living earth of Native Tradition.

It is not possible to study and examine Elders in the conventional sense simply because that is not the "way." One learns about Elders by learning from them over a long period of time, by becoming comfortable with a learning-by-doing model. Their counseling and teaching focus on learning from one's experience. Thus, through respectful and patient observation, evidence of remarkable, incisive intellect, of tested wisdom, of sharp and comprehensive ability, allied with excellent memory recall, and of well-developed discursive ability, is eventually perceived.

Further signs of Elderhood are found in their level of trust of both life itself and of their own experiences, by being into true feelings (i.e., into the spiritual side of feelings, without sentimentality), by the art of being still, quiet, unafraid of darkness and nothingness, by the ability to laugh at one another, as well as at self. All that is so because they are trained in the lessons of how the very nature of our being is in at-one-ment with the cosmo-genesis. And so, they hold to the land, ceremony, medicine, linked to the past, in Spirit.[17]

What is the "secret," if any, behind those admirable multibehaviors? My experience suggests that it is their knowledge of and skill in "primordial experience."[18] Primal experience for true Elders, in my view, is centered in the pervasive, encompassing reality of the Life-Force, manifest in "laws" — the Laws of Nature, the Laws of Energy, or the Laws of Light.[19] In other words, true Elders are familiar with Energy on a vast scale, in multiple modes, e.g., energy as healing, creative, lifegiving, sustaining. Both the experience and perception of such manifestations, the manifestations themselves, reveal that all is one, is natural, and is the realm of creative Spirit — the mysterious "Life-Force" (the Wakan-Tanka of the Sioux). There is no "between," between the God-Creator, Source and Sustainer-of-life, and the Cosmos, the environment, all life forms, and Native soul.[20]

Such outstanding qualities, levels of insight and skill, testify to an inner and personal, fundamental, consistent and unchanging process, to a capacity to respond to life as its conditions invariably change. "We have always survived. Our history tells us so."

Elders are an invitation to taste existence within the functioning of the natural world, to experience the mystique of the land. They are, Berry says, in ". . . fascination with the grandeur of the North American continent . . . ."[21] They acquire knowledge and insight into the nature of the universe. For centuries, they have wondered over the revelation of the universe . . . .

It strikes me that their "wisdom" is rooted in Immanence and Transcendence, i.e., this wisdom is attuned to the Immanent in time and space, in the dimensions and seasonal rhythm of the universe, and to the Transcendent, the Above of the confines of historical space and time. This timeless positioning makes for the Story, as carried down through the ages to it being retold and reshaped presently, leading to the discovery of new forms needed to transform current conditions of Native individuals and groups, and thereby of humankind.

Elders hold the secrets of the dynamics of the New Vision. They are propelled by the past, are drawn absolutely to the future. Theirs is a bio-concentric Vision, i.e., a vision of earth and community — an ecological vision of an enduring Mother Earth and the People, a relationship intertwined in a single destiny. In other words, Elders hold a depth insight into the structure and functioning, and manifestation of the entire ecological process.[22]

The powerful and awesome beauty of Elder vision and experience includes the contemporary state of the ecology — a deep point of agony for the state of Mother Earth and Father Sky is in a worldwide, unprecedented state of ecological devastation and disintegration.[23]

Elders have, what Berry calls, "an earth response to an earth problem."[24] "We need only to listen to what Mother Earth is telling us," the Elders repeatedly utter. Their "earth response" is the Story that has never ceased, that carries the dream of the earth as our way into the future. In a sense, this Story holds the "genetic and psychic encoding" needed by humankind for survival.[25] Their "earth response" is processive through and through, and the only immutable reality is the Life-Force itself.

True Elders are so, and do what they do because they have shamanic personalities, that is they have a non-romantic, brilliant sensitivity to the dimensions and patterns of manifestations of the natural world, in its most challenging demands and delights. As humans, as one of the earth's life-forms, they are capable of relations so that all others can equally flourish. Their power and personality hold the ability to shake us and lead us out of the current global cultural pathology, and bring us along into and through a healing and restructuring at a most basic level. They facilitate healing because they have sensitivity to the larger patterns of nature, in its harsh and deadly aspects as well as in its life-giving powers, always in balance with all life-forms.[26]

More can be said about Elder perception. Once again, their perceived world is radically, entirely relational, that is, all realities are constituents of that perception. These are what Fontinell calls "fields" of being[27] and what Fox refers to as "isness."[28] Therefore their "faith," if that is an appropriate term, or their "knowledge" and their "wisdom," is of these "fields." Theirs is a "faith" founded in what they experience. Characteristically, their "faith" is a fundamental mode of experience, rather than an intellectual grasp and understanding of concepts. It is also perforcedly a "knowing" which is ongoing, an open-ended task because, for one grounded in Nature, there can be no once and for all determination of just what is authentic (as opposed to that which is apparent, absolute revelation).

Elders should not be considered as concerned, therefore, with a Western sense of "belief," i.e., a going beyond that for which there is evidence at the present moment, but as having "faith," i.e., experiential knowing, an integrating experience ". . . whereby all modes of experience are brought together in a relatively cohesive whole which is expressed in the life of the person, thus rendering human life meaningful.[29]

I suspect that the traditional Elder capacity to accommodate change, upon contact with Western Christianity forms, readily led them to become Christian, but in a way that allowed not only transformation of perception, but sustained a full continuity with the faith of the People.[30] My hypothesis is that conversion was a simple instance of new growing out of the old, forming a new syncretism congruent with their "faith."

Summary

I concur with Gravely who says that a true Elder is not classifiable as a ". . . passive informant on the traditional past . . . ," but as ". . . a creative theologian, open to the possibilities of his situation, to new ideas and symbols, and to a dialogue between the traditions."[31] Elders manifest consistency in the life process and in relationship to several worlds, moving in and out as shamans are wont to do, with seriousness and humor, with persistent attention and awareness.

Elders possess keys to a classical journey of human and earth ecological transformation. In this era, they are being called upon to reinterpret and to apply the Tradition, the Story, in a new way. There is urgency to this for Mother Earth is no longer looking after herself naturally, but is an earth looked after, and badly, by man. Elders are now so engaged.

Some Issues

Every turn in this paper raises questions, or issues, which deserve more extensive exploration, but which an overview description such as this precludes. Nonetheless, in this last section, aspects of either a practical or academic concern are reviewed.

The rapid decrease in numbers of true Elders is most alarming. Who is to replace them? For some decades now, significant numbers of communities across Canada have lost all traditional Elders. Many individuals, forced to seek out Elders in other tribal traditions, initially encounter some difficulty because of differences in ways. This is a two-way pressure on both Elder and seeker.

The range of kinds of Elders also is bothersome. An Elders' prediction states that these times of emergence are to be marked by chaos and confusion before changing into a time of light and peace. Certainly a significant part of this difficult phase is attributable to "instant" Elders, overnight wonders who, with limited ceremonies and an abundance of cliches, confuse and stall many in their personal journey. The mantle will fall to those spiritual people, less evolved, of less ability and knowledge. "True" Elders are those who have gone through painful encounter with spiritual realities, and who become thereby, in the perception of the People, intermediary between their respective cultural communities and the spiritual forces of the universe, and defenders of the community's psychic integrity. They are those who have enacted and sustained a personal relationship with Nature.

Elders are a national issue because of their qualities and rarity.[32] The needs of the People require guiding wisdom as assurance of a continuing, living Native presence in Canada, and for during the time needed to acquire a "faith" about the real possibility of survival.

The practical requirements of establishing and maintaining a relationship with Elders are not readily perceived. First of all, at the level of individual need and change, much time and patience are required. There are no shortcuts to attitudinal and spiritual change, no possible end-runs around phases of inner change. A complete and enduring commitment is required. Secondly, the "return" is not only to "primal roots," to the living core of the Tradition itself, but is conditional on personal achievement, so as to arrive at presenting to the world an authentic mode of living.[33] And, that is not an easy matter.

The "knowing" of Elders is problematic to those who, for a range of reasons, were not schooled in oral tradition. Elders as "knowers" know intimately, directly, and are non-dualistic in their perceptions and understandings. Western trained people are inherently scholastic and dualistic in perception and thinking. True, the sense of identity of Elders is marked by an ordered consciousness. However, at the same time, it is unbounded by space and time, all the while remaining in direct consideration of both dimensions of historical time and space. Again, attainment to that state of development is a basic challenge.

Problematic also, and for that same kind of mind, is that Elders have consistency, continuity and clarity of insight and skill regarding paradigmatic alteration (i.e., reinterpreting the Story) which, in my view, as Grim declares ". . . germinates understanding of the creative role of imagination and intuition in human history."[34] Elders are positioned, I would suggest, to contribute to facilitating to what Wilson calls "quantum leaps" in developing new models of thought.[35]

It would seem that presently there are growing numbers of Western academic approaches hinting at hitherto unknown possible amenability with Native mind. Keutzer, commenting on the work of such physicists as Bohm, Einstein, Capra, etc., suggests that such physicists are becoming students of consciousness itself.[36] Their concepts of "flow" and "hologram," for example, and statements that "everything is alive," are very suggestive. To Keutzer's list, I would add the names of such theologians and historians as Fox and Berry, and of the physicist-philosopher Swimme.

A corollary to the issue of "knowing" is that of mysticism (currently a much abused and misapplied concept, in my view). From a Native spiritual standpoint, as I see it, mysticism is a question of becoming/being rooted or grounded in relationships with all constituents or dimensions of reality. I like Fox's description of mysticism because it is congruent with my understanding of Native spiritual experience. He holds that ". . . the essence of the mystical experience is the way we are altered to see everything from its life-filled axis, to feel the mysteries of life as they are present within and around us."[37] That's Indian!

To arrive at a direct experiential understanding of that definition is a primary learning task. To discover how ceremonies, for example, mediate helping energy and teaching takes some doing. Prayer, ritual and ceremony ground one in life for "It's all deah, in de sereemonees!"[38]

To acquire an awareness of all earth forms as having a life of their own, to become aware of all as Spirit-bearing, as Spirit-expressing, takes some doing. To become steeped in, adept in Native mysticism is to enter into the beautiful, the truth, the Oneness, in balance against all negativity and absence. It is to activate and sustain personal discovery which leads to a true sense of self-understanding, to a sense of future time through awareness of the past — which leads to learning how to intuit the close relationship between one's culture and one's genetic impulses.

Elders have teaching challenges to deal with. One is with regard to non-Natives. They are aware of the currently unfolding prophecy that "The White brother will come to the Red brother for teaching." There is acceptance of the non-Natives who come to them. However, they find themselves struggling with a different mind-set and affectivity, as well as with language barriers. Also, because of the knowledge level of both Native and non-Native seekers, so many are not grounded in a sense of the real but mysterious power of nature in mountains, rivers and lakes, rocks, life-forms, all as enmeshed in the web of the universe. So, the legends and stories require pedagogical adaptation. The stories have to be retold, reshaped and refitted to meet contemporary seekers' changed and changing needs.

Such encounters are but necessary moments in the retelling and reshaping of the Story, as in the case of the 1972 Declaration above. New legends as well as forthcoming across the continent, sparked by medicine Elders' dreams and visions. Tradition through Elders is converged on the present, revealing forgotten depths of perception and understanding.

Present Elder endeavor is in a tensional context. They are aware of the tensional exchange between the Story of the People and the need for a new direction, as we have seen. They are aware of the tensional exchange between immanent direction within living matter itself and the transcendent source of the creative impulse. They are aware of the tensional character of awakening, of the inner dynamics of spiritual and socio-political life.

Conclusion

We look to Elders for the way words are used, for the structural devices they employ, for the teaching and counseling approaches they utilize, for the philosophical and spiritual perspectives of the world, experienced and envisioned. We look to them to show us the ". . . the archetypal essences appearing in animal forms . . . ." as Brown says.[39] In other words, to show us the Way.

We look to them to tell us about the "Moose."

Daniel Deschinney, a Navajo Blessingway singer, explains how a Navajo experiences the sacred mountains' inner forms, and says:

> When a Navajo experiences the sacred mountains' inner forms kindling new strength within himself, he says "'I am invincible. I am beautified.' To be invincible is masculine. To be beautified is feminine. These two concepts together are a powerful entity. There is no strength from only one. Power comes from the interaction between them. When you have strength, you recognize your oppor-

tunity, you know what you must do, and you have the grace to do it.[40]

Notes

[1]The author is an Alberta Metis of Cree ancestry. His Ph.D. training and experience are in the areas of Native development, psychology, and education at all levels. His work experience includes teaching, addictions counselling, community development, and research. He has been apprenticed to Elders since 1971.

[2]Erdoes and Ortiz, p. 39.

[3]Begay, p. 28.

[4]See Berry, Brumble, Steinmetz.

[5]Brumble, p. 34.

[6]See Brown 1982, p. 119, for similar views.

[7]Carter in Rothman, p. 71.

[8]The late Elder Abe Burnstick, Stoney Nation, Paul's Band, Duffield, Alberta, was pre-eminent as an orator and teacher.

[9]Brumble, p. 42. See also Buller, Gould, and Lincoln.

[10]See the writings of Fox, Hausman, and Steinmetz.

[11]This position I take regarding the difficult issue of oral literate mind versus print literate mind finds support in the views of Geertz and Jules-Rosette, for example. Geertz holds that the main task in interpreting cultures is one of "explicating explications" (Geertz p. 18). In other words, it is imperative to acquire the feel for the "homely in homely context," for to fail to do so is a failure to place common sense thought within context of its use. The development of the "thickest descriptions" possible becomes therefore both an ideal and necessary objective.

It also means, as Jules-Rosette points out, dealing frontally with the problems of subjective interpretation (p. 563). The "veil of objectivity" masks an inability to grasp another interpretive system, or style of perception. Objectivity has "totally falsified our concept of truth" (Polanyi in Jules-Rosette, 1964, p. 289) - the "veil of objectivity" is as a protective shield of one's own oracular structure. It covers what G. Wilson calls "profound parasitic lay assumptions" (p. 118). This difficulty is illustrated by the case of Casteneda. His construct of reality was so impenetrable that drugs were needed to forcefully assault it to allow him to receive spiritual insight.

[12]For more detail about the creative capacity of Native culture see Couture 1987, pp. 180-184.

[13]Declaration rendered by Elder Louis Crier, Cree Nation, Ermineskin Band, Hobbema, Alberta.

[14]Observation made by the late Elder Charlie Blackman, Chipewyan Nation, Cold Lake Band, Cold Lake, Alberta.

[15]See Hultkranz in Capps, pp. 86-106. Refer also to the Berry and Fox writings.

[16]See Couture, o.c., pp. 180-182.

[17]See Cordova, pp. 23-24; Buller, p. 166.

[18]Huston Smith claims that "... there is, first, a Reality that is everywhere and always the same; and second, that human beings always and everywhere have access to it." (p. 276).

[19]Couture 1989, pp. 22-23.

[20]See entire article Couture 1989.

[21]Berry 1987a, p. 185.

[22]Berry 1987a, p. 185.

[23]See *Akwasasne Notes*. This internationally established Iroquois journal of social comment, over two decades now, has reported on ecological deterioration abundently and consistently. With special attention to aboriginal regions worldwide, its regular columns, in cause-effect terms, describe the autistic relationship between the ecological vision and the industrial vision.

[24]Berry 1987a, p. 186.

[25]See all of Berry 1987b, pp. 200-215 for a provocative, insightful, discussion of this concept.

[26]See Berry 1987c, pp. 211-212, and Kelsey, for more detail on shamanic personality and qualities.

[27]Fontinell, p. 138.

[28]"Isness" as term is frequent in all of Fox's writings.

[29]Fontinell, p. 140.

[30]See Gravely for discussion of the adaptability of Black Eld.

[31]Gravely, p. 11.

[32]See Phillips, Troff, and Whitecalf 1976, and Phillips and Whitecalf 1977.

[33]See Berry in Hausman, p. 7.

[34]Grim, p. 235.

[35]Wilson, p. 55.

[36]See Keutzer article.

[37]Fox 1972, p. 77.

[38]Elder Abe Burnstick.

[39]Brown 1983, p. 7.

[40]Quoted by Johnson, p. 47.

References

Begay, J. (1979). "The Relationship Between the People and the Land," *Akwasasne notes*, Summer, 28-30.

Berry, T. (1987). "Creative Energy," *Cross currents*, Summer/Fall, 179-186.

_____ (1987). "The New Story: Comment on the Origin, Identification and Transmission of Values," *Cross currents*, Summer/Fall, 187-199.

_____ (1987). "The Dream of the Earth: Our Way into the Future," *Cross currents*, Summer/Fall, 200-215.

_____ (1987). "Twelve Principles for Reflecting on the Universe," *Cross currents*, Summer/Fall, 216-217.

Brown, J.E. (1982). *The spiritual legacy of the American Indian*. New York: Crossroad.

_____ (1982). "The Bison and the Moth: Lakota Correspondences," *Parabola*, May, 8 2, 6-13.

Brumble, D. (1980). "Anthropologists, Novelists and Indian Sacred Material," *Can. Ev.*

Amer. St., Spring, 11, 1, 31-48.

Buller, G. (1980). "New Interpretations of Native American Literature: A Survival Technique," *American Indian cultural research journal*, 4, 1 & 2, 165-177.

Capps, W., ed. (1976). *Seeing with a Native eye*. New York: Harper and Row.

Cordova, Viola. (1938). *Philosophy and the Native American. The people before Columbus*. Albuquerque: Southwest Indian Student Coalition: University of New Mexico, 23-26.

Erdoes, R., and A. Ortiz, eds. (1984). *American Indian myths and legends*. New York: Pantheon Books.

Couture, J. (1987). "What is Fundamental to Native Education? Some Thoughts on the Relationship Between Thinking, Feeling, and Learning," in *Contemporary educational issues. The Canadian mosaic*. L. Stewin, S. McCann, eds. Toronto: Copp Clark Pitman, 178-191.

Couture, J. (1989). "Native and Non-Native Encounter. A Personal Experience," in *Challenging the conventional essays in honor of Ed Newberry*. W. Cragg, ed. Burlington: Trinity Press, 123-154.

Huston, S. (1953). "Philosophy, Theology, and the Primordial Claim," *Cross currents*, 28, 3, 276-288.

Fontinell, E. (1988). "Faith and Metaphysics Revisited," *Cross currents*, Summer, 129-145.

Fox, M. (1972). "On Becoming a Musical, Mystical Bear. Spirituality American Style." New York: Paulist Press.

_____ (1983). *Meditation with Meister Eckhart*. Sante Fe, N.M.: Bear and Co.

Fox, M., and B. Swimme. (1982). *Manifesto for a global civilization*. Sana Fe, N.M.: Bear and Co.

Geertz, C. (1973). *The interpretation of cultures.* Selected essays. New York: Basic Books.

Gould, Janice. (1988). *A review of Louise Erdrich's "jacklight." The people before Columbus.* Albuquerque: Southwest Indian Coalition: University of New Mexico, 11-14.

Gravely, W. (1987). "New Perspectives on Nicholas Black Elk, Oglala Sioux Holy Man," *The Illif Rev.,* Winter, 44, 1, 1-19.

Grim, J. (1987). "Time, History, Historians in Thomas Berry's Vision," *Cross currents,* Summer/Fall, 225-239.

Hausman, G. (1986). *Meditation with animals.* Albuquerque, N.M.: Bear and Co.

Johnson, T. (1988). "The Four Sacred Mountains of the Navajos," *Parabola,* Winter, 40-47.

Jules-Rosette, Benetta. (1978). "The Veil of Objectivity: Prophecy, Divination, and Social Inquiry." *American Anthropology,* September, 80, 3, 549-570.

Kelsey, M. (1978). "The Modern Shaman and Christian Belief," *Transcend,* 22, 1-6.

Keutzer, C. (1984). "The Power of Meaning: From Quantum Mechanics to Synchronicity." *J. Hum. Psych.,* Winter, 24, 1, 80-94.

Lincoln, K. (1980). "Trans - to the Other Side of, Over, Across," *American Indian cultural & research journal,* 4, 1 & 2, 1-17.

Philips Donna, R. Troff, H. Whitecalf, eds. (1976). *Kataayuk*: Saskatchewan Indian elders. Saskatoon: Saskatchewan Indian Cultural College.

Philips Donna, R. Troff, eds. (1977). *Enewuk.* Saskatoon: Saskatchewan Indian Cultural College.

Rothman, T. (1987). "A What You See is What You Beget Theory," *Discover,* May, 90-96, 98-99.

Steinmetz, P. (1984). *Meditation with Native Americans. Lakota spirituality."* Santa Fe, N.M.: Bear and Co.

Swimme, B. (1987). "Berry's Cosmology," *Cross currents,* Summer/Fall, 218-224.

Wilson, G. (1987). "What is Effective Intercultural Communication?," *Can. Eth. St.,* 18, 1, 118-123.

Wilson, R.A. (1985). "Quantum Leaps," *New age,* June, 52-55, 80.

13

Biculturalism:
Reflections on an Objective for University
Education

Evelyn Moore-Eyman

The indigenous population of the Province of Alberta includes some 40 000 legal Indians, some of them white women who have "married in." For all of these, the federal government has special responsibility. Something approaching twice the number are self-identified non-Status Indians and Metis for whom the federal government takes no present special responsibility, although an offer to that effect was made at recent negotiations on the Canadian Constitution. In the 1981 Canadian census, 27 565 of the total of more than 100 000 Indian people claimed a Native language as their mother tongue. The number in Alberta was second only to the Native language speakers of the Province of Quebec.

Schooling on the Reserves

The circumstances of Alberta Indians vary widely. There are, on the one hand, the large southern reserves of the Plains Indians and on the other hand, the Indian and Metis families in the small and isolated groups of the northern bush. The urban Native populations are growing. Most Native people are extremely poor, but eight of the 43 reserves have new-found wealth from oil. Schooling is similarly diverse. There are reserves with schools, and a few are Indian-controlled. Others are federal schools. Some reserves bus all of their children to public schools.

There are 27 rural public schools in one very extensive jurisdiction (The Northland School Division), where the children are almost all Native. The provincial government, in 1983, created school councils for each of these 27 local schools. A representative from each school council travels once a month to form collectively the board of the school division — a division spreading from east to west of the northern half of the province. This new structure has brought about a kind of Native control in that only one of the original 27 board members was non-Native. Though little changed immediately in the schools, there is considerable excitement about the future of this new provincial route to political efficacy for Native adults in Alberta.

Recent government reports have called for broad change in Native education in Alberta, although it is only the most recent, that of the Committee on Tolerance and Understanding, which recognizes fully the deplorable state of Native education. In Canada, until the 1960s, Indian education was conducted almost exclusively by the churches but with government grants. In the 1960s, the residential schools, which were the prevailing institutions for denominational education, were closed by a change in federal policy and were replaced in some cases by day schools in the communities. More often than not, these changes were necessitated by the bussing of students to provincial schools or by a combination of these arrangements. Thus, a new official policy of integration of Native children into provincial schools resulted, but in fact, it was a continuation of the assimilationist thrust of the century of church education. For instance, no provision was made for instruction in Native languages, little was done about Native culture as school content, and the community adults continued to be alienated and remote from the schools. The children continued to absent themselves, and with the R.C.M.P. no longer rounding them up for incarceration in the residential schools, many were now more successful in removing themselves from schooling. A community committee at Fort Chipewyan found in 1980 that 15 grade seven children were attending school and 26 were "running wild in the village" — a Native village which had European education for a century.

The University Response

Each of the four universities of Alberta has in the last 12 years developed some response to the situation in Native education, e.g., the Department of Native American Studies at Lethbridge or the initially reduced-time teacher education program of the University of Alberta via the Morning-Star Project at Blue Quills. The University of Calgary was first in the field of Native education in Alberta, and took the "support services" approach on the unanimous and insistent advice of the Native Steering Committee. Thus no special degree program was devised but a "Native place" was created on campus (the students named it the Red Lodge) and staff were hired to assist students, almost all of whom had less than regular university admission qualifications.

There was one Native graduate of the University of Calgary when the project started in 1972 and there were 86 in 1983-84. Graduates in a number of cases have taken up to three of the four years of a degree program in near-home communities where the office of Native Student

Services has organized University Outreach Programs. University lecturers have travelled to the local sites where the students have been supported by resident tutor/advisors. Full three-year programs were completed at Hobbema (Cree), the Blackfoot Reserve (Gleichen) and at Fort Chipewyan. In addition, the programs have built bridges between the communities and the university in such a way that there has been a steady flow of students to the university in subsequent years. By 1990, there were nearly 150 first degrees earned by Native students at the University of Calgary, with a number of students going on to graduate school.

Since 1971, the official policy of the Government of Canada has supported both biculturalism and multiculturalism. The biculturalism referred to, however, is French/English, i.e., the biculturalism of peoples derived from two segments of European culture. This type of biculturalism has been subject to much study both in Canada and the U.S.A. and the concept of European/Native biculturalism has virtually been neglected.

The general bankruptcy of past policies for Native education has, however, led some Canadian Native leaders to formulate policies of biculturalism for their circumstances. The Goodstoney Band of the Stoney Indians (Nakoda Sioux) have recently built a beautiful building within sight of the Rocky Mountains to house their Nakoda Institute which is dedicated to the development of biculturalism. It is a place where Indians and whites are welcomed to learn of Stoney culture. It is envisaged as a place where university classes may be conducted, as they have been elsewhere on the reserve for a number of years, but in future it is hoped with Native instructors.

Biculturalism, by which the practices and advantages of a second culture are *added* to the repertoire of behaviors of the first culture, but without replacing that first culture, has had a *prima facie* acceptability to staff and associates of the University of Calgary (Snow, 1977). Staff at the Red Lodge have been guided by biculturalism as an objective, to the extent that such biculturalism is at present understood. Thus, the Red Lodge is maintained as a Native enclave legitimizing a Native presence for the students on campus. There are Native speakers' programs, a Native film series, a major annual pow-wow involving Indian Elders, and a great deal of informal discussion. Mainly through experiences associated with the Red Lodge, it seems that most students who graduate leave with a more articulated view of their own Indianness than when they arrived at the university. They are generally fluent in their Native language when they leave, and more secure in their Indian identity.

Recognizing how little the literature assisted in understanding Native/European biculturalism, in 1981 the staff of the Native Students Services turned to a number of associates who were believed to be bicultural and asked them to share their experiences in a small study conference. Arthur Blue, then chairman of the Native Studies Department at Brandon University, and himself a Native person, acted as a facilitator. Those selected as participants were all people who were in some way active in their Native communities and at the same time judged to be effective within the city. Urbanized Indians, even though they retained their language and had family on the reserves, were not included unless they were known to be actively involved with their home communities.

The meetings proved to be an emotion-laden sharing of deeply felt experiences so much so, indeed, that one participant announced that the discussions had crystallized his intentions. He would now leave his university employment and return to live permanently on his reserve.

Extracts from the taped sessions follow.

Stories of Native Life

My parents formed my philosophy, made me the way I am. My grandparents especially influenced me; my grandfather was a chief many years, a very proud man believing that to be an Indian was a great thing. He wanted to be understood as bicultural. He accepted education and Christianity but respected what he was. He participated in the Sundance and in the rituals, although most have now disappeared. What people know me to be is due to him.

My mother was an educated woman. Father believed in work though he was not educated. People should not be workaholics, but to work is important. I attended a mission school taught by French nuns and priests. I have encountered three cultures. I entered school with Cree. Then, all children learned their language. Acculturation started when I entered school. I don't want to downgrade the teachers. The teachers taught the best English they knew (most were French). Boys learned to work as men, girls to be good mothers. My parents believed in education so I finished high school. I had to go away to school and there encountered discrimination, but not much. Discrimination exists where you look for it. Everyone finds it at times.

The nuns were good to me and treated me fairly. Then I went to university — out in the world. There, 30 years ago, I found that two things mattered; my race and my religion.

I am ashamed, but I tell it so that my children will be better people. I did not tell people I was Indian. If people knew you were Indian you were excluded. Now I know that was very wrong, but perhaps it had to be done to survive. (Later the storyteller told the conference she had always tried to pass as Ukrainian).

Another confession! As a teacher, I taught children not to be Indian but to acculturate. Today I am another person. Today we are proud to be what we are. I try to teach that brown is beautiful, but it is hard because acculturation has gone so far.

I have five children; they have gone to schools both on the reserve and in our nearby town. We send our children to provincial schools because we think they offer more but in a way this is wrong. If we controlled our schools much more could happen.

In our family we have tried to raise our children to be bicultural. I have a good husband who says I talk too much and I should accept things. However, I believe if we see a wrong we should right it.

This is my confession.

QUESTION: *Could you tell us what it was that brought about the change in your attitude?*

ANSWER: My (real) attitudes have not changed; I took my feelings along with me — maybe I was a hypocrite. [There was a sympathetic laughter at this point]. Today universities are different; today universities are good places.

(Note: This individual has served on the senate of the University of Alberta and was leading member of the small group of Indian women who were responsible for the establishment of the services for Native students at the University of Calgary).

Another participant, who has since died, told the study conference of how as a youth, newly out of the residential school, he set out to relearn his own lost cultural ways. He was sufficiently successful so that in recent years he had been sought after in remote communities to teach the traditional rituals to groups who had lost them. For example, he taught the ceremonies of thanksgiving for survival of the winter and for the bounty of the summer.

Another one of the informants, a former student at the University of Calgary and now a graduate social worker and already a grandfather, told of his long years on skid row and of his "finding himself again" through returning to learn matters of the spirit from his grandfather and from his aunts on the Poundmaker Reserve in Saskatchewan.

Another graduate, by then about 40 years of age, told of her capture by the R.C.M.P. in the northern bush when she was six years old. Two of her brothers escaped the raid and it was 20 years before she found either of them again. The rest were incarcerated in one of the church-run residential schools, and although it was in the same region as her family, she never saw her mother again. Their father came to see his children but was turned away, being advised that it was not in the children's best interest for him to see them. Her children gone, the mother's life collapsed and she was killed within three years in a drunken brawl. For the next 10 years our friend was out of the residential schools once only — for one period of three weeks.

As in all residential schools, the children were forbidden to converse in their own language. These children, from a very permissive child-rearing culture, were beaten for this and other offences. This student learned that her guilt as an Indian included responsibility for the Jesuit Martyrs who had died thousands of miles away and in a distant past. For the next 20 years after her schooling, she wandered a good deal through Canada looking for her brothers and sisters. She was reconciled with her father (whom she thought to have deserted her) just before his death. On graduation as a teacher, in part through the support of the Native Students Services of the University of Calgary, she returned to one of the communities near to her family home and found herself teaching the children of former schoolmates. This was for her an intense and exhilarating experience because for the first time since she was six she now had the experience of being home. She still spoke her language and used it with joy in the community in which she taught.

In the life stories shared by each bicultural informant and in the subsequent lively discussion there was found to be one overriding pattern among the Canadian Native informants — each had been educated for assimilation (in some cases forcibly) but each, over varying periods of time, had come to an overt commitment to the primacy of the first culture. Most indicated great pain before this self-acceptance and reconciliation with society was achieved in the third and final stage of this sequential accomplishment of biculturalism.

Analysis

Those who know Polgar's 1960 study of "concurrent socialization" of adolescent youths on the Mesquakie Reserve (one of the rare studies of Native American biculturalism) will recognize a fundamentally different process operating in Alberta, i.e., one that is sequential rather than concurrent. With the possible exception of one informant who did not attend residential school and whose reserve is adjacent to the city of Calgary where she attended high school, the Native informants demonstrated aspects of a tertiary socialization (to Indian society), a re-socialization to Indian culture often consciously and deliberately sought.

Most informants commented on the stressful nature of this sequential socialization and re-socialization and found Blue's analysis of stress situations relevant to their own cases. Blue's recommendation for relief of stress through "renewal" under the guidance of the Elders was echoed also in most of the life stories (Blue, 1982).

The Native informants, whose experiences were similar in many respects, were otherwise a diverse group. The age spread appeared to be about 30 years and they spoke three different Indian languages. There were both males and females in the group and members were both Status and non-Status Indians. The education level ranged from the elementary education of the former residential schools to graduation at the master's degree level. Informants came from the northern bush and the southern plains. All had been exposed to instruction in Christianity; however, the extent to which Christianity is now rejected was believed to vary considerably within the group. A study of the extent of the rejection of the Christian religion when Indianness is reaffirmed could prove to be a very significant one, but it was not attempted in this initial conference.

As already indicated, the informants were a small selected group who were chosen for their apparent biculturalism. Their successful diversity reinforced the conclusion demonstrated at the conference that it is indeed possible for individuals to be successfully bicultural in Canada in the Native and dominant cultures. It appears also that, to the extent that this group is representative, Native biculturalism has been achieved in a three-level sequential rather than in concurrent fashion. This process has been accompanied by suffering, at times intense, and relieved only in the final phase of commitment to the first culture.

Recommendations

Any university policy inferences from this study conference must of course be of the most tentative kind, but the following are representative of those in the discussions and most relevant to a university support service:

1. University support services for Native students should do whatever can be done to help Native students resolve their personal search for identity and, where the students opt for biculturalism, should assist the reassertion of "Indianness." A number of processes already operating could be facilitated and assessed for this purpose, e.g., the taking of university programs to the Native communities (the various university outreach programs), retreats with Elders, students' participation in Native political organizations, Native studies seminars,

etc. The legitimization of Indianness within the university by the provision of a Native centre or Native studies department should also be assessed in this light. Perhaps most potent is the staffed Native students' drop-in centre, providing as it does a milieu for students to work out with their peers over a four- or five-year period the implications of their identity. It is both interesting and significant that many students finally graduate from the University of Calgary apparently more committed to their Indianness than when they arrived. A recent survey indicating that the overwhelming majority of graduates returned to work with their own people is some confirmation of this conclusion. (Moore-Eyman 1981)

2. While standards of admission to universities are a contentious issue with both Indians and non-Indians, the whites hold to the position that while even the schools continue antipathetic to Native biculturalism (with resulting very low numbers of Native graduates), qualifications in an indigenous culture should form part of the Native students' package of qualifications. Thus, those universities maintaining academic (and of course social/cultural) support services may legitimately admit students with less than full matriculation at least for those professions for which competence in the culture is essential to service to the client (e.g., in teaching and in medicine). Thus, only in the forseeable future will there be any approach to proportional Native participation in universities.

It must not be assumed that the process of sequential biculturalism identified at the conference is a model for the future merely because it has existed in the lives of living people. As in the cases of the conference informants, every present student reaching the university has come through assimilationist schooling. That is the existing situation, but it is not necessarily the future situation and visionaries and leaders in the Indian world are currently seeking schooling alternatives beneath the banner slogan of "Indian control of Indian education." If through this means, or any other, the pressure to assimilate is pursued in Canada, Polgar's concurrent socialization in the future may offer a less deeply painful route to biculturalism than the three levels of sequential socialization identified by the study conference participants and observable in the lives of so many Native students.

Certainly, until the schools are transformed, and probably thereafter, Native enclaves on-campus should be available and participation in them an option for all university students who identify themselves as Native.

References

Blue, Arthur W. (1982). "Stressors and Response in the Native School Child," in *With head held high*. Evelyn Moore-Eyman and Carole Benner, eds. Calgary: The Native Students Services, University of Calgary.

Blue, Arthur W. and Meredith Blue. (1989). "The Trail of Stress," in *Multiculturalism in Canada*. Ronald J. Samuda, et. al., eds. Toronto: Allyn and Bacon.

Moore-Eyman, E. (1981). "You *Can* Go Home Again," *Education Canada*, Spring.

Polgar, Steven. (1962). "Biculturalism of Mesquakie Teenage Boys," *American anthropologist*, April, 217-235.

Snow, Chief John. (1977). *These mountains are our sacred places*. Toronto: Samuel Stevens.

14

Teaching in a University Native Outreach Program

John W. Friesen

In 1972, the University of Calgary began an outreach program involving students at the Stoney Indian Reservation at Morley, which is located 50 kilometres west of Calgary, Alberta. Later, the program was expanded to include several other Indian reserves and by the fall of 1990 the university had graduated 150 Native students, many of whom had taken training in the outreach program. In addition, the Native Student Services resources available on campus, and part of the Native Centre, have sustained many Native students and served to foster a very positive influence toward higher education in their home communities.

Intent of the Program

The motivation for designing off-campus university opportunities such as the Outreach Program originated with Native leaders. They reasoned that an onsite university operation would reduce the formidable elements of attaining a higher education in an urban setting, and provide a kind of downhome atmosphere to the process. The need for leadership training was premised on the assessment by Native leaders that to function effectively in the modern technological world, all the skills and knowledge that might be attainable should be developed by their youth. It was also felt that a localized version of university education should incorporate local content and relate better to community goals. This plan was not in any way to be interpreted as reducing academic standards, but rather as fulfilling them with a view to operationalizing the concept of cultural relativity.

Initial outreach endeavors of the University of Calgary met with many unforseen obstacles that hindered the fulfillment of envisaged goals. The first outreach curriculum was devised on the basis of the availability of instructors and students for instruction. In the program conducted at the Stoney Indian Reserve at Morley, students often encountered a weekly schedule (or course choices) without an idea of what would transpire (Brooks, 1977). Later this disorganization was overcome, new problems arose, and these too were resolved. After 18 years of operation, the Outreach Program appears to have settled in as a regular institutional component but with sufficient inbuilt flexibility to meet new challenges.

One of the practical aspects of an onsite university program has to do with the maintenance of tranquility for student family life. Since most of the students involved in the initial years of the program were parents with children, they were delighted to find that they could complete three of the four years of a degree program without having to leave their families, relocate them or try to function in the context of two different living environments, one at college and the other in weekend trips home. Most of the sites served by the university are too far away to encourage commuting, although individual Stoney and Blackfoot students have undertaken such efforts from time to time.

The original curriculum of the outreach program was geared to the preparation of teachers with the three-year local component to include a practicum opportunity. Several students chose not to complete the three years onsite, or opted for other majors by transferring credit for courses they had taken to different faculties, social work being a heavy favorite. Undoubtedly, local needs in social work motivated such moves. Courses provided were sufficiently general in nature so that a teaching major could be pursued by the student in the final on-campus year. Most of the first graduates chose to become elementary teachers, although their choice may also have been precipitated by the local market.

Despite their best efforts to relate to the Indian community, people not familiar with reserve life find it difficult to feel effective in those settings. Thus, the need to prepare Native teachers was a push factor for the program, although that attainment in no way assures success on the part of their students. In addition, university graduates often find undue pressures when they return to work at home in terms of the way they are expected to model behavior for younger people, or even to share the financial benefits of their attained profession. Still, when it comes to sensing "where the student is at" for readiness to learn, the Native teacher has several culturally related advantages. The pupil may be addressed in the Native language on occasion (if the Native teacher is from that reserve and speaks the language) and the teaching of social studies, for example, can be made relevant by using local examples. Perhaps the most important advantage is in demonstrating to younger people that Native people can be successful in academic and professional endeavors and yet be part of a functional Native culture.

Role of the Tutor/Advisor

After several years of involvement with the Outreach Program, one has the opportunity to work with a variety of support persons in the office of tutor/advisor (hereafter called tutor). Essentially, this office represents a kind of "affirmative action" component in that the person is available for special assistance and consultation in ways that the university student on campus may not experience. A close examination of resources available to the average student on campus will reveal, however, that most such students are either not aware of available assistance or deliberately choose not to seek it out. At the University of Calgary, the Student Services offers a wide variety of help in the form of counselling, study skills, and effective writing. In fact, a convincing case could be built for the argument that on-campus students have a much better opportunity to obtain needed help than those involved in the Outreach Program. A particularly strong argument could certainly be made with regard to library resources which are minimal at best on outreach sites.

The role of the resident tutor is multidimensional. As an academic assistant the tutor attends the various classes offered in the Outreach Program, takes notes, helps with written assignments, and, if requested, goes over the notes with students after hours. One tutor I worked with kept the class for an hour or two at the end of each day simply to review the highlights of the lectures. In the practical realm, this same individual often accompanied the bus driver when picking up the students so they could have extra time en route in discussing academic matters.

Much of the tutor's time is taken up with personal matters, such as listening to people in conflict situations. Outsiders rarely comprehend the challenges faced by Native people who aspire to academic careers and then try to fit such thinking and activity into the milieu of reserve life. Reserve life tends to be much more relaxed than an academic lifestyle allows, and pressures to participate in family affairs instead of studying are immense. It takes a very special person to help the student put it all together in a meaningful yet effective way, and the qualifications for the job are primarily personal rather than cultural, academic or professional.

Vignettes of Outreach Life

Instructors in the Native Outreach Program have the opportunity to add a dimension to their academic careers not easily obtainable in the traditional academic setting. Two of these challenges pertain to travel and lodging. In the case of a reserve close to the university, it may simply mean packing a lunch and driving to the teaching location. Sites requiring an overnight stay or perhaps a longer duration may mean living out of a suitcase or bunking in with local residents. In the program conducted at Fort Chipewyan in northeastern Alberta the arrangement called for the instructor to spend a week on site and the next back on campus. Some instructors remained on site for longer periods of time. It was quite the experience to trade environments on such a basis, one week pulling a toboggan loaded with books and supplies for one mile to the teaching site, in temperatures registering 46 degrees below zero, and the next spent in riding to work in a well-heated automobile in much less severe temperatures.

Weather conditions do more than inconvenience travel. When I was at Fort Chipewyan, it was necessary to change locations several stimes during severe weather to find a building that could be properly heated. We used the community building as a third location for one program, and even then we found it necessary to move to three different areas of the building as the heat diminished and the facilities showed the strain of constant cold. When the water froze and outside toilet facilities were left as the final avail, it was the last straw. Repairs finally had to be made.

Weather conditions are not the only challenge in the north. Library facilities are definitely limited, and it may require some effort to find needed technical equipment. This sometimes means finding the movie projector which can be in use at any number of locations, i.e., the primary or secondary school, band office, nursing station or alcohol rehabilitation centre. As a last resort, I personally bought a secondhand movie projector, slide projector and overhead projector and stocked them in the car for use on locations near the city of Calgary. In northern locations such as Fort Chipewyan, I relied on the luck of the draw in finding the equipment.

In one rather humorous situation when we found it virtually impossible to darken a room to see a movie, the students procured a large rock to use as a hammer, some old blinds and a few nails and literally shut out the light by covering the windows through a manipulation of this set of supplies. This same group of students located a set of travel posters from sunny spots around the world—Florida, southern California, Greece and Hawaii — and plastered the walls with them to lend warmth if not imagination to the classroom atmosphere.

A special advantage of teaching in the Outreach Program is that of working closely with a smaller group of students than is possible on campus. Often the informal times before, between and after classes are special times of learning for both instructor and student as personal insights are shared about academic and personal matters. Eating lunch together is perhaps the most relaxing time and since outreach students tend to be a little older, the exchange can often be quite collegial.

Oftimes, special problems arise in which the entire group can participate; for example, if a car won't start, everyone tries to help out; if someone has forgotten lunch, everyone shares a little of theirs; and planning a party to celebrate the semester's end, particularly at Christmas, is everyone's concern. In the program conducted at Old Sun College on the Blackfoot Reserve east of Calgary, it was possible for the instructor to accompany students on a bus for field trips to various area schools. A two-hour bus ride can become pretty boring unless some form of entertainment is invented to pass the time. A lively singsong of country and popular tunes with the occasional Christmas carol thrown in can greatly aid in such a situation. When a group becomes a "choir" a special bond of unity develops that will prevail throughout a student's academic program and, hopefully, even long beyond that.

Struggling for Relevancy

Most outreach instructors try very hard to incorporate local themes and interests in the curriculum, although the details of such a quest has to be left to the individual instructor. In the case of a drama course, one instructor devised a video film with her students which was shown on local television a number of times and earned a permanent place in the University of Calgary film library. An English instructor relied heavily on Native-produced materials in teaching about grammar and syntax, and in education, students were sent into the local community to discover what concepts of schooling prevailed among various community functionaries. A special essay on school aims included interviews with local band council members, business people and educators, and attendance at school board or education committee meetings. Results of these surveys often surprise students, perhaps because they tend to take matters for granted when it comes to the operation of their local schools — obviously their impressions in that regard differ little from the perceptions of most Canadians.

A special assignment undertaken by a group of students in the Fort Chipewyan Outreach Program was to gather opinions on education from community functionaries with a view to planning improvements. At that time (1982) the community was examining the feasibility of uniting two school campuses into one, i.e., the Indian Affairs school and the Northlands School Division facility, and there was concern that the new arrangement should serve to foster the ideals of education in a more effective manner. Specifically, the student project centred on seven concerns (Friesen, 1984):

1. What are the commendable elements of schooling currently functional in Fort Chipewyan?
2. What are some of the educational needs presently not being met by the schools?
3. What role do or should parents play in teacher selection and school operation?
4. How can additional input from community personnel enhance the curriculum?
5. What is the present function and effectiveness of the local parent-teacher association?
6. What might the role of the nonprofessional educator be?
7. What are the factors that lead to a high drop-out rate and low attendance at school?

In all, the students contacted individuals representing 30 community agencies, and the results of the research are sufficiently interesting to merit a summary. On the positive side, schools of Fort Chipewyan were commended for initiating a community newspaper, encouraging community use of facilities, employing local university students as substitute teachers, promoting Native culture through the teaching of arts and crafts, and hosting such events as community dances. In addition, various respondents expressed appreciation for the concern which teachers demonstrated regarding student achievement, and mentioned the fact that school staff had been very cooperative over the years with regard to encouraging parent-community involvement in the schools. It was soon obvious to the researchers that even though the profile of the schools was positive with regard to concern for local education, the follow-through with regard to student successes did not produce very enviable results.

The Fort Chipewyan schools did suffer some criticism with regard to failing to maintain academic standards or providing a relevant curriculum. Community residents also commented negatively with regard to the "product" of schooling in terms of employability of students upon completion of their education. On the surface, the criticism appeared to have some validity, but even a peripheral examination of the economic scene at Fort Chipewyan reveals a lack of jobs insofar as preparation for the economic market is concerned. Unless the high school particularly sees its mission as one of preparing students to live elsewhere than in Fort Chipewyan, it can hardly be faulted. With trapping, fishing and hunting on the decline in most northern settlements, the only option for people is to seek employment in nearby oilfields. With that market in as subdued a position as it currently is, there is even less reason to blame the school and less optimism to be raised with regard to future employment.

The plea for enhancement of employment opportunities through schooling has echoed throughout Native communities for decades. In 1971, the Indian Association of Alberta requested the allocation of funds so that a continually increasing number of students could avail themselves of the opportunities for training in order to pursue a life's work with the greatest effectiveness (Indian Association of Alberta, 1971). This report complemented the work of the provincial Task Force on Intercultural Education in 1972 which stated the need for job preparation for Native people in vocations which would utilize their particular talents and interests and allow them to remain in their own communities insofar as it would be economically feasible (Task Force, 1971).

When the much-quoted document of 1972, arguing for Indian control of Indian education was published, it was more specific with regard to Indian vocational needs, but failed to address the issue of *providing* an economic base for the fulfillment of those needs. The report called for adult programs to include business management, consumer education, leadership training, administration, human relations, family education, health, budgeting, cooking, sewing, crafts, Indian art and culture, and suggested that such training should be carried out under the auspices of the local Band Educational Authority (National Indian Brotherhood, 1972).

The dilemma of seeking to emphasize vocational preparation for Native people for the northern marketplace is countervened by a lack of opportunity. There are no major industries in such regions and even though the business and job components of educational programs may be stepped up there is no place to receive graduates when they have completed their work. The exception has been with regard to teaching, social work and other "people" professions.

In a very real sense the problem is one of politics and economics, and the best of efforts, educationally, will not improve the situation. The irony is that well-prepared youth are forced to leave their respective communities to practice their skills, thus raising the question of education comprising an interference factor to Native life rather than a help. The *relevance* of the training to local needs will not make a difference; in northern communities there are much larger economic questions that require an urgent answer. Some of the bands further south have managed better along these lines. The Bloods, located south of Cardston, Alberta, for example, have developed successful industries in housing development, jewellery, ranching and potato growing.

The development of receiver systems for Native university graduates is not sufficiently addressed in current commissions and reports, two of which come to mind in the Alberta context. The Committee on Tolerance and Understanding devoted an entire report to the question of Native education in the province in 1984, and though the mission of education was identified as having to address the questions of enhanced self-esteem among Native students and the ability to develop critical thinking skills, no suggestions about how these might be deployed in an economic or vocational context were offered (Committee on Tolerance and Understanding, 1984). The report does indicate that an effective educational program should prepare students for specific professions, i.e., counsellors, home-school liaison workers, teacher aides, and language and cultural specialists, but all of these are within the context of educational institutions only.

A second relevant publication is the Native Education Project of 1985 which offers a policy statement for governmental consideration based on the viewpoints of Native people representing a wide variety of reservations and professional posts. The primary focus of the report is with regard to the appropriateness of modern education to Native needs and recommends the incorporation of Native values and lifestyle content in the curriculum, and the involvement of Native parents in educational decision making (Native Education Project, 1985). No attention is given the question of finding employment for Native students when they finish their training or to attempt to utilize them in local Native communities.

Students in the Fort Chipewyan program discovered that parental involvement in educational matters was minimal for several different reasons, and they could not merely be labelled as being disinterested. Many of their contacts suggested that the habit of a few outspoken individuals to offer their opinions at meetings drove the more timid persons away. It is important to speculate that the movement toward local control currently highlighted in most Native communities will not assure additional local input unless the matter of proper representation is resolved. Parents who are interested enough to involve themselves in educational operations should also be guaranteed a platform so that their concerns might be heard. It was disheartening for the Fort Chipewyan students to find that only six persons from the local community showed up for a public meeting called to share the results of their research, but on the positive side it also motivated them to work harder to promote education on the home front.

Two decades have passed since the practice of unfair and erroneous representation of Native culture in school curricula has been pointed out, and considerable headway has been made to incorporate more accurate accounts. Much of the information has been accumulated and presented by Native people with a view to assisting Native students to develop a more positive outlook toward their cultural background. In the Fort Chipewyan project, student researchers found their audience divided on the issue of including Native data, and part of the concern had to do with a worry about adhering to provincial standards of education if other than the traditional content was treated. A similar topic has emerged at the college level at times, and outreach instructors have wrestled with that challenge in every course offered on-site.

Educational investigations of every kind inevitably have a way of coming down on the well-publicized phenomena of student absenteeism and the high drop-out rate in Native communities. There is no singular answer to these unfortunate happenings, but traditional investigations render comments about lack of motivation, lack of employment possibilities, alcoholism, and the controversy about inadequacy of positive role models. Similar conclusions may be drawn at the college level with some programs reaping much better results than others. Although not scientifically verifiable because a formal evaluation has not been accomplished for the Calgary program in the last 15 years, there appears to be a correlation between program success and access to, and familiarity with, urban centres. This has been the case with regard to two reservations on which courses have been offered for the last several years, but it is not so with regard to a reservation that meets the criterion of proximity to an urban setting; the unexplained factor there appears to be the availability of a high source of personal income. With adequate monies coming in regularly from oil and gas revenues, students from that reserve feel that higher education has little to offer them and only a few university graduates have emerged in the community. One might also observe that even though the reserve has been fortunate in having access to a large income, little of it has been directed toward moneymaking ventures so as to assure trained youth a place to ply their trade.

The Native Centre

The transition to campus life for the final year of a degree requirement can be quite traumatic for Native students, particularly so if they have never experienced urban life in any dimension. Recognizing this challenge, the University of Calgary has taken appropriate action to establish a "resting place" for Native students on campus known as the Native Centre. Lodged in the Student Union building, the Centre is responsible for several subprograms such as the Outreach Program, the Native Student Services, and the Health Science Project on the Blackfoot Reserve. Its facilities include the Red Lodge, which is a student drop-in centre; a series of offices for the Director; secretary, tutoring and advising services; study carrels, a computer room, and a study room. The decor of the area portrays elements of Indian culture with a variety of pictures and paintings of Native art hung in conspicuous places. Notices of rodeos, pow wows, conferences, and Sundances hosted in the province periodically decorate the bulletin boards, and their regular appearance gives testimony to the high level of activity directed toward the revival of Native culture today.

The Red Lodge is a favorite place for Native students at the university, both as a haven for relaxation and for educational assistance. Many times, seminars, films and discussions are held in the lodge over the noon hour and it is the gathering place for the Native Students' Club which is affiliated with the facility. Working with the club in promoting a sense of community and cohesiveness, the Native Student Services regularly sponsors educational/cultural events and participates in Indian Awareness Week on campus. The executive has also tried to offer personal services in the nature of where to obtain financial assistance or find practical help. A visit to the Red Lodge readily reveals the personal element in its operations; a large blackboard situated at one end of the room conveys personal messages from students, e.g., "Allan, please call Terry before class because I need my psychology book back!" Other items pertain to announcements of social events, job opportunities and academic deadline reminders. In short, it is a nice place to visit.

The nature of help required by students who frequent the Native Centre is usually an admixture of personal and academic. The tutors provide individual and group counselling, and advise on academic matters, but they may also make referrals for personal problems. The process is generally quite informal and the day-to-day exchange of the tutors and students is very friendly. Students can and do make formal appointments to obtain assistance, but the staff tries very hard to foster a fraternal atmosphere which puts students at ease in both formal and informal settings. Extracurricular socializing often takes place in connection with the Native Centre, featuring picnics, potlucks, etc., in which both staff and students participate on a fraternal basis.

The Centre staff are constantly engaged in tasks that will make their work more successful, most of them involving student participation, and many of them drawing on the insights of an advisory group. Establishment of and participation in seminars and conferences has enhanced staff skills considerably and there are several individuals who have now been with the program for at least a decade with the result that their experience has been proven invaluable to the program. Two such offices are those of the secretary, who effectively transmits messages across the various sections of the Centre, and the Indian Affairs Branch counsellor who maintains a vital tie with the federal Government. A serious attempt to have Native people on staff has been partially successful in that at least one Native person has always been functioning in the program. Combined with other efforts, the program now has retention rates of over 80 percent compared with only 20 percent in the initial years (Gallant, 1984).

Evaluating the Outreach Program

In the initial years of operation the role of Native Student Services and the Outreach Program were carefully observed and formal evaluations were undertaken. It became clear that the operation was basically a success, and with the occasional change in the makeup of staffing or financial shifts, the attached Office of Educational Development was discontinued and formal evaluations ceased. Informal evaluations have occurred periodically; for example, students have referred to their experiences in their papers, and related discussions have reflected a similar positive note (Moore-Eyman, 1982). The fact that requests for additional outreach programs have come from various reserves also attests to the popularity and success of such a venture. There is no question that the university's role in Native higher education has been significant.

On a more specific note, considerable advantage could be derived from a thorough evaluation of the Outreach Program as well as the Native Centre. Specifically, such an evaluation should tackle three fronts — Native community liaison, staff utilization and student needs. The first focus would be directed toward determining community concepts of university endeavors, that is, the degree to which community concerns are being met by current programs. There is some indication that a gap still exists between university and community with regard to successful liaison. University opportunities need to be publicized in the marketplace as well as in school in order to acquaint individuals with new possibilities in training. Also, the development of a stronger support system for students in process needs to be investigated because community residents are sometimes uneasy in the presence of their university members and the latter often feel misunderstood by family and friends. An evaluation should look at ways of building better bridges of understanding between the university and Native community so that students are not caught in midstream. Emphasis on obtaining community opinion as to how to accomplish this goal should be a priority.

After nearly 20 years of operation, even the best of organizations run the risk of stagnation, sometimes in structure or function. Staffing at the Native Centre, including that of the outreach programs, has adopted a fairly established format. While the inherent effectiveness appears to be evident, an analysis of staff roles is appropriate. Without such examination, staff energies and talent may be misdirected or even become redundant. Evaluative procedures need to glean suggestions from at least three important constituencies, that of faculty, staff and students.

The underlying objective for the Native Outreach Program is the provision of adequate educational opportunities for Native youth. While these needs have comprised academic, economic and personal dimensions, they have also changed with the times. Thus, the provisions of a decade ago may no longer be relevant. As university programs change, the student is affected. Economic trends in the cities are reflected in terms of accommodation needs, transportation, and family life needs. Still another factor is the personal element of Native education; most Native students still experience culture shock when moving from the reserve to urban centres. It is not advisable to rest on the laurels of the past in devising appropriate adjustment maneuvers and therefore the process may require an additional look.

In the final analysis it is always good practice to examine periodically those academic procedures which have a high degree of personal significance attached to them, and the Native Outreach Program is no exception. In fact, because of the implications it conveys in terms of the future of Native culture, it is of the utmost importance. As Bruce Sealey has stated, "To a great extent education will be the key that allows [Native] people to enter the mainstream of society and operate within it as equals" (Friesen and Lusty, 1980). Whether or not the Native people choose that option or continue to thrive in the reserve setting, their chances of success will be significantly improved through higher education. To that end, the Native Outreach Program of the University of Calgary has played a significant role.

References

Brooks, Ian R. (1977). *Fourth evaluation report, Native student services*. Calgary: University of Calgary, Office of Educational Development.

Committee on Tolerance and Understanding. (1984). *Native education in Alberta*. Edmonton: Government of Alberta.

Friesen, John W. (1984). "Challenge of the North for Teachers," *Canadian journal of Native education*, Vol. 11, No. 3, 114.

Friesen, John W. and Terry Lusty. (1980). *The Metis of Canada: an annotated bibliography*. Toronto: Ontario Institute for Studies in Education.

Gallant, Emily. (1984). "Native Student Services," in *Field experiences in multicultural education*. John W. Friesen, ed. Vol. 2, University of Calgary.

Indian Association of Alberta. (1971). *Proposals for future of education of Treaty Indians in Alberta*. Edmonton: Indian Association of Alberta.

Moore-Eyman, Evelyn, ed. (1982). *Understand with head held high: papers of a study conference on Canadian Indian biculturalism.* University of Calgary: Native Student Services.

National Indian Brotherhood. (1972). Policy paper presented to the minister of Indian affairs and northern development.

Native Education Project. (1985). *Native education in Alberta's schools.* Edmonton: Alberta Education.

Task Force on Intercultural Education. (1971). *Task force report.* Edmonton: Government of Alberta.

15

The Role of Native People in Canadian Multiculturalism

John W. Friesen

Multiculturalism in Canada has recently gained a great deal of attention, but its practical implications have yet to be worked out. A case in point pertains to the Indian people whose quest for equality and cultural recognition has often been slowed by attending legal complexities. At a superficial level, it is customary to speak of three groupings of people in connection with multiculturalism in this country, namely the Aboriginal peoples, the founding nations of French and English, and immigrant groups. The latter are usually pegged in the expansion period of western Canada from 1870 to 1914, but in light of continuing developments it may be wise to project a fourth grouping, namely the newcomers who have emigrated in recent years and in significant numbers. The "boat people" are a case in point.

Outlining the fundamentals of multiculturalism will provide a framework for this discussion, although it is easy to overgeneralize because each group is so unique. This makes the operationalization of multicultural principles a very localized matter because the historical, cultural and legal nuances of each situation must be taken into account. In general, the principles of multiculturalism fostered by government and other institutions are:

1. to promote policies that guarantee equality of opportunity for all citizens;
2. to originate and revise policies that operationalize access to government services for all citizens;
3. to preserve the linguistic, cultural and religious heritage of all Canadians;
4. to encourage all ethnocultural groups to share the richness and diversity of their cultural heritage with the general community;
5. to encourage policies that facilitate preservation of the heritage of all citizens and recognition of the contribution of all members of society; and

6. to provide assistance in clarifying for the public, government policies relating to multiculturalism within a context of full, equal and responsible citizenship for all citizens.

Statements like the above are fairly commonplace in Canada and they are often articulated in a variety of institutional settings.

Emergence of Multiculturalism

It is generally recognized that the official policy of multiculturalism in Canada was enshrined by the words of the Hon. Pierre Elliott Trudeau on October 8, 1971, when he rose in the House of Commons to declare:

> Every ethnic group has the right to preserve and develop its own culture and values within the Canadian context. To say that we have two official languages is not to say that we have two official cultures, and no particular culture is more 'official' than another. A policy of multiculturalism must be a policy for all Canadians (Friesen, 1985,1).

Trudeau's words did not originate void of any previous considerations for, as Sandra Gwyn points out, the story really began on December 17, 1962, when Prime Minister Lester Pearson announced in the House of Commons that he would establish a Royal Commission to examine the issues of "biculturalism and bilingualism" in Canada. By 1969, when the Commission's work was finished, resentment against recognizing only *two* of the nation's cultures and languages sparked a debate that ended in compromise. Canada would have *two* official languages, but would recognize "the multicultural character of Canada" (Gwyn, 1974). It was this conclusion, framed in the form of a resolution by the "Thinkers' Conference on Cultural Rights and Freedoms," that entrenched the idea of two languages and no "official" culture in the minds of many Canadians. There are numerous indications that subsequent federal government action supported this policy.

To operationalize the notion of multiculturalism within a bilingual framework is no mean feat, since language is so much an expression of culture. We need only look at the enrollment figures in French classes by people of all ethnic backgrounds to see what this means in terms of the potential decline of their own cultural familiarity or affiliation. Anglo Canadians who seriously take up the challenge of learning French also run the risk of facing the ire of French Canadians who fear that bilingual Anglos have an unfair advantage over their own children in terms of political and economic opportunity.

All this is really only the tip of the iceberg. Canada's ethnic makeup is basically a bewildering array of peoples clamoring for differential rights, without a particularly benevolent attitude toward granting the same on behalf of others. Most studies of these groups have avoided the thorny questions of rights, leaving those to the legal and political realms of society and government to hammer out.

Dominant ethnic studies have tended to concentrate on ethnic identity and survival, history and demography, ethnic relations and educational matters (Anderson, 1982). The single almost classic exception is Kallen's book, *Ethnicity and Human Rights*, which begins with the biological roots of human rights, traces the development of rights with reference to ethnocultural groups in Canada and concludes with applications to the rights of individuals generally (Kallen, 1982). Kallen asserts that Aboriginal peoples in Canada have been relegated a third-class citizenship because their Treaty and Aboriginal status have been ignored under multicultural policy. What they possess unique only to them in terms of looking at the various ethnocultural groups in Canada is the right of "original possession and use of the land long before the arrival of the so-called charter groups." That right is complemented by the extraordinary rights which have been granted to a series of other cultural groups over the years of Canada's duration by government and in that sense is not unique. What will be argued by Aboriginal peoples, then, is that theirs is a *prior* or primary right and thus it takes precedence over all rights subsequently granted to others. It is a right that originates from an entirely unique category not unlike that of a nation dealing with a nation.

Determining Multicultural Policy

Some observers argue that despite having a rather large multicultural directorate in the Canadian government, its effect is dramatically diminished by the fact that multiculturalism per se has no status in the cabinet. Its budget is limited and, when cuts are to be made, multiculturalism is an easy target. Lupul claims that in department charts, the minister floats like a loosely connected dirigible to one side of the secretary of state, while the directorate is well hidden beneath the undersecretary of state, five assistant undersecretaries and layers of other bureaucrats (Lupul, 1982). It is therefore highly unlikely that this underpowered office can be expected to produce very much by way of an impact policy in Canada or effect much by way of identifying or alleviating unfair practices. The needs of the Aboriginal peoples have not yet gained a high priority and their concerns are usually relegated to the Department of Indian Affairs and Northern Development (DIAND).

While the effectiveness of Canadian multicultural policy may be debated, it must be acknowledged that some helpful activities *have* been carried out. In the 1971 policy statement, the government pledged itself to supporting *all* of Canada's cultures and, "resources permitting" (the catch phrase that saves all governments from action), seek to assist the developments of those cultural groups which have demonstrated a desire to continue to develop. The government also volunteered to participate in helping groups to overcome racial and cultural barriers, encourage cultural exchanges and provide special language services to newcomer peoples. On these counts there has certainly been action, as may be attested to by the role of such agencies as the Ethnic Studies Advisory Committee, the National Film Board, the National Museum of Man, and the Department of Manpower and Immigration, to name only a few. Funding for educational programs and research has also occurred, although when these have reference to Native communities, they are generally referred to DIAND.

There is a legitimate concern that the Royal Commission which laid the groundwork for the multicultural policy failed to be specific about which groups might be logical and rightful beneficiaries of the policy, and the acknowledgement of two official languages and many cultures only served to further muddy the waters. The commission's failure to deal more specifically with the cultural question allowed the issue to be swept under the carpet. What evolved was a subtle policy of assimilation of cultures which Native leaders in Alberta so aptly objected to in the Red Paper of 1970. They refused to be treated as ordinary citizens and rejected the notion that they should receive services through the same channels and from the same government agencies as for other Canadians on the ground that they were "Citizens Plus" (Citizens Plus, 1970).

It is this right, emanating from an historical agreement "set in the very sun" that constitutes the ground of the Indian interpretation of multicultural policy. In a very real sense it is not at all multicultural nor pluralistic; it is, in essence, *extraordinary* to the regular ongoings of Canadian society. That kind of contracting, as pointed out earlier, has been fairly typical of government-ethnocultural dealings in the past, although, practically speaking, no citizen or subgroup of society should be regarded in exactly the same way in any context. To suggest this is to ignore the reality of individual needs and differences, and the force and intensity of cultural configurations. In a legal sense, however, the implications are more severe, for they affect the future of all Canadian cultures in very crucial ways, i.e., land claims, language maintenance, etc.

Operationalizing Multiculturalism

Government efforts to recognize cultural specialties in the form of functional needs have been inconsistent and often contradictory. Concessions which minorities have wrenched from the hands of both federal and provincial governments have not always been exemplary of the philosophy of cultural appreciation. Some contracts were negotiated simply on the basis of immediate need, while others were formed without consideration for the resultant implications. Some were even cancelled, though such action violated basic human rights. Yet in each case, differences of need were recognized and accommodated, thus laying the ground for the current policy. At the very least, these happenings have established a Canadian precedent for the acknowledgement of extraordinary circumstances. In the case of Native education, this factor is foundational to all other developments.

A brief look at some of the instances of government action with regard to recognizing special circumstances will illustrate the thrust of this paper. To begin with, there is the contentious issue of French language rights in Manitoba. Despite the fact that the *B.N.A. Act* spelled out that the granting of language rights is a federal matter, in 1890 the province of Manitoba felt constrained to make English the official language of the people. Periodically, the issue flared up in the province's history, but it was only in 1979 that the Supreme Court of Canada was asked to render a vote on the matter and the decision was to abolish the bill of 1890. The subsequent government was required to translate all provincial laws into the French language within a period of five years and correct a wrong that has affected the French residents of Manitoba for nearly a century. The conclusion to be drawn from this pertains to the manner in which special rights can be ignored or overrun by insensitive governments or citizens. Penny pinching-oriented politicians might take objection to the expenditure of large sums of money for the translation of Manitoba's laws since the francophone population comprises only five percent of the province's total, but federal jurisdiction is paramount. In the unfolding of multicultural developments, however, no single basis for either the granting of rights nor their fulfillment may be identified.

Two Anabaptist groups in Canada, Mennonites and Hutterites, have a different story to tell. Lured to Canada in 1874 by the campaign speeches of Mr. Clifford Sifton, Minister of the Interior, who wanted to populate the West, the Mennonites were given two special promises. Put in writing by the Secretary of the Department of Agriculture, the Mennonites were assured that they would be allowed to establish their own schools and run them without government interference and, secondly, their young men would not face military conscription. These arrangements meant a great deal to the group and constituted part of the rationale for their original migrations from Europe to Russia 100 years earlier. After an investigation of school practices in Manitoba by a provincially-appointed commission, the right to have private schools was taken from the Mennonites and they were required to send their children to public schools. The same action forced the closing of Roman Catholic Separate schools.

In addition, when World War I broke out, the clause in the federal order-in-council that granted freedom from conscription was changed by the addition of the words "except in times of war." When the Mennonites received the news, they combined their disappointment with that experienced by the closing of their schools and some 5,000 of the Old Colony variety of Mennonites fled to Mexico where they procured similar assurances from that government about their requirements. Others sought refuge in the neighboring province of Saskatchewan where similar circumstances about schooling evolved, and they moved to the Peace River country of northern Alberta. The Mexico group eventually lost the leases on their lands when oil was discovered and they begged to be allowed to return to Manitoba. This was arranged and a quiet acquiescence was made to government demands with regard to compulsory public schooling (Friesen, 1977).

Hutterites migrated to Canada much later, arriving in 1918 in the province of Alberta (Dariusleut and Lehrerleut) and soon thereafter to Manitoba (Schmiedeleut). Since one of their priorities has always been the socialization of their children to adopt Hutterite ways, they managed to work out an arrangement for schooling to take place on colony premises. This, along with other of their quaint ways, has often made them the object of public scorn and jealousy. A fairly standard form of agreement has been made between individual colonies and local school boards which arranges for the Hutterites to pay the costs of their children's education through that component of their land taxes. If this base of funding falls short, colonies must raise extra funds to make up for the difference. If there is a surplus, the monies stay in the coffers of the local tax office and may be used for other purposes. The tax fund is used to pay for teachers' salaries; colonies provide the school building and furnishings, pay for utilities and supplies and, if needed, provide a teacher's residence as well. Teachers are usually off-colony people (except in rare situations), and their efforts are supplemented by a locally selected German teacher who provides additional Hutterite education before and after school and on Sundays (Hostetler, 1977).

Opposition to the Hutterite arrangement for schooling occasionally arises in communities where there is resentment against the practice of communal living. Hutterites also prosper economically. The grounds on which presentations to government are made for a dismantling of the special educational consideration, however, are usually that Hutterite children need to be given an opportunity to experience "true Canadian living" or that they are being shortchanged in terms of learning what it is like to function in dominant society. So far, these "commendable" concerns on behalf of Hutterite children are quickly shown to be the camouflaged form of jealousy that they are. What is probably less well known is the fact that "home schooling" is really the right of every Alberta family and the Hutterites are citizens who have claimed that right. What initially appears to be a special right to them is really only a case of colony concern and initiative.

Of a more serious consequence is the matter of Hutterite land purchases. Originally they, like other citizens, were free to exercise this right until the Alberta Social Credit government passed a law in 1947 that restricted such for Hutterites only. The law specified that colonies could buy a maximum of 6 400 acres for a new colony only if the site was at least 40 miles from an existing colony. In 1960, the law was amended to eliminate the 40-mile clause and allowing no sales to Hutterites without hearings before a community property control board and approval by legislative cabinet. This law has since been repealed because it violated the subsequently passed *Bill of Human Rights*. Ironically, while Hutterites, who are Canadian citizens, were forbidden to buy local lands, foreign firms gobbled up prairie lands at a rate far exceeding Hutterite purchases.

Another group that migrated to Canada from Russia in 1899 were the pacifist, vegetarian, communal-living Orthodox Doukhobors who settled in the eastern side of Saskatchewan near the Manitoba border. They were not informed of the vicissitudes of the Canadian way of life when they filed for entry (many of which beliefs were in opposition to their religious beliefs), and shortly after their arrival they ran into a series of conflicts. One of these emanated from the fact that the communal way of life they established was not favored by government officials. In all, 61 villages were built in the Kamsack, Blaine Lake-Langham, Swan River-Pelly and Buchanan-Canora areas which were overseen by a general board.

When their leader, Peter Verigin, arrived in 1902, he oversaw the operations which prospered and which endeared him to his people. It was therefore a great shock when the Doukhobors discovered they would lose their lands unless they registered them individually with the federal government instead of as a corporation. This included swearing allegiance to the Crown, an act that violated their belief of separation of church and state. Some Doukhobors did choose to go that route and registered their lands; they became known as the Independents. The Orthodox followed their leader to a site he had purchased in the Grand

Forks-Castlegar district in the B.C. Interior. Doukhobor homesteads were immediately confiscated by government and placed up for bid by incoming settlers who lined up at the claims office several days before the official offering of the lands. Many Doukhobors were understandably angry at these proceedings since no compensation was made to them either for their buildings or for the cost of landbreaking. They left the prairies emptyhanded, long remembering their experiences with governments that "give and take away." Quite clearly, the case illustrates the fact that special agreements may be made with ethnocultural groups by government, but they can just as easily be violated (Friesen and Verigin, 1989).

The experience of a group that prevailed when put upon to make themselves scarce are the members of Calgary's Chinese community. The Chinese presence in Canada was initially motivated by push and pull factors. In simple terms, China was not a pleasant place to live a century ago, having lost wars with Britain, France, Germany, Austria and other countries. With each defeat, the standard of living was lowered, and a restlessness emerged among the citizenry. On the other hand, gold had been discovered in North America and attracted many Chinese to California and later to places north.

Prime Minister John A. Macdonald encouraged the influx of Chinese for the purposes of building the railroad, but when its completion came about, their immigration was stopped. Eventually, many Chinese moved inland, arriving in Calgary in 1886. They soon established themselves in business and their premises quickly provided common meeting places for their friends and families.

Annoyance with the Chinese presence in Calgary's downtown has been expressed from time to time, most recently in relation to urban renewal of the city's downtown core. However, successful campaigns to maintain Chinatown in its present location have been launched by local Chinese leaders over the past two decades so that the community's status and geographical location have been assured for years to come. One of their members, Mr. George Ho Lem, was elected to a seat in the House of Commons in the interests of having the voice of his community heard. Chinatown in Calgary is a rare multicultural arrangement and a sign of cultural persistence to the extent of gaining public and governmental approval, albeit reluctantly (Friesen, 1983).

The above examples indicate that variations in government policy and ethnocultural reaction are well-entrenched in the nation's history. These sometimes contradictory occurrences have formed the basis of the present multicultural policy and underscore the fact that it cannot be meaningfully operationalized on a comprehensive basis. They also strengthen the case for Native claims for recognition of their extraordinary rights.

Multicultural Policy and the Native Community

Many details are yet to be worked out in the present Canadian multicultural policy, some of them rendered quite complex by the inclusion of Native cultural considerations. One of the most obvious has to do with the identification of an ethnic group. One cannot be certain that established groups like the French, Scotch, Welsh or Irish are truly "ethnic." And what of Mennonites, Jews, Mormons or Americans who settle in Canada? Are these groups ready to identify with that designation of their lifestyle? If this is the case, what does it imply for their rights, privileges and extraordinary claims, if any?

Generalizing the objectives of multiculturalism on a universal scale is a complex matter, even when the universally accepted values of freedom of speech, justice and guarantee of equality of opportunity are being promoted. When the specifics of each situation are calculated, the task becomes onerous. This has been shown with regard to the cases just described. Native peoples bring to account an even longer list of factors to consider — historical, geographical, cultural, economic and legal. Historically, they possess the right of first occupancy; their geographical speciality emanates from the fact that they occupied a different continent from that of their invaders who originated the multicultural policies, and culturally they constitute a group that respects the balance of nature and sees technological advance in a corollary context. Economically, they occupy the lower levels of the economic ladder and legally they are still the object of special laws which identify them as a group and set them apart from the larger society (Berry, 1981). These characteristics certainly establish the case for extraordinary considerations in the Canadian context.

Multiculturalist policies in Canada were originated quite in isolation from Native concerns, partially because matters pertaining to the Native community have generally been considered the domain of the Department of Indian Affairs. As applications of the concept were made to practical areas such as schooling, however, concerns about the treatment of Native children in the classroom have arisen. Quickly, the notion of the culturally different child was enlarged to include Native education. At first this was done without any regard for the historical, geographical, cultural, economic and legal considerations outlined above, and it is only as multiculturalists have become more sophisticated in their practice that the unique factors pertaining to Native peoples are taken into account. Now it is an area about which few practitioners feel qualified to make comment, thereby necessitating Native input.

Pacheco suggests that multicultural education programs specifically come in two varieties, compensatory and functional. The first type is understood to mean the designing of special programs or units of work for those students who are considered to suffer from disadvantages due to their home cultures being different from that of the school. Its underlying assumption is that unless these disadvantages are remedied, the educational opportunities of the minority child will be undermined. A corollary consideration is that multicultural programs can have value for all students, regardless of background, with the components of the program set in the framework of the psychosocial, stressing awareness, tolerance, understanding and pride in one's heritage. The second kind of program (functional) is intended to aid the student in developing the ability to function in a culturally pluralistic society, one in which there is parity among various cultural groups (Pacheco, 1981).

Initial multicultural efforts in the Native community were clearly of the compensatory nature, intending to school Native children in the ways of the non-Native world — to provide them with equal opportunity, it was said. More recently, probably greatly due to the input of Native people, the trend has been toward bicultural education, that is, allowing the Native child to develop in ways that enable effective functioning in both worlds. The bottom line is that the individual may choose where, in the final analysis, his or her heart will find a resting place in terms of cultural loyalties. This approach lessens the impact of covert assimilative forces, even though it will not be entirely clear of these intents. It is all very well to emphasize the neutrality of the bicultural approach, but if these programs are spawned without meaningful dialogue and/or origination in the Native community, they are still, at best, a form of external determination of Native destiny.

A principle much extolled by educational multiculturalists is that of assisting the student to develop pride in his/her heritage and in his/her community. A way to foster this orientation is by way of including curricular information about the local community. The extent to which departments of education are serious about this may soon be tested with regard to the Plains Indians Survival School in Calgary whose staff have developed a Native-centred curriculum which does not fit neatly into the rubrics of provincial departmental examinations for high school students. The question now is whether the province's educational officials will take seriously the principle of reflecting community themes in school curricula for ethnocultural communities or simply enforce compliance with standardized provincial curricula. If the former approach is adopted, the situation may necessitate the inauguration of total local control of schooling, including selection of teachers and curriculum content as well as the establishment of an overall philosophy and operational procedures. Educational difficulties cannot be resolved in isolation from the community whose members and leaders should really originate these components. Outsiders who wish to assist with the process need to become servants of the Native community and act in an advisory capacity only. Regardless of their academic or professional qualifications, they must acknowledge their inadequacies regarding Native culture and values, which of necessity must constitute the foundation of any proposed changes for Native society (Bowd, 1977).

Multiculturalism and Local Control—Today's Challenge

Multiculturalists usually promote the principles of cultural pluralism in terms of experiencing equality of status in Canadian society, with a meaningful choice of lifestyles and freedom to practice esteemed cultural traits. The provision and guarantee of basic human rights is a vital part of the package (McLeod, 1984). Any proposal to project these rights beyond those "normally" granted to citizens, however, is quickly blocked by a series of constraints.

Milton Gordon, an oftquoted American writer on the subject, straitjackets the right of minorities in a pluralist setting in specific terms. He postulates that cultural pluralism as a social arrangement is committed to maintain freedom of individuals and groups to practice separatism though perhaps at some sacrifice in terms of material standard of living; to permit subgroups to maintain a separate economic system as long as this does no damage to the general welfare of society; to permit subgroups to carry on their own educational system though they must bear the extra expense; and to make all subgroups responsible for contributions to the general welfare of society (Gordon, 1964, 16-17).

This background of restrictions, if applied to the Canadian scene, impacts most severely on Native communities. No other subgroup features as diverse a set of circumstances earmarking their identity. Preferentially, most ethnocultural communities appear content to integrate into society and to placate their identity-maintainers with a variety of festivities featuring food, dance and costume displays. Others vie for the maintenance of their identity by developing second language schools. These practices usually apply to immigrant groups.

In the case of the "founding peoples," French and English, both have the advantage of official language status and a familiarity with the basic institutions of dominant society which they designed. Also, most Canadians speak English. The French have the added protection of federal bilingual policies which are often strengthened by the support they receive from the Anglophone community members who aspire to second language mastery on the part of their children. Reasons for this support are often quite unrelated to the cultural factor in that Anglophones see facility in the language as an added opportunity for advancement in the arena of the civil service. Native people, on the other hand, are quite left out of the picture. Thus, if the restrictions on cultural pluralism outlined by Gordon are too quickly enforced, the Native community stands to be most affected in a negative sense. While comprising the component of Canadian culture that could benefit the most from a recognition of multicultural principles, the Native community is also very different from dominant society insofar as values are concerned. Indian cultures are traditionally past- and present-oriented and collaborative. Dominant society is future-oriented, individualistic and activity-centred. Indians strive to live in harmony with nature. Their non-Native counterparts seek to exploit, dominate and control nature (Frideres, 1988). How can these value schemes be reconciled in any workable manner?

Berry posits four kinds of results when distinct ethnocultural societies make contact with dominant society. These are: integration, segregation, assimilation and deculturation. The results of assimilation are inevitable absorption by the dominant world; integration suggests both the maintenance of the integrity of one's culture and identity and the movement to become an integral part of the larger societal framework; and segregation implies a withdrawal away from larger society. Deculturation, however, deserves special attention in this context because it concerns those cultures which are essentially out of touch, culturally and psychologically, with the larger society. When imposed upon by the larger society, the result is tantamount to ethnocide. At best, it brings about the classic situation of marginality (Berry, 1981).

The official Canadian government policy on multiculturalism endorses the right of "every ethnic group to preserve and develop its own culture and values within the Canadian context." The Native response to this challenge is to try to avoid the pitfalls of deculturation by embarking on the path of local control. If it is to be effective, however, it must be a policy that is originated, planned and played out by members of Native culture themselves. There is little assurance that this will happen in light of the many factors that have figured in Native destiny. This includes the traditional role of DIAND, the fact that funding for Native ventures will continue from external sources, the nature of societal institutions with which Native people will deal in restructuring the directions of their own culture, and the overwhelming impact of advancing technology.

If the past is any indication, however, the Aboriginal peoples will survive by inventiveness, adaptation and creativity (Couture, 1985). In terms of policy, their efforts may comprise the best test to date of Canada's multicultural commitment. What is even more important is that Native cultures be *encouraged* to persist. Their successes will assure Canadians of the opportunity to discover different ways of living in the contemporary world (Porter, 1972). That possibility would not only lend credibility to the word multiculturalism, it might also provide mankind with an alternative to some of the very destructive directions of today's technological society. Multiculturalism in this sense would truly offer us the best of both worlds.

References

Anderson, Alan B. (1982). "Canadian Ethnic Studies: Traditional Preoccupations and New Directions," *Journal of Canadian studies*, Vol. 17, No. 1, Spring, 515.

Berry, John W. (1981). "Native People and the Larger Society," in *A Canadian social psychology of ethnic relations*. Robert C. Gardner and Rudolf Kalin, eds. Toronto: Methuen, 214230.

Citizens Plus. (1970). *A presentation to the Government of Canada by the Indian Chiefs of Alberta.* Ottawa: Government of Canada.

Couture, Joseph E. (1985). "Traditional Native Thinking, Feeling and Learning," *Multicultural education journal*, Vol. 3, No. 2, November, 416.

Frideres, James S. (1988). *Canada's Indians: contemporary conflicts.* 3rd edition. Scarborough: PrenticeHall.

Friesen, John W. (1977). *People, culture & learning.* Calgary: Detselig Enterprises.

Friesen, John W. (1983). *Schools with a purpose.* Calgary: Detselig Enterprises.

Friesen, John W. (1985). *When cultures clash: case studies in multiculturalism.* Calgary: Detselig Enterprises.

Friesen, John W. and Michael M. Verigin. (1989). *The community Doukhobors. A people in transition.* Ottawa: Borealis.

Gordon, Milton M. (1964). *Assimilation in American life.* New York: Oxford University Press.

Gwyn, Sandra. (1974). "Multiculturalism: A Threat and a Promise," *Saturday night*, January, 1517.

Hostetler, John A. (1977). *Hutterites' society.* Baltimore: Johns Hopkins.

Kallen, Evelyn. (1982). E*thnicity and human rights in Canada.* Toronto: Gage.

Lupul, Manoly R. (1982). "The Political Implementation of Multiculturalism," *Journal of Canadian studies*, Vol. 17, No. 1, Spring, 93102.

McLeod, Keith A. (1984). "Multiculturalism and Multicultural Education," in *Multiculturalism in Canada: social and educational perspectives.* Ronald J. Samuda, et. al., eds. Toronto: Allyn and Bacon, 3049.

Pacheco, A. (1981). "Cultural Pluralism: A Philosophical Analysis," *Journal of teacher education*, Vol. 28, 1620, quoted in "Multiculturalismpluralist Orthodoxy or Ethnic Hegemony," M. Bullivant, *Canadian ethnic studies*, Vol. XIII, No. 2, 122.

Porter, John. (1972). "Dilemmas and Contradictions of a MultiEthnic Society," *Transactions of the royal society of Canada*, Vol. X, Series IV, 193-205.